The Mud Daddy Chronicles:

Raging Bass, Mystic Muskie and Twinkie Tiramisu

By David Lowery, John Eckberg, and John Erardi

Illustrations by Ran Mullins

Mystic Mud Publishing

© 2015

Kindle Edition March 2015
Print Edition June 2015
Manufactured in the United States of America

Cover Art by Ran Mullins

Print Layout Design by:
Nick Bauer
Bloomington, Indiana

"The One Enthroned in Heaven laughs."

Psalm 2:4

Table of Contents

Cast of Characters
or
Dramatis Personae

David Lowery was an award-winning editorial writer and columnist with the Austin American-Statesman in Texas. He earned his Mud Daddy credentials by actually enlisting in the Army in the middle of the Vietnam War. "I'm not sure what I was thinking when I did that," he said. "It seemed like a good idea at the time."

John Eckberg was an award-winning business columnist and reporter at the Cincinnati Enquirer. He earned his Mud Daddy marks by completely rewiring a '60 Chevy bread truck converted into a camper for a cross-country trip after high school graduation. No big deal except that he and his pal, Jerry Sliger, were broken down in a KOA campground outside Lincoln, Nebraska, and had to hitchhike to the library for a Chevy car wiring diagram, then back again. They rewired the truck with no clue if it would really work. It did, and they pressed on with their search for America. That, too, seemed like a good idea at the time. And it was.

John Erardi was an award-winning former columnist and sports writer for the Cincinnati Enquirer. Erardi, three-time Ohio Sports Writer of the Year, earned his stars early in his career by wrestling a bear at a shopping mall. Entering the ring with a bag of circus peanuts – supposedly Victor the Wrestling Bear's favorite treat – Erardi found he had a big problem – Victor. The match ended when Victor grabbed the backpedaling E-man, dragged him across the ring and held him nose down in a pool of bear piss. Erardi isn't sure what he was thinking when he accepted the assignment, but it was definitely not a good idea.

Introduction

Cooking is easy and fun. Fishing is, too. But living a full life takes work, particularly if circumstances limit your time and income, as it does with most of us. For more than three decades now, the three of us have gotten pretty good at spending a long weekend together each fall, fishing, drinking, talking, lying, cooking and making the most of our time together in God's great outdoors. This annual get together – called the Mud Daddy for a reason that will be explained later – is supposed to be first and foremost about fishing. At least that was what it was about when we started it all those years ago. Think about it – three or four days of unapologetic goofing off times the more than three decades that we've been doing it and that equals a full summer of freedom pilfered from the world of work and the nagging, day-to-day responsibilities of life in America: mortgages, jobs, bills and patio furniture that needs to be cleaned…kitchen sinks that need to be unclogged.

The following pages hold an account of our time together: anecdotes, stories, recipes and tips, as well as strange, synchronistic journeys into the Mystic, which we call The Vortex for lack of a more concrete term. Within these pages you will experience and hopefully learn from our pitfalls and pratfalls. You'll discover the rewards and penalties that come from driving to a strange, faraway lake to set up a campsite in the black of night and a downpour – only to realize that you forgot the tent pegs. Mud Daddy trips often include cranky resort owners, leaky aluminum boats with balky motors, too-small flashlights with weak batteries and cabins advertising views of distant mountains when the actual view is of an asphalt parking lot filled with boat trailers. The waters are usually foreign, the waitresses in the greasy spoons have big hair and bigger attitudes and the marina owners seem to speak another language. But always there is the exhilaration and promise of fish – an emotion that only part-time fisherman feel upon the cusp of a quixotic adventure.

We always fish old-school, starting out with lures (no live bait) and without the benefit of guide or fish finder. Inside these pages we'll explore the how and why of our strategy, if strategy is the right word for a Mud Daddy.

When we catch fish, it's a testament to our true grit. When we fail, which is regularly, the effort goes into life's ledger as a success anyway. We understand that fishing is more about being together and trying to catch fish rather than actually boating them. Every fish caught becomes a manifestation of grace, a gift from the Lord and an unseen world. Going fishless always lends itself to an exploration of deeper meanings: Haven't I been a good man, maybe I should try to be a better man.

We're unsure now how the first one actually came together. We know that it started out as a lark – more like having a beer after work on a Friday afternoon and then realizing that the one-bar, one-drink episode has turned into six beers and a few shots at a half-dozen hole-in-the-walls before staggering out into the night in search of a cab.

The Mud Daddy usually involves at least three of us and evolved after we found ourselves sharing adjoining cubicles in the newsroom of the Cincinnati Enquirer in the early 1980s.

David Lowery, a true son of Virginia, was born and raised in a small town near the North Carolina border and came to Cincinnati from Richmond, Va. as a general assignment reporter seeking poetry and illumination in the most mundane of newspaper tales. Lowery soon figured he was as smart as any of the bears in the Enquirer zoo and set out to climb through the newsroom ranks. In the process, he became an editor at many top newspapers – Cincinnati, Atlanta, Seattle and Austin. The nickname Doc stuck because he could edit copy like a surgeon.

John Eckberg, who grew up in Akron, Ohio, developed a love for fishing and for words in fourth grade thanks to the book Kon Tiki. He came to Cincinnati because the Enquirer was the only daily newspaper he could find that would hire a reporter whose experience was on a weekly newspaper. It helped that one of his pensive columns had landed on the opinion pages of the New York Times.

His nickname would become Slim, although he also answers to Big Cat (because Slim claims to move like one on the tennis court), Slick, The Big Swede, Johnny X and MC Johnny-John. He often quotes Marvin Gaye when bosses do something stupid ("Makes me want to holler, throw up both my hands…."), wonders if he's not a black man trapped in a white man's skin and expects some day to write a book White Like Me.

John Erardi, like many men before him, set down roots in the town where his wife, Barb, grew up. He came from a traditional Irish/Italian household of two sisters and two brothers in upstate New York and has forgotten more about major league baseball and the players who people that sport than most sports reporters will ever know. His black book has the name and phone number of over 300 former and current Big League Players. Need to talk to Jesus Rafael Aristimuno, who played nine years in the minors from the Clinton Pilots to the El Paso Dodgers and a few cities in between and who scouts Venezuelan ballplayers like a hungry man hunts hamburger helper? Erardi can hook you up. Because the handle Erardi sounded obtuse and also degenerates into 'Rardi when spoken in haste or slurred after a beer too many, "Hey 'Rardi" soon became Hey E-Man, Big E or E-Dog.

From time-to-time, these events also brought together Bob Rankin, a life-long pal of Lowery's and career D.C. journalist, who was to be dubbed Junkyard Dog or Raging Bull, and Bob Drews, a childhood friend of Slim's who will forever be known as Drewsie.

Anyhow, it was mostly the three of us. We realized one dull afternoon that we needed a break from the grind of our jobs.

Casting crankbaits for an entire weekend and maybe drinking to excess, we knew, would offer plenty of time to ponder some of the essential and timeless questions men have asked over the ages: Is quickness the same as speed? Does good pitching always stop good hitting? Is it true the best players take it one swing at a time? How do they stay within themselves? What, exactly, does it mean to stay within yourself? On and on it goes, usually with answers ending in paradox because some questions don't have answers, they have believers.

Big E believes the best players don't try to do too much, though he has no idea what that means. Doc believes quickness and speed are different, but he isn't convincing. Slim believes fish never bite beneath power lines, but he can't prove it. To know about how this tradition began, you have to understand a little more about us.

David, now called Doc by his Mud Daddy pals, began fishing before he began school. It's a scene straight out of the opening of the Andy Griffith Show. His grandfather, R.S. Lowery – everybody called him by his middle name, Stebbins, because Lowery men had always gone by their middle names – would walk with him to a bridge over the Bannister River below Stebbins' house in Halifax County, Va. Stebbins had had a heart attack when he was about 50 years old and took that as a sign to stop working. Some called it laziness, but Stebbins didn't mind. So he had a lot of time to fish and David frequently joined him, a little guy who had to stand on a cinder block to cast over the railing to the tea-brown water below.

They fished for catfish in the loafing river, always ruddy from the red clay runoff of the tobacco farms along its course. Stebbins liked to use shrimp for bait. He'd leave it out in the sun to spoil and make sure it was extremely stinky for the catfish. People don't like stinky shrimp but catfish love it. David didn't know people ate shrimp until he was in his teens, and even then he had to get up some gumption to try it because the smell of the bait lingered in the crannies of his mind. David and Stebbins fished the Bannister in the spring, summer and early fall, using spinning reels and stiff rods, a big sinker to hold the line tight to the bottom with the bait floating in the current. They caught a lot of stuff: pan fish, eels, carp and now and then some catfish, which went home for dinner.

After the shrimp odor, getting gored by the catfish barbs while taking the fish off the line and the ripe odor that fills kitchens when fish are cooked, David didn't have much appetite for eating fish. He fished because he wanted to be with Stebbins, and he wanted to be doing something that seemed grown up. David was soon was hooked himself, thanks to that always-surprising thrill that comes with the tug when a fish takes the bait. Every fisherman since Ovid and before knows of and lives for that wonderful throb of life that comes from something as simple as a line, a hook, some bait, the deep mystery of dark water and a fish.

Stebbins and David fished farm ponds, too, but never big water, never the reservoirs and man-made lakes scraped from the American heartland or created when dams were built across rivers. As David got older, he went out less and less with Stebbins. Then they built a new, higher bridge over the river and the old one became inaccessible. By the time he was a teen, David had stopped fishing with Stebbins and with the onset of girls, cars and rock and roll, he pretty much stopped fishing altogether. He picked it up again in his mid-20s, when he took up backpacking through the Southeast to fish mountain lakes and streams. David would pack an open-face reel, a short rod that broke down to fit in a backpack and enough lures to occupy a few hours. He caught a few trout, smallmouth and pan fish, but that hardly mattered. He was fishing to be fishing where he was fishing – not to catch fish.

David went back to that bridge over the Bannister a few years ago. The river doesn't look like much now. It's smaller than he remembered, but still lazy and crawling red through what once was rich tobacco land. The tobacco is gone now. The farmers bought out by Congress. But the Bannister is still there. And so are David's memories of it and his time with a line in the water, Stebbins by his side, and a bag of rotting shrimp.

John "Slim" Eckberg came to love fishing through a story. His father, Stanley and dying mother Sarah Nell, who had cancer at the time but her three boys didn't know it, had taken the family (Slim was the youngest and about eight at the time) to a cabin on the northern shore of Lake Michigan. Stanley had gone off one morning to fish with a friend, Paul Johnson, who with his wife, Libby, had made the 12-hour trek north from Akron, Ohio, to Brevert, Mich., as well. When he returned in late afternoon, Stanley told the story of a fish they had caught. It was a massive thing, Stanley said, holding out his arm to about the same level as Slim's flat-top haircut – maybe four feet off the floor. Slim gazed in wonder at a fish so huge in a lake that he might have swum in. Oh, no, Slim thought, I'm gonna die someday soon from a Muskie attack.

The giant Muskie battled relentlessly, Stanley told them, wallowing like a long pig there atop the water before leaping into the sun and then diving only to resurface again and again. The fish finally gave up and was reeled to the boat, now a broad but limp slab of fish alongside the leaky wooden watercraft. Stanley said they used a net to get it up over the rail but it was so heavy and large that both men had to haul it in, the fish half in and half out of the net. Muskies, Slim knew, were monsters of the fresh water. His father had told him of their rows of razor sharp teeth. They looked like they were smiling, Stanley said, but you knew they were not happy. And almost nobody ever actually caught one.

Once they got the creature in the boat and they got the lure out of its mouth – a giant red Daredevil spoon – it began to revive. And did this fish ever come back to life, Stanley recalled. It flipped and flopped there on the bottom of the boat and when Stanley's fishing buddy put his foot on it to keep it down, the fish squirted out from underneath his shoe and slid across the floor of the boat, right under Stan's seat, and now with more than a little force. The creature slammed into a pair of wide open tackle boxes. Here it exploded into a true fury of tail and malevolence. Lures flew everywhere, Stanley recalled. Lines were a mess. The fish was flopping around, hitting hooks on lures on the deck of the boat – all the while gnashing and slashing at air with that terrible razor jaw. It was mayhem. The men had no choice but to reach down and bare-hand the thing into the water to get it out of the boat as fast as possible.

The fish was soon gone, back to the deep of a U.P. lake. From the first time he heard the tale, Slim knew he had to catch one of these monsters and that someday, maybe, he would. After Sarah's death, Stanley had three boys to house, clothe and feed, so there was little time for fishing distant waters. But the family became Stanley's little platoon, and for this crew, fishing at the nearby Nimisila Reservoir near Akron offered a chance each week to let his rambunctious crew cut loose in the woods or get muddy on shore. The lake was a flat stretch of water south of the city limits, and it mostly held bluegill and not too damn many of those but Stanley never gave up on his quest for bass.

Once a year Stanley took his brood camping and – what else? – fishing. They regularly traveled to big lakes in upper Ontario, to the Upper Peninsula of Michigan and to the Boundary Waters of Minnesota to chase and sometimes catch big bass and long pike that seemed to Slim to be more snake than fish. At night the boys would have to clean their catch, which almost always turned into a gut fight (pick up fish gut, flick it at your brother's face when he's not looking, then run like hell). The quest for that massive Muskie would stick with Slim his whole life. So would fishing. Slim has seen much of the world in his time since then, and on his travels, he tries to fish: from a lost lake in the woods of Sweden to the tumbling Soca River in Yugoslavia, where Hemingway opened A Farewell to Arms; from a pasture stream in the Pyrenees of Spain to the Fox River in Michigan, which Hemingway describes in his Nick Adams Stories; from the rich crystalline waters of the Sarapiqui River in Costa Rica to the headwaters of the San Juan River above Pagosa Springs, Colorado. Fish – both caught and uncaught – haunt Slim's dreams. And he still hasn't landed that Muskie.

Big E first got hooked on fishing at Stiefvater's Camp on beautiful Fourth Lake near Inlet, N.Y., in the Adirondack Mountains, where the family would vacation for a week at the end of summer when the boys' baseball seasons were over. The hook was set deepest in early September 1964, when the St. Louis Cardinals were making their annual run at the National League pennant, which that year culminated in the World Championship, their first since Stan the Man's days. Musial, a great lover of fishing, never had a bigger haul than the Erardi brothers had one night during a rainstorm in ADK. They rigged their poles with big nightcrawlers, and retreated to the warmth of Stiefvater's party room, where rested the resort's lone TV – black and white, of course. It had to be a Saturday night, because the Miss America pageant was on from Atlantic City – and that meant it had to be the final night of the week-long stay, Sunday being departure day for the two-hour drive back to Syracuse.

Every commercial break, Johnny and his younger brother, Greg, would sprint for the dock through the rain, and find another rainbow trout at the end of their lines. They reeled in their blue-and-pink trophies, keeping the biggest ones to pack on ice for the trip home, where a big fish fry awaited. On and on it went that night, fish after fish after fish; they caught over 30 of them, good-sized ones, always over a foot, sometimes approaching two. Horsing in those big beauties was an adventure every single time, because the boys had thrown their lines out as far as they could – a far piece, given the heft of those huge sinkers, always set about 18 inches below the hook in the famed "New York rig."

Big E's no meteorologist, but he later learned that the weather conditions were perfect for rainbows that night. It had something to do with warm fronts, raindrops and barometric pressure. Big E's never seen those conditions duplicated, at least not when he's had a line out, although he does wonder sometimes, when the rain's falling hard and there's a warmth to the air.

"I know it may never happen again like that," he says, "but it doesn't keep me from going back out to see if it might."

The other fishing moment that has stuck deeply with him over the years was on Jamesville Reservoir outside Syracuse, where he went fishing for the first time with his youngest brother, Frank.

On the very first cast from their johnboat, Frank nailed a two-pound bronzeback while demonstrating top-water retrieve with the versatile spinner bait, chartreuse, of course. The rainbow adventure was purely serendipitous, the largemouth largely scientific. Together, they've kept Big E on the water the past 44 years.

Socrates said the unexamined life is not worth living, so for us a Mud Daddy is a weekend-long opportunity to examine our lives, to dive deeply into our innermost selves and to do it on a libation-fueled holiday of fun and adventure. Along the Mud Daddy Way, we've picked up some angling strategies that we will share. For example, cranes on the shore mean little fish in the shallows, and little fish in the shallows mean bigger fish on the nearby shoals. We also look for the seams – between shoreline vegetation and rock, sand to clay, clay to gravel, sun to shadow, cliff to hillside – because life is always more interesting in the seams.

We will also offer some instructions for après-fishing activities. Firing a potato gun is a great way to break the monotony of a hot afternoon when the lake is dead. Homemade rockets constructed from plastic bottles, cigar tubes, duct tape and Styrofoam packaging bring great guffaws, and they are marvelous to behold as they scream into the blue beyond. A box of Trivial Pursuit questions fills the rainy hours and lends fuel to the hotly disputed question: Who's the biggest dumb ass in the boat?

Mud Daddy Grub

Early in our Mud Daddy adventures, it became clear that it would take more than angling ability to stave off hunger. From the first trip, the food menu grew in importance, and as Mud Daddy I evolved into MD X then MD XX and, we hope, into the fog of the future, we concentrated as much on food and drink as we did on fishing. It is a good thing, too, because many an outing has ended without enough fish to feed us even one meal.

Our recipes are special for what they are not. They are not for the gourmet or chef wannabee with a Jenn-Air grill in the kitchen island, a Viking refrigerator, a pantry full of every conceivable condiment and spice and cabinets and drawers overflowing with pots, pans, cutlery and utensils. The Twinkie Tiramisu, for instance, is fine enough for a flaming finale at any five-star Milan restaurant – as long as the Milan is in Indiana, Kentucky or Texas and not Italy.

Think Chicken De Mountain Dew, not Chicken Devine.

The fare in this book serves folks who find themselves in less-than-perfect circumstances preparing dinner for four hungry people. These are recipes for cooks who might have forgotten or misplaced a thing or two when preparing for the weekend – like spatulas, big pots, plates and frying pans. You name it, we've forgotten it at one time or another. We give you lists, suggest menus and offer insights into what to expect when convenience store pecan twirls are used to stuff baked apples. You'll find a recipe for a dazzling Frittata Mundatta, as well as Grinnin' Parrot Cobbler and pan-poached fish nuggets, cooked when there isn't a drop of oil to be found. We offer some unusual cocktails, too.

Mud Daddy recipes are for real men and women – but mostly men, we'd guess – who venture into the outdoors with a Swiss Army knife on their belts and optimism in their hearts; pals who face the deep woods, wild rivers and out-of-the-way lakes of our nation with aplomb, humor and faith that everything is going to turn out all right – even without a spaghetti pot. The actual ingredients and preparation are not as important as the attitude. For more than three decades, we have improvised in some peculiar ways and in some daunting places. We've made coffee without a coffee filter. Cooked fish without oil. We've used an orange as a TV antenna. And we've watched candles cobbled from a suburban garage sale glow in the deepest dark of the woods because it was too wet to start a fire. Along the way, we've always managed to pull off a wilderness meal that is tasty and filling and a trip that is always – well, almost always – great great fun.

The Vortex

Webster's defines it as: 1. A whirling mass of something, especially water or air, that draws everything near it toward its center. 2. A situation or feeling that seems to swamp or engulf everything else.

To us, The Vortex is an enigmatic reality we first identified after several Mud Daddies. Maybe it's a message from On High, a serendipitous signal that we are on the right path toward knowledge. Maybe not. The Vortex most often reveals itself as strange animal occurrences and/or the unexpected confluence of unusual events too cosmic to be pure chance. How else to explain this: after the three of us had not communicated for months, Doc pulls an Ohio baseball cap from its lonely drift on a lake in Missouri. On the same day, E-Dog calls Doc in Austin – not knowing he was on a fishing trip - to ask about a new Cincinnati Reds draftee from Texas. An hour after that call, Slim emails Doc that this is the year we go fishing for Muskie, in – that's right – Ohio.

All that happened independently. Nobody knew what the other was doing.

The Vortex is a strange and mystical force. How else to explain that – only moments after a lengthy discussion of faith and religion – one of us catches a trophy bass with bare hands? How else to explain the historical sign post detailing a battle between pioneer Daniel Boone and Indian ambushers, a skirmish that led to the death of Boone's teenage son, when only moments before, E-man had told the same story as he drove down a highway that he had never been on before? The answer? The Vortex! In the following pages, we will offer an impressive body of evidence that The Vortex is real – and you better watch out.

We will also sound an ominous warning for anglers in this great nation. Fish that once were abundant in natural areas in the United States are under attack: pesticides, herbicides and fertilizers have upset the natural balance; overdevelopment and urban sprawl have left an indelible mark on backwoods lakes and streams; acid rain from power plants in the Midwest is real and has decimated lakes throughout the northeast; global warming, alien fish species, overflowing city sewer systems, decades-long drought ... the list of threats to our natural areas is long, imposing and terrible. When the Mud Daddy began, we journeyed to the Shenandoah River, memorialized in song by flatboat men on the Missouri River in 1800, and found the stream virtually pristine and the fishing just fine. Within two decades, that same stretch of bucolic waterway was virtually devoid of fish, biologists would report. In 2005, biologists found, more than 80 percent of the smallmouth bass and red-breast sunfish were gone. By 2007, a Virginia fisheries biologist couldn't even find a red-breast sunfish in the river.

After reading this book, you'll understand The Mud Daddy Way if you never remember a single recipe exactly, but are able to make meat loaf without a pan or a plan. You'll get what we're writing about if you recognize that success isn't duplication, but improvisation. You will be a Mud Daddy peer if you can cook bacon on a charcoal grill without torching your eyebrows and causing a three-alarm grease fire; if you can create a rocket from clear tape, a cigar tube and a slab of egg carton foam using only a Swiss Army knife and some wisecracks; if you can pose your own imponderable questions regarding the sporting life and debate those queries with intensity, humor and understanding while never allowing facts to get in the way of your opinion and never conceding that you might be wrong; if you can bullshit somebody into thinking you know the difference between Venus and Saturn in the night sky above.

After reading and studying these Mud Daddy chronicles carefully, one should come to understand that it's not the ingredients, nor the measurements, nor the gear, nor the boat that makes a Mud Daddy rewarding – it's the willingness to get out there and do it. To organize a trip, fuss with the details, head to someplace strange, try something unusual, to think through a problem and come out on the other side at the end of your personal Mud Daddy still breathing and with all body parts attached and fully functioning. What the Mud Daddy Chronicles hopes to convey is that life is an adventure, and fishing, food and fun ought to be a big part of it.

The Mud Daddy Chronicles:

Raging Bass, Mystic Muskie and Twinkie Tiramisu

Chapter I - The Curse

The Mud Daddy officially began in September 1982, when the three authors and "Slim" Eckberg's Akron buddy Bob Drews embarked on a three-day canoeing/camping/fishing expedition on the South Fork of the Shenandoah River in Virginia. That first outing gave this annual trip its name and included all the elements that would come to mark a Mud Daddy in the decades to come: adventure, bloodshed, mishaps, near disasters, unexplainable vortextual occurrences, strange wildlife encounters, periods of miserable fishing, periods of excellent fishing, tremendous fun and great food.

Mud Daddy number one began with an all-night drive from Cincinnati to Luray, Virginia. For reasons now unclear, we decided that the best place to leave one of the cars was in the parking lot of an Ohio Highway Patrol branch headquarters in Central Ohio. It never occurred to us that there might be a better place to leave the vehicle, particularly since we were hauling along vast quantities of alcohol, a few already opened and partially consumed. But E-man made an illegal left-hand turn into the headquarters, we dumped the car and continued on our way.

Two hours after daybreak, we stopped at a rural bait shop/convenience store to buy some hellgrammites and "Mad Toms," the minnows Lowery's brother advised were best for catching smallmouth bass on the South Fork of the Shenandoah River. We had never fished Mad Toms before; didn't know a thing about them, in fact, but we were experienced with other species of baitfish and thought nothing of it. We were taken by their name but never wondered how they got it. We ordered a bucket of Mad Toms and some hellgrammites. The guy waiting on us nodded and disappeared into the back. We stood around for what seemed an awful long time pondering the jigs, poppers and crankbaits on the wall. Finally our guy emerged with the weekend's ammo, and we proceeded to the canoe livery.

The Shenandoah is a wild, scenic river that slices through the Blue Ridge Mountains of Virginia about two hours from Washington, D.C. Rolling hills surround scenic valleys of farmland and pasture. The river turned and twined past islands and summer cottages, the water tumbling over rocks and shoals and stretching out smooth and slow across the flats.

After launching the canoes, we found our first challenge was not the fish in the river but the Mad Toms in the bucket.

They were vicious little bastards, essentially miniature catfish, and clearly pissed-off. When we grabbed them, they squirmed like crazy, and their tiny fins jabbed us like little needles. With fingers bloody, red and swollen, we managed to get a few on a hook, and just below the first rapid, Doc and Erardi caught several decent-sized smallmouth bass. "This is going to be great," crowed Big E. He had no idea what lay ahead. The good fishing soon ended, and we realized the Mad Toms were not only painful to rig, but ours were too big for the smallmouth to feed on. The ones we had were huge, some almost six inches long, giving any smallmouth pause.

We wanted the bass to eat them, not battle them.

"What's up with these minnows?" Slim wondered aloud. He had yet to get a bite on one.

"We've been had," laughed Lowery, who Big E had taken to calling Le Docteur. "They saw us coming at the bait shop and sold us the ones that that no one else would buy 'cause they're too big. The guy probably has these critters haunting his bait tank for years. All he needed to see was the Ohio plates and he knew he had some suckers – and not the ones in the fish tank."

"So that's why the bait shop guy took so long," Slim recalled, with some admiration for a fellow scammer.

There was empty talk of retribution on the way back home, but we had to chuckle at our own naiveté – swindled by a backcountry mountain man who knew a thing or two we city boys didn't.

And we still had the hellgrammites to contend with. Hellgrammites are multi-legged little devils with stingers or pinchers near their heads that are down-right nasty. When Drewsie tried to retrieve one from the cup, it clamped to his thumb with some ferocity.

&%$#@&*%#* he yelped, flicking it across the boat and giving the thing its first flying lesson.

"Pick that up, Slim," E barked. "It cost money."

Slim tried. It stuck him, and away the creature went away one more time – lost in the bowels of the boat, only to appear from time to time before scurrying back into its hiding place. Nobody wanted to touch it. We had no gloves. We had no tongs. We didn't really know how to fish them, either. They were as much of a disaster as the Mad Toms.

Still, the river was lovely, the surrounding countryside stunning in the amber of autumn, and wildlife was abundant. Deer emerged from the woods to feed on the distant river bank across the flat water. Cardinals and Blue Jays stitched and swooped through every bend, and V-formations of ducks heading south winged overhead several times. At one point, a heron sailed down the river ahead of us for what seemed like miles, tree to snag to shore. Hawks worked the sky above as leaves rattled in the soft breeze or lifted away from the boughs to fall on the water in a steady drizzle of orange, ochre and tan.

Bleeding from Mad Toms and sore from hellgrammite stings, we gave up on the bait and turned to tackle. All except E-man. From a nearby bridge, he amused himself by casting those poor Mad Toms far out into the river and reeling them back at double-speed. They returned with bellies tragically pink from flopping onto the water – cast after cast after cast. Slim warned E that he was courting Karmic disaster by treating one of God's creatures in so cavalier a fashion. But E kept at it, the bait's name soon morphing from Mad Toms to Bad Toms – as in "Fish me another Bad Tom from that bucket, will you, Slim?"

He thought the fast action would bring a bass.

"Screw you. Here's the bucket. Fish it out yourself."

Then the name went from Bad Tom to Bad Daddy to finally Mud Daddy – as in "I'm gonna catch me a big ole bass with this Mud Daddy and fry up that bad boy for dinner."

Of course, there was no big ole bass. No little ole bass either.

But there was spaghetti.

That evening Lowery made his now legendary Doc's Pasta Luray (recipe to follow), a Mud Daddy staple ever since. We sat around the

The Mud Daddy Chronicles

campfire drinking Akron Sours, (recipe to follow), and laughed at ourselves for being rubes enough to buy the world's largest, meanest baitfish in the first place. But it had been a great day, and dinner was delicious. We tuned in a high school football game on the radio and toasted living life in full. It was the beginning of something that would last longer than many marriages, and carry us from youth into middle age and then into the years of silver hair and aching joints. Young men with dreams would become gray guys battling guts. But we didn't know that then. All we knew was that we were young, on a fishing trip, under a stunning firmament of stars, and we were becoming one with the universe.

The next morning, we took the canoes out again, floating the South Fork, pulling up at riffles to let tiny spinnerbaits drift down with the current and perhaps woo a feisty smallmouth from beneath some underwater root. We landed a few, but "too few to mention," as Old Blue Eyes or Doc would croon it. Later we fished the smaller North Fork of the Shenandoah. Doc waded into a small pool below a long, lazy riffle and parked himself there. He was catching many smallmouth – small ones, but fish all the same – on a tiny gold spinner with a blade the size of a toenail. E cast below him.

When Doc lost his spinner on the rocky bottom, he asked E for a favor.

"E-Man, hand me that tackle box on shore, would you? I got a small spinner in there that ought to work like crazy here."

"No problem, Le Docteur."

E turned and began to wade out across the pool toward shore. Then, bloop, he was gone. Down he went, under water, only his gimme cap visible. A strange cap, too, something from a bluefish saltwater fishing competition that had no bearing to any event in E-Man's life, though wore it with pride and aplomb. He'd stepped from a shelf into a drop-off. Almost as fast as E disappeared, he resurfaced, soaking wet and now with a deep gash in his shin and more pain than he wanted to admit.

"Damn, E, that was cool. You OK?"

"Went down hard on my shin, but I think it's good."

Hobbling back to shore, E checked out his bloody wound and then returned to the water to fish. Doc and E both worked the pool until the water reached to their chest. E would cast, hobble a little farther and cast again. This went on until the autumn sun fell below the trees and hunger could no longer be ignored.

"Let's check out," Doc said, looking at Slim, who was wearing a pair of nice flyweight waders, a birthday present, and fishing a fly in a pool below them.

"Yeah, but I got a problem," Slim replied with nervous laughter, his brow now creased.

"Heh, heh, I got in too deep," he continued. "My waders are filling with water. If I stumble and go down, boys, I gotta tell you right now that I could drown."

He was talking loudly now so his pals could hear him above the ripples of the river. His voice carried more than a hint of worry.

Doc watched Slim, now bouncing on his tiptoes, bump toward shore a few times as he began to drift downstream. It wasn't working. The water was moving fast, and the current splashed into the waders, making a bad situation much worse. There was nothing Doc could do but watch. Slim was too far away now for him to do anything about it. Slim was bouncing for his life, and would soon be gone – either safely ashore or underwater in the heart of the river, drifting away like a discarded four-ply tire, bound for Maryland and the other side of the rainbow.

"Yep, that seems to be the situation," Doc shouted back, amazed at this life-and-death pageant now unfolding before his eyes. Slim kept trying to hop toward shore. He liked life. He didn't want to drown on some stupid fishing trip. He debated whether to drop his expensive gear (a $30 rod and reel combo is expensive by Slim's standards) and try to peel off the waders. But how, exactly, does one do that in chest deep water? Dive under and peel them off? Or would that be the wrong thing to do, a final, fatal mistake? So Slim continued to moon walk and hop, finding that he could make headway by cutting on a diagonal toward shore. He hit solid ground. Stumbling out, he looked like a float in a Macy's parade, brown waders ballooning with water and his face above it all, now white with fear after his bunny-hop dance with death. Doc stared at Slim in amazement until they both broke out in relieved laughter.

"That could have messed up your whole day," Doc told Slim.

Meanwhile, E-Dog was in excruciating pain. Rock and debris, tiny pebbles, bits of leaves and God-knows-what-all-else were embedded deep in his shin bone, and the exposure to the river water bacteria couldn't be a good thing. And we still had to get back to the campsite. Instead, we made the call to stay in a motel. This might be surprising to some, but it is totally within the bounds of Mud Daddy protocol even if we planned to camp because accommodations like a TV, a bed and a shower have great value to us.

"We ought to stitch that up," Slim offered en route. "I can do it with a No. 10 hook and some 4-pound test." E laughed weakly through his pain.

"Don't think so, Slim. Thanks for the offer though."

E eventually agreed to go to the emergency room in Luray, but only if they could pick up a pizza on the way back to the motel. Drewsie drove to the pizza shop with Doc along for company while Slim remained with E at a Doc-in-a-Box emergency room. When the patch-up job was done, we returned to the motel, pizza in hand. Drewsie and Doc talked about seeing a group of midget cheerleaders in the pizza joint.

"Man," Slim said. "I would have loved to see a bunch of midget cheerleaders in a pizza shop in Luray, Virginia. That doesn't happen every day."

"We're not talking about dwarfs, you moron," Doc explained.

"What do you mean?"

"You know, pee wee football cheerleaders. Kids, you idiot."

"Oh," Slim replied, now doubly disappointed.

We headed out Sunday morning, driving up and over the Blue Ridge, bound for the Ohio River and home. A driving thunderstorm struck as Doc maneuvered the rental car up the twisting, two-lane mountain road. Doc accelerated – slightly, he swears – on a hairpin curve, and the big Ford went into a full 360-degree spin. It was out of control, and all Doc could do was hang on to the steering wheel as the car lurched and twirled across the pavement. It finally came to a halt, facing the leering precipice. No guardrail, only trees and rhododendron bushes and oblivion below.

We stared at the sharp slope and the hundreds of feet of steep mountainside. It looked pretty – and deadly. No one spoke. No one breathed. No one had a thought that wasn't a silent prayer.

Doc blinked hard and took stock. He'd never go to another strip club.

Slim silently swore to give up beer.

E promised to go to Mass weekly for the rest of his days.

The back wheels were still on the highway, the engine was still running, the car was still in drive. Without saying a word, Doc gently shifted into reverse, accelerated slightly and eased his left foot off the brake. The car backed off the precipice, and Doc slowly swung it around back into his lane. He dropped into drive and moved up the mountain again. The danger passed, Doc was greeted with a torrent of abuse.

"You could have killed us!"

"What the hell were you doing?"

"Can't you drive in the rain, you damned idiot!"

This wasn't good-natured joshing, either. It was hard-core abuse, driven by intense fear. Doc took it like a man. When the insult tsunami subsided, he looked around, smiled and said, "That was a helluva driving job wasn't it? I saved all your sorry asses. Damn, I'm good!"

"I could use a beer."

"Wonder if there are any places that serve and have performance dance nearby."

"Mass can wait till next week."

Back in Cincinnati, we looked at E-Man's wound again. His leg was swollen and inflamed and causing him some serious anguish. The next day, he couldn't put any weight on it, and the stitched area was full of puss. Off to another emergency room. At the hospital, they found the shinbone had tiny chunks of limestone debris ground into it that the doc-in-a-box had missed. Later, Doc wanted to know if E had kept some as a memento. He had – a tiny piece of slate long since lost, however. E took three days off from work, walked with a cane for two weeks (he performed a "Cane Dance" center stage at his sister-in-law's wedding) and somehow remained vertical for his 30th birthday, insisting he mustn't concede to defeat.

E-man made a resolution on that trip. He would never again fish with a Mad Tom, much less cast one until its belly was pink. Slim made a vow, as well. He would never again wade with tennis shoes over the stocking-foot waders, opting instead to glue a rubber-backed bathroom rug to the soles, thereby creating a pair of poor man's wading shoes.

The biggest lesson of this first Mud Daddy trip was also established: What goes around comes around. Don't abuse little animals even if they are just bait for dinner because payback is hell, and there ain't no getting out of the way.

The Akron Sour

The Akron Sour is an official cocktail of the Mud Daddy. It is vigorous yet simple, a tasty treat after a hard day of fishing. It works well as a pre-meal cocktail, an after-dinner drink or a morning wake-me-up. Created by Slim Eckberg in 1982, the Akron Sour came to be out of necessity and has been with us ever since. Using field expediency, Slim wanted a fishing trip eye-opener, but it has served us when the beer went missing, when the weather was too miserable to stand, when the fishing was atrocious. The legendary Akron Sour, truly a Mud Daddy original.

1 jigger tequila (or Maker's Mark if tequila has been exhausted)

2 jiggers orange juice (or Gatorade if that's what you have left. Mountain Dew works, too)

1 lime (or substitute equal amount of Mountain Dew)

Squeeze the lime into the orange juice and tequila before dropping it into the glass. Serve before sunset and again after.

Pasta Luray for Four

Doc's pasta recipe was an early Mud Daddy staple that we've resorted to on numerous occasions for a solid, hearty meal. There are many variations on this theme. (Big E's Neapolitan variation appears later). The following recipe is the one Doc says is the foundation of his iconic pasta dish.

> 1 lb. ground beef
> 1/2lb. Italian sausage (or chopped up pepperoni stick in a pinch)
> 1 onion
> 1 green pepper
> 6 garlic cloves
> 3 bay leaves
> 1 tsp. oregano
> 1 tsp. thyme
> salt, pepper
> pinch of sugar
> 1 large can stewed tomatoes
> 1 large can tomato sauce (or a jar of prepared spaghetti sauce if you're lazy or unprepared)

Brown the ground beef and sausage together. Drain grease. Chop onion, pepper, garlic as fine as possible. Add to the simmering meat and mix. Sprinkle a pinch of sugar. Add salt and pepper to taste. Place tomatoes and sauce in a pot, add meat and bay leaves and other spices. Simmer 1 hour, stir occasionally. Serve over thin spaghetti. Slosh some Italian red wine into a cup. Drink it. Pour yourself some more. Drink that, too. Eat while sitting around a campfire as the autumn leaves rustle in the night. And thank the Almighty God that you're there and not in your office in front of a computer. Not talking on the phone with an impatient customer or client. Not mowing a lawn on a sweltering afternoon. Not listening to a neighbor's dog bark to greet the dawn. Not anywhere else but in the here and now with a plate of spaghetti on the table in front of you and an ice cold beer nearby to wash it all down.

Chapter II - The Tradition

Sometimes things just go right. They fall together in an almost perfect way, what psychologist Abraham Maslow calls a "peak experience." They're those special moments and situations that will never be forgotten, moments fraught with emotion and meaning, moments that can seem vital to our existence because, well, because they are. In 1983, we decided to get serious about making a fall fishing trip an annual outing. We coined it the Mud Daddy in deference to Big E's malapropism the year before, when he called our "Mad Tom" baitfish Mud Daddies.

"Well, if these trips aren't Mud Daddies, then what the hell are they?"

We agreed.

Slim found Laurel River Lake in deepest Kentucky on an AAA map. Big-E was on board all the way, and Doc recruited his best friend from his earliest newspapering days in Richmond, Va., Bob Rankin, aka The Bull. After spending a year writing the Great Unpublished American Novel ("Hammers and Anvils"), Rankin had signed on as an editorial writer at the Miami Herald. Doc was a newlywed, and he and Rankin caught up on old times at Arnold's Bar and Saloon in Over-the-Rhine in Cincinnati, the oldest continuously operating bar and grill in this fine American city. Later, everyone met at Bogart's, a former movie theater converted into a concert hall in a neighborhood near the University of Cincinnati, to hear Third World's soulful reggae. After closing the place down and packing up a ton of gear in Slim's Toyota Tercel Moonbuggy – an early kind of SUV – we left about 5 a.m.

"This thing looks like it's doomed to tip over," Rankin observed from the back seat. "Are we safe?"

"Of course not," Doc answered. "Did you come all this way to be safe? It's out of your hands, my friend. And besides, we have this little gauge here to let us know if we tip."

Slim gestured at the inane meter on the dashboard, a gyroscope that had a picture of a little car on it that tilted to and fro with a jolly little motion.

"When you roll over, what do you need a gauge for? To tell you that you're upside down? You already know that," Bull said.

"Yep," Slim wryly replied. "Sweet, isn't it?"

On the trip down, with UB 40 on the tape player, the conversation never lagged. To an outsider it would have sounded like four guys with attention deficit disorder just released from a Trappist monastery. There was so much to express, to discuss, to analyze, to be amazed by.

"Where we going?" Bull asked, finally.

"Uhm, not real sure," Doc replied. "Where are we going?"

"I think it's called Laurel River Lake but don't know exactly where we're camping, probably a campground near the lake," Slim announced. Eyes rolled. Slim had been in charge of finding a place to hunker down, and with his pronouncement "I don't know exactly" that told everybody else in the car everything they needed to know: accommodations were doomed.

We drove through the morning and got to the lake before lunchtime.

"Hey, Bull, what you think about Doc getting married?"

"Bout damn time somebody tied his ass down. He needs to be saddled with responsibilities like the rest of us. Who you like in the Series, E-Man? I'm saying the O's."

"Most definitely the O's. Too much pitching for Philly. Whatcha been listening to down there in Miami?"

"John Mellencamp is what I'm saying," Slim interjected before Bull could answer. "Cornfield soul. Can't beat it. The guy just rocks."

So it went, back and forth, rocketing from wives and kids to music and sports to what lures were fascinating to us at the time. At the marina on Laurel River Lake, Slim went into a rap that either amused, baffled or infuriated, depending on the attitude of the person on the other end. In this case, the marina manager already had had a dose of the Slimbagger by phone, so he was ready.

"So, what are they hitting on?" Slim inquired. No answer. That only slowed Slim down some because he sure wasn't finished. Long pause – 20 seconds of silence.

"Are they holding off the points?"

Nothing. So, Slim gave it just a tiny pause this time before launching into the next question.

"Near the stumps back up inlets? Or out on the breaks, those underwater humps?"

The manager laughed, shook his head and handed out the paperwork for renting two john boats, Kentucky fishing licenses and a camping permit. Slim got nothing.

When the paperwork was completed, we loaded about 500 pounds of gear, food and libations into the boats and motored away. Laurel River Lake had a few islands outfitted for camping, with tent sites, picnic tables and fire rings. Already impatient from the paperwork, we beached the boats at the first island campsite we found and unloaded everything. It was a nice spot under tall maple and pine trees with a 180-degree view of the sparkling water.

We filled a cooler with beer, a flask with bourbon and carried our tackle down to the boats. Setting up camp would come later. Doc was practiced with the six-man tent and could throw it up by himself. Slim would handle the food while Bull and Big E scoured for downed tree limbs and built a fire. All that could wait. Now it was time to hit the water.

Unlike many Mud Daddies to follow, the '83 expedition started out with excellent fishing. Within the first hour, Slim landed a nice largemouth bass on a silver Rapala. Doc followed up with a largemouth of his own, smaller, but still respectable, and on a glitter-smoke grub.

Laurel was a calm, deep blue on the main channel. The inlet we were fishing was shallower, shading toward green and surrounded by pines and hardwoods in daring fall colors. The scene was so soothing, so perfect an autumn day that no one wanted to say anything for fear of spoiling it. That's how men know they are enjoying the company of good friends. They don't feel the urge to fill the silence with gab. Long silences don't feel awkward. Good friends can be lost in their own thoughts, and it's okay. When silence is good, you're among friends.

Doc soon took care of that.

Aiming his crankbait shoreward, Doc neglected to consider his back-cast. It is but one of his several character flaws, and a particularly dangerous one for those in a boat with him. A flying treble hook caught Rankin's "Junkyard Dog" gimme cap he'd purchased at a truck stop on the trip down, and it plopped into the lake with Doc's bait.

"Damn," Rankin protested. "That's not funny. Why don't you watch what the hell you're doing!"

"You could put somebody's eye out like that," Slim mockingly reminded Doc, invoking the admonition from his fifth grade teacher Mrs. Stevic, when she caught Slim shooting paper-wads at fellow students. (Later, down at the principal's office with his partner-in-crime, Drewsie, they heard the same put-an-eye-out recrimination from the principal, Mr. Hauenstein, to which Drewsie replied with a robust, "So!" Slim cringed and knew they were both screwed with that wisecrack. It earned them a 30-day sentence of no recess. And for that period of time, no one in the class was permitted to talk to either Drewsie or Slim, an order that lasted about a day because even then Slim was simply too ebullient for his 10-year-old classmates to ignore.)

"Somebody's going to get hurt around here," Slim warned. "If it IS a Mud Daddy, there will be bloodshed."

"Nice hat grab, though," E offered. "You don't see that move that often. Very nice, Doc."

"It's not funny," yelped Rankin again, thereafter known as "The Raging Bull" for his feisty demeanor. Or the "Junkyard Dog," in honor of his reaction to the errant back cast, a nickname soon shortened to just Bull or Dog. The fishing was good enough that Slim had some fish to dress. The killing task usually falls upon Slim, who has his ritual. He looks the fish in the eye – Is that terror there? Anger? Resolution? – thanks the fish for giving up his life, whispers to himself the Lord's Prayer or perhaps the 23rd Psalm, then makes a swift cut through the spine below the head at the word Amen. Some cuts are swifter than others. The fish thumps in your hand at the end.

Mud Daddy recipes are generally not for great cooks, as they would likely be appalled, but are for men who appreciate the simple truth that preparing a meal in the wild is usually done on the fly. Our efforts at cooking in the great American outdoors proved that no matter the meal, a river or lake makes a wonderful and timeless backdrop and that flexibility in epicurean style will always require creativity and more than a bit of whimsy. This night would be no different and offer the first of many more culinary improvisations to come.

Where's the oil? We had none. Someone – most likely Slim – had forgotten it.

So that night Slim cooked some bass fillets in an unusual way. He poached them in lemon, Chardonnay and parsley, a succulent repast, accompanied by more white wine followed by Akron Sours or whiskey neat sipped around a roaring campfire as the World Series game was tuned in on a Realistic transistor radio. Who needs oil anyhow?

A philosopher once asked, "How many moonbeams are in a locomotive engine?" There was a similar feeling of wonder by our wilderness campfire, the countless stars above, the cigar smoke curling through the pine boughs and on the radio the 1-95 Series between the Orioles and Phillies. Beamed to us high on a Kentucky hilltop, it felt as if the outside world didn't exist, and that somewhere grown men were playing a boys' game and the count was 3-2 with a guy at second and it was all just for us.

As the evening wore on, the temperature dropped. We saw our breath in the firelight. We shuffled around the fire to stay warm as we listened to the game. We took a picture. It was magical because sports are integral to the Mud Daddy and somehow, hearing that '83 game on the radio, surrounded by deep woods and good friends, was more involving, more special, than watching it on television ever could be. We hung on every pitch that night, offering our own versions of what was, or should be, happening. Bull was an O's fan of longstanding – he owned a foul ball he caught off Ken Singleton's bat at a game that he and Doc had attended a few years earlier. Big E is a sports writer of no small fame. He played college baseball, has a brother who pitched for the Seattle Mariners organization and knows the game like only an expert can. Their color commentary was easily as entertaining as what came from the sportscasters on the radio.

Fishing the next morning was eminently forgettable. Little if anything was landed, and a lovely fall day was spoiled by long hours of fruitless casting, working the points, trying the drop-offs, throwing to the shallows, unsnagging snags. Any day fishing beats any day working, they say, and it's true. But fishing hard in the hot sun with nothing to show for it carries its own kind of frustration, a frustration born of the ever-present realization that time is slipping away. Our fishing minutes on these trips are limited, so every moment counts, the present minute more important than the previous one and the future minute more important than all the others combined because time is dwindling with each cast. When those minutes are filled with empty motion, desperation soon sets in.

As our questions were posed and observations debated, a Darwinian pageant played out in the murky waters below. Stupid fish get caught; really stupid fish get caught by us. What's going on in those tiny fish brains must be a welter of conflicting signals: instinctive fear, intense predation and frantic efforts to mate. Much like life above the water line, we agreed.

There was nothing to be done but return to camp, eat, drink and tune in the next World Series game on the radio. But the sunset proved too spectacular to ignore squatting deep and red on the lake and turning the water into an Old Master's painting. We took both boats a short distance off shore, casting into the shadow line where the sunset on the water faded to the gloaming of the nightfall still to come. No one expected much. We were there for the aesthetics more than the fishing. But a strange thing happened. We started hooking fish. One after another after another.

"Is this a crappie?" Slim asked, holding up a black and white fish wider than his hand.

Doc said he thought so. Then he got one, too. Then we all did. As darkness descended and the lake went black, the four of us pulled in too many crappie to count. As it is with fish, the run ended as suddenly as it began. The fishing died, and the lake went black. Since we'd already eaten, we released all we caught. We returned to the camp for food, wine, Akron Sours, cigars and the next Series game.

"That was strange," Doc said. None of us had ever experienced a crappie run like that before.

"We should remember this place," Slim said.

But we didn't. We never found that island again, though we returned to Laurel River Lake several times, and we never were in the middle of a crappiefest again anywhere. It was one of those perfect and perfectly strange moments, one of Maslow's peak experiences.

Big E slept outside that night. No tent for him. Maybe it was the snoring of men too much under the influence of drink. We like to think that he simply didn't want to end the day enshrouded in plastic, that he wanted to live in the moment of a glorious outdoor adventure even while sleeping in the bone-chilling cold, frost gathering on the leaves all around him. Perhaps he needed to drink in more of nature – to have a spider drop from a tree at 4 a.m., crawl across his face and sip from the corner of an eye as he slept. Or maybe some timeless current called to him from deep in the Milky Way, a primeval pull of billions of stars in the amazing night sky, a tug that Big E was powerless to resist.

Most likely it was the excessive flatulence inside the tent.

Bull was up early the next morning and stumbled down to the lake for a few last casts. He woke the rest of us up with a whoop. Standing on the shore with rod held high and bent nearly double, he fought and eventually landed the biggest bass of the weekend, a nice largemouth that went close to three pounds. Throughout the weekend Bull had had the worst luck of any of us, but he didn't quit and plain dumb luck gave him the nicest bass of the Mud Daddy. Good for him. There is a lesson in there. Maybe several. The first lesson is this – that's a Mud Daddy for you. Another might be that no matter how errantly a Mud Daddy begins, by the time it's over, it's all good.

Laurel River Lake Poached Fish

Here is one of Slim's "go-to" recipes for cooking bass (or crappie or bluegill, for that matter) in the wilderness. It's simple and, like most of our recipes, it's not the ingredients that go into it that matters so much as the setting and the heart.

Fish filets (bluegill or bass)

A giant handful or two of dill or parsley

Two or three sliced lemons

About a cup of Chardonnay or dry white wine

Water – about half cup

Salt and pepper to taste

In a large frying pan make a bed of the sliced lemons and the herbs, wine and water. The fluids should just crest the level of lemons and herbs. Bring it to a low simmer, then lay the salted and peppered filets onto the lemon bed. Cover with lid or foil. Simmer three to six minutes, only until the fish flesh flakes. Eat on crackers for an appetizer or as a main course if you have enough fish. Perfect approach for small fish. No muss. No fuss.

Things You'll Never Hear on a Mud Daddy

- Haven't you had enough of that?
- You're not going to leave the dishes like that are you?
- You're not going to try to do that while driving are you?
- You're not going to leave the place looking like this are you?
- You're not going to wear THAT are you?
- You're not going to wear that with THOSE are you?
- Do you really think that shirt matches your pants?
- I'm not going anywhere with you dressed like that …
- How do I look?
- Does my hair look okay?
- Doesn't this look cute?
- Does this match my outfit?
- Are you sure about those shoes?
- Why would you think that cream of mushroom soup mixed with hamburger over noodles is a great entre?
- Don't eat stuff that has been dropped on the floor.
- You're not going to eat THAT are you?
- Haven't you had enough (cigars, beer, whisky, food, etc.) for one day?
- Don't you think that three pieces of cake is excessive?
- You're not going to try THAT in here are you?
- What do you mean the floor doesn't look dirty?
- Why don't you dry the dishes instead of letting them air dry?
- Haven't you watched enough (football, baseball, hockey, cheerleading) today?
- Do you HAVE to swear like that?
- You're not going to try to GRILL the bacon are you?
- You're not putting the (worms, shiners, minnows, hellgrammites, mad toms, etc) in the cooler with the food are you?

Chapter III - The Brookville Skunking

After the second Mud Daddy in 1983, it became clear that some of us would have to go to extraordinary lengths to go fishing because of distance and family commitments. Children were infants or toddlers. It looked like the burden of making a Mud Daddy work would fall to Doc. Did that mean these trips meant more to him than to the others? Perhaps. Who knows? The reason that the heavy lifting fell upon Doc was simple enough: E and Slim chose to stick to writing and reporting in Cincinnati, while Doc thought his career should take a different direction.

Slim was working his way toward being a columnist, and Cincinnati was the best place to make that happen. Big E was angling to be a sports writer, and Cincinnati was the perfect fit for him. He could cover the Reds, the Bengals, U.C. football and basketball and a big-time golf tournament or two. But Doc was destined for management. He was always complaining about editors and bosses, so it was natural that he decided to stop bitching and do something about it. In a roomful of editors, he would look around and think, "I don't see how I can do any worse." So he became an editor. At the Enquirer, he became an assistant city editor after only six months as a general assignment reporter. A year after that he was promoted to deputy city editor, managing the city reporting crew, including Slim and Big E. Rather than chafing at Doc's rise, and his at least titular authority over them, they sought him out for assignments and editing. If anything, their relationship with Doc grew stronger. But Doc wanted a bigger venue than the one Cincy could provide. And bigger venues were courting him. He would be limited at the Enquirer but not elsewhere. That meant moving on to become an editor in far-flung Seattle, then Atlanta and later to an even more responsible role as managing editor in Austin, making critical news decisions for the next day's Austin American-Statesman: a forgettable house fire that was probably an arson; a car wreck that led to the death of a drunken husband; a city council committee meeting on neighborhood revitalization; or a county commission initiative to reduce spending on health care. In other words, determining which story was less dull than the others for the morning newspaper became Doc's mission in life.

So Doc would separate the wheat from the chaff in Atlanta, Seattle and finally Austin, while Slim and E-Dog labored in the trenches of the first amendment, actually researching and writing dull stories that marked the state of journalism in our time. Doc's new role as editor would take him far away from conservative Cincinnati, where Republicans outnumber Democrats by about four-to-one, while E and Slim, both avowed liberal/progressives, would wallow in the misery of conservative politics and lifestyles on the banks of the Ohio.

Doc's career moves meant that he would be the one who would have to travel more than the others if he were going to make a fishing trip each year. So as sure as a dog barks at another dog, that's what he did. The travel would take planning, whining, saving and a little luck. But it usually worked out, though a couple of the early Mud Daddies were far more improvised than the control-issue manager in Doc would have preferred. The first improvised trip came in 1984, when Doc returned to Cincinnati with his wife and newborn son, Jason. Doc slipped away with Slim and Big E for a one-day fishing excursion trip to Brookville Lake in Southern Indiana, about an hour and a half west of Cincinnati.

The autumn day dawned cold and gray as we poured ourselves into the car. It began to rain on the drive west, and we knew it probably meant a wet and uncomfortable outing in the boat. But, we were young men at the time, in our 20s and 30s, and able to persevere, and besides, we were doing something that few of our urban contemporaries in Cincinnati even attempted anymore – we were going fishing! At the time there was still a bit of romance and adventure in that gesture.

Great American writers fished: Hemingway, McGuane, Harrison, Washington Irving, Melville and Thoreau, among others. As writers and fishermen we would walk in their footsteps – chase the same fish they chased, tell versions of the same stories they told, hear the call of a pack of hounds in the distant hills, wonderful music that they surely heard as well. Ours was a noble and rewarding quest, and if the fishing was lousy, there was always the company of friends.

The Indiana water was big – huge, in fact – and we knew nothing about the lake, now swept by a chilling early autumn wind. We had no trolling motor, no fish finder, no life preservers beyond meager seat cushions, and no anchor. But we had an overwhelming desire to enjoy what time on the water we could manage and under whatever conditions nature threw at us. That is, as long as there were no white-caps, the foamy chops that sometimes pre-tell the disastrous and frightening three-footers to come.

As the boat churned to a far-flung bay that we reasoned simply had to hold fish, we confronted that timeless angling question: what lure to use? Each of us had our "go-to" bait. But under adverse conditions, what lure would be the first out of the tackle box? This is never an easy decision. If you go to your "go-to" lure too early, then what do you go to after your "go-to" has gone – lost to a submerged tree limb or rock – or was unproductive? After all, how many times can you cast the same lure, feeling no tug of a hooked bass or tentative bump of bluegill, before it's time to move on to another? How many minutes – even hours – must pass before the "go to" goes back into the tackle box?

Slim tied on a lure he had long ago dubbed The Producer, a five-inch gold Rapala with three treble hooks and a nice lollygagging roll in the water. Its hand-carved cousin caught fish for old men in Sweden and Finland eons ago, and it caught fish for Slim's father, Stanley, in Michigan, Canada, Minnesota and any place else he fished. It caught fish for Slim in Canada. It caught fish for Slim in Ohio. It caught something on virtually every lake that Slim had ever fished, and that's why it was his "go-to" lure. It would surely catch fish here. Slim sometimes fell asleep at night thinking of that lure and its wobbly return through the water.

E-Man went with his favorite crankbait, an orange Rattle-trap, a sharp, thick slab of plastic with a noisy BB inside that had a swift little shake and ran deep, enticing strikes because the damn thing just looked scared, like a piscine Barney Fife on steroids. E-Man had caught fish with it all over Northeast America, but mostly in those natural lakes of upstate New York. He didn't care if a stub of monofilament crested from his knot, either, as the stub might bring action that in turn would bring fish. Who could say?

Doc tied on one of his favorites, a glitter-smoked grub. It had a lead-head jig, and the tail looked particularly inviting, scooting through the water just like a shad or other small baitfish, the tail wiggling and flipping in the wake. He let it drift on the cast – a countdown to get it as deep as he could. And he would be the first to send a cast arching toward shore as we chugged from spot to spot.

Soon, each of us would be tying on another lure, then another and yet another as the morning faded into afternoon. Because we were not catching fish, we told stories from our lives.

Doc told of his grandfather, R. Stebbins Lowery, who was a fox hunter. Not like the red-coats-and-horses fox hunters seen in paintings or British movies, but a back country fox hunter. He raised long-legged fox hounds with names like Chopper and Blue and Digger, and he cared for those dogs like they were his children. He and his buddies would meet after sundown at someone's house, often Doc's grandad's because it was near the Bannister River. They'd bring their dogs in home-built cages that rested in the pickup truck bed, take them down to the river and turn them loose. Then the men would stand around listening to the hounds bay and yip. Sometimes they'd build a fire if it sounded like the dogs were onto something good. They could identify their dogs by their baying, and they could tell what was happening in the deep woods by the sounds they made.

"Sounds like ol' Blue is onto something," one would say.

"Nah. He's running a deer I bet. Dang it."

"Listen, I believe Chopper has run one to ground."

"Sounds like he treed a coon to me."

He never saw them shoot a fox, or even shoot at one. They just liked to get out of the house, get in the company of other men and listen to their dogs. Once in a while the dogs would bark in such a way that the men knew they had run a fox to ground. If it happened only a hilltop away, they might try to smoke him out. That took some work, because the fox would come up in a foul mood. Once cornered, a fox is a ferocious little beast and it was always exciting to see a caged fox spit and snarl and growl.

When it got late or the dogs weren't scaring up anything or had run too far to be heard, everyone went home. The dogs would come straggling back the next day or the next week. Stebbins lost a few to the highway traffic, too. And now and then a fox would tear one of the dogs up pretty bad. There were many lessons in the way those country men hunted fox, Doc finally declared.

It said a lot about the love of the outdoors, the immutable nature of the dog and the fox, and the camaraderie of men. One lesson he never forgot. When one of Stebbins' dogs came home torn up, the old man looked at his grandson and told him what had happened.

When the fox is exhausted and can't find a hole – when it knows there is absolutely no escape – it will turn on the dogs. It's in its nature, Stebbins said. A desperate, doomed fox goes down fighting.

"I think there's a lesson in that," Doc concluded.

The day was dying and the fishing never improved. Then the waves kicked up into white caps, and with them came the inevitable moment of doubt.

"I don't care how big this lake is. There's no fish in it," Slim announced. Of course there were fish below, but it was the pronouncement that he and his brother, Dale, had first made long ago after horrible afternoons of no-fish ennui on family vacations.

"You might be right," E-Man replied. "Or maybe you just haven't put us on 'em yet, Slim."

"Me? Why am I always the captain anyhow? Here's what I mean. I cruise this johnboat and get us tight to the shore and you guys each get three casts in before I can cut the motor, find my rod and get one cast in. It ain't right," Slim complained.

"Yeah, yeah. Can you get us over to that stick-up?" Doc asked.

After another hour of fruitless casting, Doc finally uttered the question that had been on everybody's mind most of the morning:

"Would a football game with a cold beer and hot hamburger in some Indiana bar and grill be a better way to pass the time?"

Even though we hadn't hit the water until almost 9 a.m. and were off the lake by 3 p.m., registering the first of what would be many more skunkings to come, we knew that with this trip to Brookville, the foundations of a tradition were intact. Fish? Maybe. Fun? Definitely. Could we keep these trips going, given the restraints of time, money and distance? Hell yes, we would.

After only three such tours, already a beguiling pattern was in place: a drive to a strange lake, sit in a boat with a beer or two or three and chatter like jays. Sprinkle whiskey and laughter over the entire weekend. We didn't know much about the particular lakes or the fishing, but we did know this: there are worse ways to spend a day. We had come to appreciate every last little thing about the Mud Daddy. Bad weather couldn't drown our enthusiasm, bad boats inspired us to improvise and bad fishing gave us a shared experience and galvanized our resolve.

When we left Brookville, we weren't sure how often we would be able to fish together in the years ahead. There were a lot of miles between Seattle and Cincinnati and Miami. But we knew in our hearts that fishing together made life richer, so we would keep trying to make it work. However much trouble we had to go to for a long weekend together, it would be worth it. And by now, on this choppy lake in Indiana, we understood that in our souls.

Slap-Your-Daddy Fried Fish

This simple recipe for fried fish works well anytime and anywhere. It is especially good on camping trips because the ingredients – except for the fish, of course – can be prepared ahead of time. Just about any fish can be prepared this way – bass, crappie, bluegill, catfish. Try it; you won't be disappointed. Make up a bag of seasoned flour before heading into the wilderness of Kentucky or wherever your wandering leads you (amounts are estimates, use your judgment, assuming you have judgment): ½ cup all-purpose flour, ½ cup cornmeal, 1 teaspoon salt, ½ teaspoon pepper, ½ teaspoon paprika, ¼ teaspoon onion powder, ¼ teaspoon garlic powder.

Roll the filets in milk until they're soaked, then put them in this seasoned flour until evenly coated (or what would pass for evenly coated on a fishing trip). Pour two tablespoons or maybe a little more of corn oil (packed in a small plastic bottle that hasn't yet leaked, assuming you are at a distant campground; just buy a small bottle otherwise) into the skillet, (assuming you have not forgotten to bring a skillet). After the oil is hot, place the fish in the pan and cook until flaky, usually no more than two or three minutes a side. Serve with a crisp white wine. Mutter something about fruit of the gods and eat with your fingers.

Chapter IV - Blueberry Hill

By 1984 we knew that something of a half-assed tradition was underway, an annual fishing trip with a couple of hand-picked friends. To keep our wives and domestic duties at bay for at least one weekend a year (and to escape the grind of daily journalism), Slim, E-Man and Drewsie picked the New York/Pennsylvania line and historic Chautauqua Lake for a Mud Daddy in 1985. Though this jaunt, sans Mud Daddy founder Doc, who was a continent away in Seattle, would include more golf than fish, we decided that at least one day had to be spent in a boat, bouncing on the waves of what we would soon realize was a lake improbably and impossibly clogged with weeds. Still, we figured we could fish and ponder the same social conundrums that once upon a time brought America's intelligentsia to salons in this quaint town of lakefront cottages: We would consider the meaning of grace, whether the collective will of a people offer a transcendental means to an end and whether all baseball games are lost because of coaching, not lack of hitting or excellent pitching.

We played a round of golf, while awaiting Drewsie's and Slim's high school pal, Keith Carmany, who drove down from the north woods of New York. Keith had graduated from the same suburban Akron high school as Drewsie and Slim – and had been a roommate of Slim's at Ohio University, where the partying will usually wipe out one-quarter of the freshman class. Keith and Slim, however, both survived.

Then Keith relocated to become something of a hermit in upstate New York. He needed a fishing trip and needed one badly. We rented a condominium on the Blueberry Hill golf course and were mid-round when Carmany appeared. He had commandeered a golf cart and worked his way through the course to the top of a hill on a par 5 where Slim sat to spot Drewsie's drive. Pulling from a bottle of Ezra Brooks and puffing on his pipe, Carmany watched a trio of deer emerge from a nearby glen when Drewsie crushed an uphill drive. "Watch out!" Slim yelled as the ball screamed up the fairway. Carmany, with golf absent from every gene, had no clue what Slim was yelling about, had not seen Drewsie swing and the sound of his tee-shot had not yet found us. From 240 yards away, an incredible drive by Drewsie standards, the ball bounced once and then slammed into Carmany's noggin' – with a sound like two blocks of wood clapped together. Carmany pitched forward and dropped from the cart. When his eyes opened, he was staring at the slate-gray sky.

"Hey man, you all right?"

"I … I don't know."

"Well, welcome to the Mud Daddy."

Onward we trolled through the weekend, renting two boats for the four of us and heading for the middle of Chautauqua, as most of the fingers were clogged with weeds. We caught a few little fish but nothing to fill a frying pan. Where were the fish of our fathers? And why was this lake so full of weeds? It should have been great fishing but throughout the morning we found it was anything but. All around the lake were houses, a small town nearby. We were not biologists but nobody needed a doctorate to know that decades of fertilizer and pesticides on lawns had clobbered the food chain as nitrate and phosphate run-off from the lawns flowed into the lake and encouraged weed growth. The pesticides, we knew, did a great job of killing grubs and larvae, but that also meant fewer insects and fewer insects eventually meant less food for the fish. Fish counts were falling at an alarming rate most everywhere in New York thanks to acid rain from the Midwest. Where were the fish of our fathers? They were dying.

With the fishing all-but-dead, E Man told of a New York fishing trip and of how the fishing used to be in these parts.

Most fish stories are by definition tall tales. But some, even those with some NBA height, simply had to be true. E Man's dad back in the 1950s left Henderson Harbor on Lake Ontario, with some buddies from his bowling team. E's dad was high man in the loop, a 191 average, back when that meant something and they decided to use their pot money from missed spares and strikes to hire a guide with a boat. They were on the water by 10 a.m., limited out with 24 smallmouth by 11:30 a.m. and in the bar drinking Manhattans by noon.

The guide told them he would clean the fish and be back soon because he "just knew" they'd want to go back out. What he didn't know – because he'd spent way more time on the water than in the alleys – was that It's harder to pry a kegler away from a Manhattan than it is a crawfish from a hungry smallmouth. Eventually, the guide did coax them back out – probably with a bottle of Seven Crown, some sweet vermouth and lots of maraschino cherries.

Wouldn't you know – same honey hole, same results. Only this time they were catching them even faster. They were catching them so fast they were chucking the smaller ones from the live well back into the lake to make room for the bigger ones. Another hour-and-a-half, 24 more bronzebacks, nothing smaller than a pound, pound-and-a-half, some pushing past two. When it comes to smallmouth, especially in northern waters early in the year, those are lunkers. Nobody knows how many more Manhattans those guys drank when they got back to the bar, or who was the designated driver, but there was at least some accounting.

When they arrived back home in Syracuse, they had an ice box full of 48 smallmouth. Unheard of by Mud Daddy standards and a catch that is seldom seen in these times of acid rain, Great Lakes water laced with antibiotics and all manner of heavy metal pollution, and makeshift sand bars built up from the silt of a few hundred thousand homes. The modern era has been hard on American waterways and stories like that bowling team proved it.

Slim told of a trip to Minnesota that he made as a boy with his father, Stanley, and brothers Keith and Dale. It was a grueling day as the troop had to haul their boat and motor inland from Long Lake the cabin lake over two tough portages to get to a distant larger lake that had ancient Indian petroglyphs seared into a sandstone shelf. Since the fishing was slow, Stanley told how he and pal "Yellow" Momberg were teenagers in the late 1920s way up in the deep woods of the Northern Peninsula of Michigan when they loaded Yellow's birch bark canoe onto his family's station wagon and headed off into the wilderness. They lived in Iron Mountain. It was and remains an American Siberia, and on this day they were bound for a hard haul on the Menominee River, a broad sheet of slow-moving water that breaks Michigan into Wisconsin.

From the canoe-launching site, Yellow and Stanley had to paddle against the current upriver into a meander that soon turned into a swamp. They headed for a non-descript log, checking to make sure nobody was around and watching, then moved the log, canoed though, replaced the log and paddled onward into the miasma. The hidden waterway finally opened into a broad lake, newly flooded by the construction of a power dam for their hometown. Until the dam was built, to get to this point would have required hours of painful bushwhacking through brambles and thorns. They knew the fishing would be superb, and for the entire day, it was.

On one cast, Yellow paused and looked down at the water. He had just reeled in a double train of June Bug spinners above a buck tail treble hook, when he spotted weeds trailing from the rig. Yellow reached to the water to shake the weeds off. And as he splashed the lure on the surface, there, just under his hand, a giant fish head appeared from the murk. It was the size of Yellow's own head. Both young men could see the razor teeth and imposing jaw line poised only inches from Yellow's hand. Would it strike? Slice his hand from thumb to little finger? Or maybe open up a wrist vein or two and Yellow would soon be saying hello to his Maker? Then, the head evaporated, leaving only a reflection of the blue Michigan sky, the canoe and a young man whose hand was still at the waterline - reaching toward a great mystery.

Stanley said Yellow put down his rod to snag a cigarette but his hands were shaking so much he couldn't even light the match. Slim said his Dad's eyes went distant as he told that story, lost in time, taken back to an era of wooden canoes and the hollow sound that waves made as they splashed against it, the sweet scent of forest pine on a sunny fall day, the face and quaking hands of a fishing pal named Yellow, and a giant muskie long gone.

Others may catch plenty of fish on that grand New York lake, but we did not. It was a perfect weekend for a getaway, though. On the tube in the house we'd rented, the World Series raged between Kansas City and St. Louis, the nation's first I-70 Series, which is the Interstate we'd crossed en route to Akron to pick up Drewsie on the way to upstate Pennsylvania.

E-Dog created a grid from the lid of a pizza box, and we all picked when we thought various activities that always happen on a baseball field would occur. For instance, each picked the inning when he thought the game would bring the first slide, when a manager would pick his nose, when somebody would scratch his crotch, when somebody would reach second, when somebody would hit a homerun, when somebody would reach third, when the first double play would be turned, when the first stupid fan in a stupid fan hat appeared on the screen, the first shot of a little kid eating something, the first shot of a man with his arms around his gal.

Then there was when the first grounder to second base would be hit, when the first fly ball was hit to the outfield, when there was a walk, when the camera would first pan onto a nose-picking fan or on a Centerfold-quality babe and on and on. As innings approached with an individual's choice for, say, the nose-picking category, that guy would move away from his chair to stand near the TV and yell, particularly during close-ups: "Pick it, pick it, pick it!"

Or, if it was somebody's inning for a slide, maybe some slob of a player had just drawn a walk and as he was headed down to first, the ever-hopeful Mud Daddy fan would yell, "Slide, slide, slide!"

The place had no popcorn popper, so we improvised and popped popcorn with an aluminum foil lid. It didn't work very well, in fact, it barely worked at all, the popcorn exploding through the foil and flying pretty much everywhere in the tiny kitchen, like Mickey in Fantasia with the magic buckets. The popcorn was not important, but the improvisation was vintage Mud Daddy.

Two decades later, nearly to the weekend, Carmany would remember catching fish and eating perch and smallmouth bass back there on Blueberry Hill. But whether that happened or not, well, who can say? Carmany's memory has always been something of a foggy marvel: sometimes amazingly accurate, other times nothing but magnificent embellishment. Maybe it had something to do with that golf ball. We knew this much about that trip to Blueberry Hill. We had a bona fide tradition on our hands.

The Tuneage

"When you start talking about the music you want on a three- or four-day fishing trip," Doc says, "you don't go for the classic stuff: "Blood on the Tracks," "Greatest Hits, Vol II," "Abbey Road," Elvis and such. You want something that you're not overly familiar with, something you don't hear every day; something that moves you and surprises you at the same time. Something you won't tire of too soon."

From the beginning, music has played a prominent role on Mud Daddies. We can recall songs that we sang along to on trips more than 30 years in the past: UB 40's haunting "King" (Where Are Your People Now?) on the dawn drive to Laurel River Lake in '83; Isaac Hayes' "Walk on By" on a beautiful fall drive through the Ozark Mountains in '91 and again in 2005 en route to Pickwick Lake; Van Morrison's "Did You Get Healed" from his obscure CD "A Night in San Francisco" – a chestnut discovered by the Raging Bull. It helped keep us sane during a skunking in '95.

Music that finds its way to a Mud Daddy is memorable for hitting creases outside of the mainstream, exposing us to genres or lost music found in cut-out bins that are usually overlooked. "Spanish Bombs" from the Clash or "All Lost in the Supermarket" and "If Music Could Talk" invoke strong memories of wind kicking up a campfire, cold moonrises across dark, still water, and long drives through the night. When Slim broke out his Eric Burdon CD at Norfolk Lake in Arkansas one night, it was a revelation. Not because the music was so good, but because it was so strange to hear an old man sing those anthems of our youth: "We Gotta Get Out of This Place," "It's My Life" now resonated with real meaning as youth had turned into middle-aged introspection.

Hearing Nathan and the Zydeco Cha Chas doing "Everything on the Hog is Good" made a dreary evening in Leesville, Ohio, bearable and brought back memories of boudin sandwiches on the drive to Lake Sam Rayburn in Texas a decade before. We fought the law after a night of loud Red Hot Chili Peppers in Virginia, and we believe that bass funk may be the genre of choice at Heaven's Door in the Great Beyond, a door that everybody knocks upon some dark day. Bring up Dylan, and Slim will gladly recount the time from 1980 when he tailed a trio of hippie-looking East Villagers (patches all over their jeans – they can't be from Cincinnati) to Dylan in a local hat shop.

"Bob Dylan," Slim announced as he entered the shop.

Dylan's entourage leaned in tight in a protective huddle around a guy who looked like the smallest homeless man you ever saw.

"Are you talking to reporters this time out?" Slim asked.

Nobody said anything.

Dylan looked at Slim with blue eyes as bright as a Caribbean sky.

"What kind of newspaper you work for? A good one or a bad

one?" Dylan asked.

Slim shrugged and furrowed his brow as if to say, well dumbass...

"I dunno. That's not for me to say, anyhow …"

Dylan must have liked the answer - and was surely bored beyond belief from a couple of years on The Road.

He had a ready reply:

"Sure …"

Slim found that interviewing Bob Dylan was a lot like talking to your foot. The guy had been interviewed so many times, his interview gag-reflex took over: say nothing of any importance, ignore the questions you don't want to answer. When Slim asked when Dylan was going to re-release the footage from "Rolling Thunder Review," the scrawny guy perked up a little and asked about art cinema houses in Cincinnati. One was right around the corner, Slim said. Where? Dylan wanted to know. Slim showed him. An Associated Press photographer, David Kohl, came by and had a bag holding a container of Cincinnati chili. At Slim's urging, he snapped a shot of the rock star recluse, and Dylan didn't like that at all. He got quite huffy. What's up with Bob, Slim thought. Is he Amish now? Did I miss something in his life? After protesting and taking a picture of the photographer, Dylan, to show he was a normal guy after all, then started talking about how much he liked cold spaghetti.

In a way, Slim recalled, the Dylan interview reminded him of what it's like to yakity-yak with a stranger at a gas pump. Takes but a moment. Nothing new. Slim left the interview feeling sorry for the guy: trapped in his celebrity but still reaching out to chat with a stranger on a street corner in Cincinnati

Music is the subject of many unresolved arguments: are certain albums great or merely good. Dylan's "Slow Train Coming" and "Shot of Love" always get us worked up, mostly because Sly Dunbar and Robbie Shakespeare of Black Uhuru fame are backing him up and the words are powerful and prophetic.

Slim and Doc have an undying appreciation for Steely Dan and E doesn't get that at all ("No soul," he says.) Doc can sing Steely Dan for hours – each and every word by heart. Sometimes, we just ask Doc to sing Haitian Divorce, Bad Sneakers, Kid Charlemagne, Babylon Sisters or Deacon Blues, and Doc can and will hit it word for word and note for note. It is truly something to behold. He needs professional help. It's damn near a disability.

Big E goes straight for hot soul shots from Otis Redding or Sam

Cooke with a dose of cold, steel-guitar blues. He thinks he can croon with Mel Torme or Rao Malo. And everyone digs Sinatra and Dino and Louis Prima and, of course, Van Morrison – most anything from that Irish soul singer will do. Doc is big on James Brown, Muddy Waters, the Stones, Dylan and early Police. He also goes for classic jazz when he can. Slim is a fan of anything Sting, the Clash, Chrissie Hynde (she's from his hometown, Akron, as is James Ingram of "Yah Mo B There" fame), John Lee Hooker and The Killer, Ol' Jerry Lee Lewis. His "Rockin My Life Away" is a Mud Daddy favorite. Slim even taught his then 3-year-old daughter, Rachel, to sing "Every Day I Have to Cry Some" so he could hear the song daily on the way to preschool …"Duh-Dry the water from my eyes some … Every day I have to cry, cry, cry. . ." Slim always has a Dylan and Ziggy Marley CD around. Bob Marley works, too. There is no song that gets Slim going quite like "Buffalo Soldier" unless it's "Lively Up Yourself" or "Is This Love?"

Bull is a vocal, enthusiastic blues man all the way. Maybe a little too vocal. Once in a blues club outside D.C. after a few beers (well, maybe a few more than a few), he happened to find himself right in front of the bandstand, a beer in hand, just a few feet from the guitar player who had starred for the Nighthawks back in the '70s. The guy could really play, and the band was rocking. Bull started groovin' and shakin' and shouting as loud as he could: "You got a gift, man! Don't give up on it! You got a gift! Don't give up on it!" People cleared a space for him on the dance floor so as not to get splashed. Bull was a one-man mosh pit. Then he became aware of a large hand on his shoulder. The next thing he remembers, he was outside on the street and the music was inside, behind a door.

You might want Smokey Robinson, Etta James, Dinah Washington. You might want Third World's "African Woman" or Laura Nyro's unforgettable "Gonna Take a Miracle" with Patti LaBelle. Even Todd Rundgren's "Between the Bars." Doc loves the way Rundgren does that Philly Soul.

If you are into matching geographies with music, as we like to try do, it's Mellencamp for Indiana, The Pretenders for Ohio, Elvis and Carl Perkins for Tennessee and George Strait, Willie or Delbert McClinton for Texas trips.

Doc's top albums for a Mud Daddy? Start with Miles Davis "Kinda Blue" because "you hear something new in it every time you play it."

Can't be without the Allman Brothers' "Live at the Fillmore East," Muddy Waters' "McKinley Morganfield," Otis Redding's "Live in Europe" and James Brown's four-CD "StarTime." They're the musts. He'd want Van Morrison's "A Night in San Francisco" and Isaac Hayes' "Hot Buttered Soul," too. After that it might get a little obscure: The Stones' "Aftermath," Captain Beefheart's "Trout Mask Replica" or "Clear Spot."

If he has the room, he'll take Joe Jackson's "Jumpin Jive," some Count Basie, the Police's "Synchronicity," Sinatra's Nelson Riddle sessions and maybe Neil Young's "Decade."

But by now the music bag is getting kind of heavy.

Pickled Eggs

Hard-boil a dozen eggs for about 10 minutes. Give the eggs 10-15 minutes to cool before peeling. We've heard all kinds of secrets about things to toss into the water during boiling to make it easier to peel the shell off the eggs; we don't believe any of them – or find any of them necessary. The only secret is to crack the living heck out of the egg – and use the dexterity required to tie a lure to your fishing line to peel down through the silky-thin membrane just below the hard shell. Into a small pot toss a mixture of half water and half white vinegar (enough of each to roughly fill the empty spaces of the old pickle jar that will contain your 8-12 hard-boiled eggs, which means you want about a cup of each) and add a heaping teaspoon of salt and a heaping teaspoon of sugar (you can double up on the sugar if you like a sweeter brine). Bring it to a boil then back it off.* Let it simmer 10 minutes under a lid.

Drop your peeled eggs into a large pickle jar, let the liquid cool enough so it doesn't shatter the glass, then pour the hot liquid into the jar, flavor it up with some black pepper and oregano and, if you like (as we do), add a splash some sort of heart-healthy vegetable oil (but, note, if you use olive oil, make sure not to use TOO much, because if you like to refrigerate your pickled eggs, the olive oil will morph into a loathsome lardish lump). Screw the cap on tightly for a nice seal, and let it ferment a night or a month. Then you are ready to consume this Mud Daddy delicacy.**

*Open the windows, fishermen; otherwise this is a helluva nosequet to leave your wife when she arrives home.

** Optional, but if you are smart, which all fishermen are, you peeled a head of garlic (at least) and a chunk of onion while your eggs were boiling. You sliced the garlic and onion into long, thin strips and layered them in the pickle jar between the eggs. These garlic strips serve the dual purpose of giving you garlic for your other cooking (for those times when you were so stupid as to have forgotten garlic, as we have) or when you would like a pickled-onion/garlic element to your antipasto (we do). You cannot add too much garlic or onion to this mixture.

Chapter V - Rigid Taiwanese Standards

Mud Daddy tip: *Always study the behavior of any flock of birds you might see on shore or near the water. If, for instance, they settle from a grove of trees to the ground, a pasture or swampy area, chances are that a hatch of insects has emerged nearby, particularly if the flock is a large one and it is clearly feeding. Insect hatches on shore, especially if it is a windy day, could mean a free meal for any smaller fish in the nearby shallows. Though shallow water usually means dinky fish, anytime there are small fish around, bigger fish are sure to be nearby. And if you see a bird skirting the crest of the waves, then fish are feeding on top. Cast top-water lures – and make that cast with hope in your heart.*

The day was dreary, the sun buried behind slate skies as we pulled out of Cincinnati bound for Taylorsville Lake near Louisville, Ky., which is billed as "an angler's dream come true." We'd prove that to be a lie. Within minutes of our beginning the trip in the spring of 1986, the skies opened up with a light but steady cascade, a curtain of discomfort that would surely bring a day of soggy socks and cold water dripping into our eyes. Fishermen – and in their own manner, golfers – are eternal optimists, people who will always put a bright shine on an otherwise tarnished circumstance. Most fishermen do it with platitudes: Fresh water means fresh fish. Or, Gray skies bring great fishing. And yet another: The fish won't see the line today. All these tired expressions attempt to conceal the obvious. It's likely to be a miserable day on the water.

But the beauty of a one-day fishing trip with your best friends is that it is, after all, one day more than you would have had otherwise. You leave your warm bed in the wee hours, shower under plumbing that actually works, maybe have some toasted cinnamon bread with a pair of fried eggs for breakfast and linger over the sports pages before heading off into the still-dark morning. At that point in the trip, it's too early to tell whether the elements are going to cooperate. You can't see the sky because it's dark, so hope is alive, at least until the sun has risen and the granite clouds emerge and, with them, a steady rain. If the birds are already walking about, feeding in the downpour – oblivious to it, in fact – prepare yourself for an all-day downpour. That's what we were facing.

Somewhere south of Cincinnati, it occurred to us that we had no rain gear. Now, many fishermen have cool clothing for these conditions: parkas of Gore-Tex that cost $175 or more and cover the knees, perfect for canoeing or a day in a john boat. Some have oil-finished, Filson all-season coats in a sea-otter green that sell for $215 plus shipping and handling. Or maybe something known as a Dry-Plus Signature Series parka that has room for a hand warmer in the pocket and sets back a Father's Day shopper a neat $119.95.

We didn't have any of that stuff. That kind of gear is for high-roller millionaires and the like, and we were far from that. In fact, we didn't even have one raincoat among us, that's how prepared we were for this outing. Which meant it was time to make a pit stop at the nearest Wal-Mart. Or maybe it was a Walgreen's, or for that matter, a Walter's IGA. The memory of the actual place is lost to time. What we do know is this – when we came out, we had rain gear. A bunch of rain gear. And we were happy again. We had clear plastic jackets and slip-on pants. We had an umbrella. We had bright yellow and blue ponchos that cost $3.99 each and were guaranteed to keep us dry. Damn the elements, we were ready for action on the water! In fact, under the clear plastic wrapper, which was alleged to be a convenient carrying case and had a nice white snap to prove it, was a sheet of marketing material that made a bold promise. This raingear HAD to work because it was manufactured to Rigid Taiwanese Standards! It said so right on the instructions. Collectively we pondered the phrase and its implications. Whose standards? Some assembly-line supervisor half-a-world away, watching intently as these neatly packaged rain ponchos flew into boxes bound for far flung Wal-Marts in Kentucky?

"This one…good. This one, no good. This one, good. That one, no good."

Maybe he was a fisherman. Maybe he stalked the misty forests and valleys of Yushan National Park in the dawn on his day off work to hunt the elusive golden carp – worm and hook in one hand, bamboo rod in another. Or perhaps he was a saltwater fisherman who trolled alone through a shimmering bay of the East China Sea on the skirts of Yangmingshan National Park, committed, as a poet once said, to the lonely sea and sky. Perhaps he was a man who tasted of the water's vagrant gypsy life, when he wasn't lording over a kingdom of disgruntled factory girls and plastic rain ponchos that filled a warehouse floor-to-ceiling.

Eight hours and only a pair of tiny fish later, the hoods leaked, the poncho snaps were torn asunder and useless, the underarm seams were split and the trouser crotches ripped, too. Three wet fishermen looked across a soggy boat at one another – too wet to even light a cigar – and muttered a mantra that would forever mark this trip in their memory: *Rigid Taiwanese Standards... Rigid Taiwanese Standards . . . Rigid Taiwanese Standards . . . .*

Pasties

(Sounds like paaasties – not like what exotic dancers used to wear. Serves four.)

Back in the day, before men had to wash dishes, this simple meal was popular among iron ore miners throughout the American north woods. It was a transportable meal that miners supposedly wrapped in waxed paper and put in their coat pockets where it stayed warm until lunchtime. It's a perfect fishing trip take-along lunch, particularly when made the night before. Also, "Pasties" is a common but confusing term on luncheonette signs throughout the Upper Peninsula of Michigan, where Mud Daddy patron saint Ernest Hemingway – fisherman, writer, gourmand and lush-extraordinaire – first popularized the appeal of this state's quiet gurgling brook trout streams with the iconic "Big Two-Hearted River." Here you go:

The Mud Daddy Chronicles

3 Readymade Pie Crusts from dairy case (Is there any other kind?)

2 giant potatoes or 3-4 regular-sized 'taters

2 large carrots

1 large onion

2-3 lbs. lean ground round, chopped sirloin or defatted and deboned porterhouse steak

1 tsp basil, salt and pepper to taste

1 clove minced garlic

Peel and dice potatoes into squares no larger than the nail on your index finger. Larger dices will take longer to bake. Cut carrots lengthwise into halves, then cut into 1/8-inch slices. Dice the onion any way you want (to avoid being called a Sissy Boy, hold a slice of white bread in your mouth to block fumes from your eyes to keep from crying. There's no crying on fishing trips.) Cut sirloin into one-half inch chunks. If you're using ground meat and it's not lean, pre-fry to pink and drain grease. Mix all ingredients in large bowl and salt and pepper to taste. Open up pie crust, dump 1/3 of mix onto one half of pie crust, then fold the other half over it, closing up the half-moon shape by pinching around the edges. Repeat with pie crusts until all material is gone. Cut three two-inch slits into the top of each pasty to allow steam to escape. Cook in pre-heated 350 degree oven until crust is a golden brown, about 1½ hours, maybe. Serve with Australian Merlot and purloined packets of ketchup from a self-serve counter at a convenience store. To sound real fancy while pouring, call the wine M-air-low, not M-er-low.

Mud Daddies are cultured events, after all.

Chapter VI - Soul Feeding

Mud Daddy tip: *Keep all your Mud Daddy gear in separate smaller bags that can be stowed in a duffel bag. Then, leave the big bag stashed in a backroom in your house during the months leading up to the trip. Keeping the camping gear, candles, cooking pots and pans, dining ware and silverware, portable stove and miscellaneous stuff – like duct tape, extra tent stakes, hatchet and additional rope — in a bag dedicated to the trip means you won't be as likely to forget anything when the time comes to travel. Throw in a basketball net to fill with rocks for an anchor.*

Garage sales are great places to pick up bargain duffels. Look at garage or estate sales, too, for used kitchen items like frying pans, spatulas, plastic mixing bowls and dinnerware. Keep your eye out for candles because three or four fired up all at once in a fire pit can dry out wet kindling or, if nothing else, bring the solace of a warm flame to a damp camp.

A tradition doesn't often begin with just one moment. Traditions build and evolve, sometimes with care and planning, other times haphazardly; and often without the knowledge that a tradition is even being born. But looking back, you can clearly see those moments when a mere outing has evolved into something enduring. For the Mud Daddy, that came in late September of 1986 at Norris Lake, Tenn.

In "Memories, Dreams, Reflections," C.G. Jung wrote, "Among the so-called neurotics of our day there are a good many who in other ages would not have been neurotic – that is, divided against themselves. If they had lived in a period and in a milieu in which man was still linked by myth with the world of the ancestors, and thus with nature truly experienced and not merely seen from the outside, they would have been spared this division with themselves."

What Carl Gustav is saying is that guys need to go fishing. And what he really meant was that most guys need a Mud Daddy to get their minds right and to keep their goals in sight. That's where we were in fall 0f 1986 – needing to experience nature truly and deeply on a Mud Daddy for just a few days a year to escape the quotidian demands of life and keep ourselves somewhat sane. That year, we committed wholly and completely to this enterprise. It would be our annual soul-feeding, and we knew that to miss it would bring great peril to our psyches.

"We have to maintain our image as men of free will, masters of the great outdoors and expert anglers," Slim explained when the Norris trip was under discussion. His first-born child, Matthew, was at home, and at five months old was waking up to the world and, mysteriously, never seeming to sleep. Slim knew he had to get away if only for the perspective that always comes with distance.

"But none of that is true," Doc protested. "We're none of those things."

"Of course not," Slim said. "But that's the image we want and we have to keep the Mud Daddy going if we want to maintain that image. Doesn't matter if it's not true. "Let's go fishing, Doc."

So we did. Doc had a friend who owned some undeveloped lakefront on Norris, and he gave us permission to camp on it. Doc arranged for two john boats at a local marina, and the Mud Daddy was on. It began like many others would – in utter confusion. Slim, Drewsie and E stopped to golf at a pretty but rough course in Pineville, Kentucky. An historic marker at the course indicated it was the first golf course in the United States (and where Dr. Thomas Walker, who discovered the Cumberland Gap, camped at what would become the fifth hole tee box). We wondered what the good doctor might have thought as he camped by that stream in the wilderness, if he even knew about the game of golf, and if he would have changed his mind about hunting for the Cumberland Gap if he knew that, 200 years later, his campsite would be the tee-box for a cheesy golf hole. It seems an unlikely place for the first golf course in the U.S.A, but we weren't about to argue with it.

Doc, bored by waiting at the marina, decided to bushwhack into the spot and set up camp. He left a crude map of where he thought the site was with the marina manager and hoped the group would find him. Eventually they did, as their cursing, condemnations and warnings about the evils of impatience soon found him. The imprecations floated across the water, barely audible at first, but as the trio drew near, they were quite clear and understandable to Doc, who was waiting onshore, smoking a cigar.

"Why the hell didn't you wait for us?"

"Well, you were playing golf, weren't you?"

"What are you – a wife?

"So what if we snuck in 18 holes, you chump. We got here as fast as we could!"

"Where's the camp?"

Doc pointed around the bend. It was all set up – tent, fire ring, cooking area, everything. Doc was forgiven his chronic impatience as we stared at the Cezannesque canvas before us. Norris Lake was a beautiful spread of water – a TVA impoundment – and the campsite was atop a manageable embankment, a sweet spot up at the edge of the tree line. Edog looked at it and though: driving range. He'd even brought a driver along and a shag bag of balls. The lake was sparkling blue, and there was no one for miles in any direction. It seemed a perfect location for a successful Mud Daddy. But dread descended soon enough. On that first afternoon, no one got so much as a bite in spots that looked like they should be teeming with bass. We gave up early and retired to the camp to eat spaghetti and drink beer, wine and Akron Sours while catching up on each other's lives.

The time came to light the stove. Slim suddenly announced, hey, check it out. In his hand was a matchbook and on it was a trivia question: Name the first golf course in America.

"What kind of serendipitous shit is this?" E wanted to know.

"It's like a Vortex or something."

The answer on the inside cover was some course in New York, but we knew better.

And we knew another element of the Mud Daddy had just presented itself: the Vortex, a strange coincidence that signaled we were on the right path – whatever path that was.

Just below camp we found a fairly flat spot, and used E-Dog's driver to crush tee shots far out into the lake – tall, arcing drives that laced out into the blue and then fell into the water with magnificent splashes or laser darts that went farther than any of us thought possible. We considered timing swings and trajectories to match the speed of the $20,000 bass boats screaming through the afternoon. But in a more sober moment, we figured that might not be a good idea. It was a Mud Daddy, and sometimes shit happened on Mud Daddies that would never ever happen at any other time. Nobody wanted to risk actually hitting a drive where it was supposed to go and maybe nailing the owner of a boat that cost as much as Slim's first house. As Mud Daddy luck would have it, the guy would probably be an Atlanta lawyer – somebody with a $1 million house, a closet full of alligator shoes and lawsuit language on cut-and-paste back at the office.

We'd also brought along a box of Trivial Pursuit cards, but left the game board and pieces at home. We rolled through the cards and counted the correct answers per person per card – card after card after card. The box would prove who was the dumbest.

Now, Doc was not only not so dumb, he was pretty smart, having the advantage of being raised in a small town in rural Southside Virginia in the 1950s and 60s. With nothing much to occupy his time down there in Tobacco Road, he read too much and ruined his eyesight, but retained gigabytes of useless trivia. He knows something about a lot things, from '57 Chevys to the Civil War. In his sophomore year in high school, he lucked into a scholarship to a fancy-pants (for Virginia) Episcopal boarding school, where they tried to teach him the classics and Latin, government and science. At the University of Richmond, Doc actually had to study. And a graduate degree from Ohio State makes him think he has an edge. Plus, he has traveled widely and served in the military. That always counts for some knowledge – mostly that he didn't want to spend a lot of time in the military. Finally, Doc was a student of history and a journalist his entire adult life – having read and remembered obscure details from hundreds of thousands of dull-ass AP wire stories year after year after year. And, what's more, he is a slave to college football and a student of sports history. His claim to the trivia crown is well-grounded.

But then there's this: In all things technical and most things scientific, Doc is a chimpanzee.

Slim has extensive formal education, from two years at Akron University and three years at Ohio University for a Bachelor of Science degree, a diploma he proudly displayed from time to time in the newsroom. And he has traveled the world. Three months for a sabbatical to Europe to do nothing but burn through the down payment of a house on day after day of adventure. He's fished the Yugoslavian waters of the Soca and trolled for pike on remote Swedish lakes. Slim, raised in a small town south of Akron, has seen the sun rise from the south shore of St. John, crushed drives on improbable par fives off the coast of Costa Rica and chased mystic vibes in the canyons of the Southwest USA. In his early years, he was drawn to science and folks who liked science, managed to stumble onto a championship high school basketball team because he had quick hands for steals and knew how to block out for rebounds and thereupon learned many intricate details of that game. His late father was a rocket scientist – or at least a production manager for rocket scientists, working out design problems on the guidance systems for missiles that carried nuclear depth bombs – so Slim was exposed at an early age to a lot of strange stuff. His interests as a youth ranged from origami to Kon Tiki, chess to ping pong, astronomy to agronomy. Ducking the tire factories of Akron, he headed from Akron University south to Ohio University and being an adventurous sort, with a bigger dose of Kipling's Elephant's Child in him than most, he also credits serendipity and innate intelligence for his stellar Trivial Pursuit abilities. Something has to explain it. He is a golfer, an avid reader of travel writing from the 19th century, and a shirker of all duties domestic, though a pretty good cook when the spirit wells up in him and it's not too much trouble.

Still, Slim had a problem. He didn't know a damn thing about sports specifics – names, dates, that sort of thing – but believed he knows virtually everything about sport strategy that one man can know.

E-Man, a creative soul with an Italian's disdain for all things phony, has seen most of the world through the lens of sport – specifically baseball. He is a lawyer, has written five books, which makes him smarter than the average bear, interviewed thousands of professional, collegiate and high school athletes and usually reads two books at the same time – though one of them doesn't count because it is always baseball-related. As a kid, he was educated at a parochial high school, and his insightful intelligence – and occasional contact with a Louisville Slugger and an unfailing ability to punt a football – led to a posting at the Naval Academy. However, an intense anathema to bullshit led to his departure from that august institution and into a 2½ - year sabbatical at out-of-the-way Murray State on the western Kentucky frontier. (Civilian E was back in Philadelphia partying at the Army-Navy football game when his parents scouted out Murray. His mother ordered a beer at the local fancy restaurant. When told that the county was dry and liquor was not sold anywhere, she looked at her husband, John, and, having never heard of such a thing, intoned: "Well, there's no way he's going to college here.")

But E-man knows next to nothing about five of the six categories of question on each Trivial Pursuit card.

Being competitive types, we found that making Trivial Pursuit a blood sport comes naturally. We were more amazed by what one or the other of us knows or doesn't know. How does E remember who won the Triple Crown before Yastrzemski? And why doesn't he remember Sugar Ray Robinson's record? Why does Slim know anything at all about cauliflower and a smattering about Antarctica and the Peloponnesian War but nothing about World War II other than Patton kicked ass in fast tanks? How come Doc knows Chinese Gordon died at the Battle of Khartoum but can't remember what year Hemingway won the Nobel Prize for Literature?

As day turned to evening and evening to night, we yapped it up and ended by singing – though that's too grand a word; bellowing is more accurate – Smokey Robinson songs and then some Neil Young.

During the night, a cold front roared in, bringing high winds and a drenching rain that pelted us for hours. Drewsie and Slim had trusted that they could make it through the night without a rain fly over their tent. They were wrong and danced through the downpour at 2 a.m. to get the fly up before everything inside was completely soaked. When they rose in the morning, Drewsie pointed to a spot behind the tent where the two had hopped barefoot the night before to get the rain fly up (but never staked). At his feet was a broken beer bottle left by a previous camper. The shard was three inches long and pointing straight up. Both campers probably missed it by inches during their midnight high-step in the rain.

There is no greater teacher than adversity. We hung up the wet items, fired up the camp stove, brewed hot coffee and then Slim went fishing in the downpour, pulling in two nice bass while trolling. Those fish would be a cruel hoax, however, because he soon learned that a fish caught without a Mud Daddy witness does not count. The lake would yield no more bass. Make a note. Fishing behind a cold front is futile. We cast in utter impotence until our wrists were sore. Still another lesson awaited us, one we would experience many times in the years to come.

The motor on one of the boats died. Kaput. Lesson two: Some marinas have terrible motors and leaky boats. Unfortunate traditions were a-building.

A true Mud Daddy experience is a smorgasbord of adversity, but we overcome it through perseverance, improvisation and a little luck. At Norris, the adaptation concerned tying the two boats together end-to-end with a stub of nylon rope and chugging down the lake, casting and laughing at how foolish we must look to all the Bass Masters. Once, about 10 of these tony boats were congregated near a point where the lake split into two arms. They were fishing for stripers and doing it at specific depths, we would learn. We came trolling through the glitter-paint carnival with our lines all splayed from the back of the boats, smoking cigars and drinking beer beneath the bills of our caps (pulled low because we were probably screwing up their fishing and didn't want to make eye contact.)

We were Huck and Jim, lolling on the river and loving it. Doc even hooked a fish, a pale specimen of a striper that had almost drowned as the Mud Daddy armada motored along. At first, he didn't know a fish was on but discovered he'd hooked the fish when he decided to reel in. Because the fish came in sideways, Lowery thought he had hooked a keeper.

"That's a pathetic fish you got there, Doc," observed the E-Dog with a sad look on his face. "What is it?"

"Who knows?" Doc replied, "But you're skunked and I'm not."

Doc and Slim hauled in a few small bluegills in the shallows while listening to college football on the boom box. E made his famous Frittata Mundatta, throwing everything left over from the other meals into the scrambled eggs. Slim flapped some jack cakes, and we finished off the Tequila. The tiny boom box was raffled off by cutting a deck of cards, and the debts were settled through an accounting method nobody could quite follow. Any leftover booze was parceled out (or paid for if a participant was flying and couldn't take four or five half empty bottles of wine, Tequila, bourbon, gin, vodka or a few stray six packs along in his carry-on bag). Then the Enquirer Outstanding Angler plaque was awarded to the best fisherman of the weekend – Doc.

It's an appealing circular patch with a leaping bass (something we see too rarely on these trips) stitched over blue water and the words "Enquirer Outstanding Angler" above it along the border. It's a beautiful thing to have on your desk at work. Better still, the losers have to stew for a year, steeped in dark envy, for a chance to have it adorn their workspace. It draws admiring stares and reverent questions from passers-by.

"Where did you get that? It's lovely."

"Won it on my annual fishing trip. It is nice, isn't it?"

At that point, usually, the possessor will delicately hold it up to catch the office light, turning it slightly ever so and smiling all the while.

They don't get it, but you do.

We said our goodbyes at Norris, promising – swearing – next year to go to that can't-miss lake where the fishing would be great. The fact is, four of us had fished hard for maybe 30 hours, caught a handful of measly fish and still had an outstanding weekend. It wouldn't hurt, would it, to find a lake where we might actually catch something worth eating, we agreed.

Norris had been the quintessential Mud Daddy experience in every respect. It was the outing that solidly established the tradition that was to be an unbroken string for decades and exists to this day: poor fishing, a dead boat, bad weather, Sunday frittata, football and baseball on the radio, golf balls driven off a high bank and Smokey Robinson songs by a campfire long into autumn night. Traditions don't get much better than this – unless you add a big fish or two. Either way, our souls were fed and our appetites already building for next year.

Fried Fish Like Momma Thought She Could Make

This is an excellent recipe for those fighting bluegills and smallmouth bass pulled from the picturesque Shenandoah River in Virginia. You might be camped illegally on someone's private pasture when it got too dark too soon and you forgot the flashlight and an extra pair of dry socks. Not to worry because this will save the day and make your evening.

Pack eggs in hard plastic egg case, available at any decent camping supply store and most Wal-Marts. Mix egg with water and powdered milk. Dip fish into seasoned flour, then into egg solution and back into seasoned flour or vice versa. Just don't get it mixed up. Let it congeal real good for a couple of minutes. Count fireflies or stars and drink wine. Think about the Civil War and the 600,000-plus men who dreamed in their last moments of life of how they once fished hip-deep in a cold country stream. Drink to them, in fact.

Fry the fish in hot oil three or four minutes to a side until the fish is flaky, then squeeze juice from a fresh lemon into the pan, a splash of white wine and jack up the heat. Cover with foil or a lid (for those who are really prepared) and cook for no longer than 15 seconds on high heat. (If it's black, you cooked it too long.) The heat will infuse the lemon and wine into the batter and fish. It may be the best fish you've ever eaten.

Chapter VII - Fire in the Night

The 1987 Mud Daddy was officially under way.

Slim, his high school pal Drewsie and Big E were headed through the Cumberland Gap, in Daniel Boone country, on the way to meet Doc at Lake Wautaga in deep east Tennessee. None had been through these parts before, particularly this blue-line state highway. But E knew some history and he began to tell a tale of Daniel Boone. Boone, E said, regretted little about his adventurous life on the frontier, but he mourned to the end of his days a hunting trip that ended in an ambush by Indians. His son and his son's pal were killed, and Boone blamed himself. He thought he should have been more careful by keeping the teenagers closer to the main party and by being more attentive for signs of hostile Indians – birdcalls, that sort of thing. Boone believed that if he'd done so, the boys would have lived to be men and would have, perhaps, grown to have families and sons of their own. "It really tore Boone up," E said.

Just as Big-E ended the story, they saw a roadside sign marking an historical event. They pulled over to take a look. On the marker was the story of the Indian ambush and the loss of the two boys. The three looked at one another in amazement. What kind of Kismet shit is this, Edog asked. The Vortex, again!

After engaging in typical shenanigans and banter at the marina, we settled into two boats and headed out into the big lake in the glorious fall mountain light. We found a campsite on an island far from the marina, choosing it because entry was easy from a back bay. In any direction, we had a splendid view, the hills splashed with distant thumb smudges of Technicolor foliage, the water deep green and inviting. We had upped the Mud Daddy ante considerably this year with prepared food in Tupperware, the first but not the last time we would do this, and a battery operated television, which actually worked well enough to watch the World Series and a college football game. Reception improved after Slim produced a mess of wire he brought along to use as an antenna. To ensure proper reception, he stuck an orange on one end, duct-taped the wire to the fruit and tossed it over a tree limb as high as he could chuck it.

"Oh yeah," he said, with his familiar 'can-you-believe-this-shit?' laugh.

"Trust me. I know what I'm doing."

Whether the orange had anything to do with it or not – and almost certainly not – the little TV worked.

We had changed, too. Doc had turned 40. Slim was pushing that watershed year and had a toddling Matthew at home. Careers were blooming, though hair was going gray and guts were going round. Mortgages seemed to be growing, too, and haunting each of us every month was a pile of fresh bills. Still, it was a good time to be alive and a good time to fish an emerald lake on a crisp fall day, with plenty of cold beer and cigars and good conversation covering our favorite topics: sports, wives, kids, careers, cars and more sports. We were breathing it all in, and it was good.

There are times when life can be so sweet that you feel like an integral part of a seamless world, that the entire natural tableau – the water, the trees raining leaves, the hawk circling above, the call of a mockingbird in the glen behind camp – was all there just for us and it was all good.

The fishing, however, was bad – typically bad. And frustrating, because everything else was so perfect and the lake looked like it should be bountiful. Saturday afternoon, after hours of fishing futility, Slim, Big E and Drewsie went to play golf and Doc stayed behind to catch dinner. The golfers got a late start because Syracuse (E's hometown school) was giving Notre Dame fits in a great football game.

Roan Valley Golf Course was pure mountain Zen in its beauty, deep in the Appalachian Mountains with views that never ended – pasture to distant bald knob. As the front man, Slim hit the pro shop. He figured the best look for this championship course was a yellow sweater, knee-length socks and Army fatigue pants tied below the knee. He essentially was wearing knickers, an Appalachian version of the timeless Payne Stewart look and something nobody ever wore anymore to a course. He knew no pro shop would turn away a man in knickers who had a fistful of cash, even a man grimy from smoke and ash and rubbing a three-day stubble. Standing there in the clubhouse, Slim felt like a grungy version of someone on a "Slow - Children At Play" sign, where a skipper in knickers is chasing a hoop with a stick down some suburban street.

One hole on the down side of the mountain coaxed extraordinary distances on the drives. Slim, for his part, sent a Titlest 384 yards out into the valley and blew over that par four mountainside hole by 40 yards or more – although a cart path beyond the green may have been involved, as balls sometimes take galloping hops when landing on asphalt. He had to hit a half wedge back for a three-putt bogey. Typical. It was the first memorable big blast on a Mud Daddy, though plenty more inexplicable and mystical drives would appear as the ribbon of time unfurled.

Alone back at camp, Doc found some quiet inlets and broke out a dry fly and clear bobber. In the dying daylight, the Bluegill rose to the dry fly with enthusiasm. He kept eight of the biggest for dinner and put them on a stringer. With night falling fast, Doc made preparations for the evening repast, building a fire in a makeshift ring to fight the autumn chill as he cocked an ear for the chug-chug of the john boat and loud chatter of his golfing campmates cutting across the quiet water. He heard nothing. As minutes dragged into hours and with no sign of the boys, Doc eventually released the bluegills, ate stroganoff made earlier, and kept the little fire going. Something had gone wrong – the motor had conked, or they had gotten themselves lost on the dark lake. Maybe a car wreck out on the highway. He thought he'd better make the fire bigger, so they could see it if they were near enough. He mumbled to no one as he puttered around scrounging for more limbs to throw on the fire. Doc fed the flames until they were six feet high and crackling. And he kept them there.

After an eternity, he heard the laboring motor in the distance. Then came happy voices; sounds at first, not words. Then the cry, "Doc, what's for dinner?"

"Where the hell you been?" Doc asked when they reached the fire.

It had still been daylight when they got back to the marina, but only barely. They knew the camp was somewhere down the main channel, but they soon couldn't see a thing and had pressed onward.

"I'm glad you had this fire going because we didn't know where we were until we saw it," Slim said.

"Didn't know if we had gone too far or not far enough. And these guys were hopeless," he said, waving at E and Drewsie.

"Look what we used for a light," laughed E, holding up a small flashlight with a puny beam. It was a standard D-battery variety, but useless in the smothering darkness of a huge lake where the shores are hundreds of yards away.

"They charged us $10 for this little piece of shit, plus we had to buy batteries," Slim groused. "It was the last one left." Big E said they weren't sure why they bought it, because it was still daylight back at the golf course when they left.

We laughed at the absurdity of it all – in relief as much as anything.

That's how the marketplace works. People make impulsive buys at a point-of-purchase and they don't know why. We golfers thought that the flashlight might come in handy. We kept it around for years as a reminder: the market is efficient, but heartless. And, of course, the flashlight became a talisman of another sort, one with a lesson that was lasting and irrevocable:

Don't stay on the golf course too late because the price for doing so can be steep. The prospect of a cold night on a boat lost in the middle of a Tennessee lake looking for a back bay on an endless coast was not lost on us.

Watauga Stroganoff

We could have had a delicious meal of panfish at Lake Watauga if the golfers hadn't been so tardy and so impatient and stubborn. As it was, the stroganoff prepared the previous night made a nice meal. Here's our recipe:

½ pound salami chopped into small chunks

1 ½ pound ground beef/sirloin

1 can cream of mushroom soup (garlic-added variety)

½ cup onions

½ cup sliced mushrooms

½ cup sour cream

½ cup any red wine

1 tsp. basil or oregano or thyme, or, for that matter, any combo thereof

1 pound spaghetti or flat noodle or spinach noodle spaghetti

Cook onions and mushrooms until pearly, then remove and drain. Cook beef until pink in same frying pan. Drain grease (letting a paper towel soak it up is about as easy as it gets, unless the cabin has a glass suction grease remover, which it won't). Add wine and jack up the heat to make it steam, then back off the heat to medium/low after wine reaches a slow sizzle. Add salami, soup, onions, mushrooms and herbs. Simmer for a while or until you can't stand it anymore. Add sour cream and stir well. You should have had water boiling by now. Cook the chosen noodle and find a plate.

Chapter VIII - Daughter of Darkness

Doc was on his back deck in Austin, Tex., adding new line to his reels and sharpening his hooks in preparation for a Mud Daddy that was not yet assured of coming together. Problems with logistics, money, families and work threatened to sink the trip again that year. But Doc was gearing up just in case, spending a quiet September afternoon on his deck with a cigar and his tackle. Suddenly, out of nowhere and with no warning, a huge buck vaulted his back yard privacy fence and landed with a crash in the hammock strung under an oak tree. The stag smashed the wooden crossbars and ripped the rope. Extricating himself, he shook his magnificent rack, gave Doc a knowing look, then bounded back over the fence.

"Oh yeah, it's on," Doc said, grinning as Boscoe, his sweetly goofy Dalmatian, cowered behind him.

In our years of fishing and camping, we have had bitter disappointments on the water and in the woods. Bad weather, bad boats, bad equipment, bad fishing, bad luck. But we never had bad company. And, too, we've had some outings that actually qualified as excellent fishing trips, where the bass were plentiful enough to serve for dinner. Those successes were probably more luck than skill, though we went into each venture acting like experienced anglers. The key for us was this: We always hope for the best and expect the worst. If you do this, you usually get it – the worst, that is.

We would read up on a particular lake, mail around articles about how to fish it, learn what lures work best at certain times of the year, and once there, search for the points and drop-offs and shelves or do whatever the writers said we were supposed to do. We tried to approach each of these outings with a sense of professionalism. We wanted to catch fish. And when it happened, it was unforgettable, sweet magic.

One of those successes was in September 1988 on Laurel River Lake in Kentucky – the site of a classic Mud Daddy years earlier. On that trip years before, the nights were cold, we picked up a World Series game on the radio, and we ate fish. The original three had descended on Laurel in '83 – Slim, Big-E and Doc with his buddy Bob "Raging Bull" Rankin – and the outcome had been solid.

This trip would be equally spectacular, but this time with Drewsie instead of Rankin. And much of it was due to one remarkable lure we dubbed Daughter of Darkness. A large black spinner bait with a black skirt, it was a true bass assassin. Big E threw it early and often, and at several points during the three-day tour would get a strike with the first crank of the reel. It was an awesome display of angling. We caught enough bass to serve them for dinner for two nights in a row – one of the few times that's happened.

"What a producer," marveled Slim as he pulled his john boat up to the one with E and Doc, having seen all the action they were into.

"What do you call that?"

"Daughter of Darkness," Doc smiled behind his cigar. "What else?"

"Oh, yeah. That's it, Le Docteur," Slim laughed.

There is a somewhat rambling story behind the name of that spinner bait. It began in Newport, Kentucky, at a club – it may have been the infamous Talk of the Town – where we had repaired to view some interpretative dance. One of the beautiful artists moved to Tom Jones' classic hit "Daughter of Darkness" in her routine, which involved a small carton of half-and-half, lots of incredible motion and attire too scant to count as attire.

So when Big E's black spinner bait worked its magic on Laurel River Lake, the name was a natural. The lure seemed too big. Each cast landed like a small grenade. She made a lot of noise and threw up a lot of water going in, but that didn't seem to matter. One crank of the reel and E was fighting a bass.

Slim cooked the fish that night in traditional corn meal, eggs and milk.

The duties of cleaning fish usually fell to Slim, and he had a ritual for it. It was after all, as Dylan sang, a world of steel-eyed death, so as much as he hated the killing part, Slim looked the fish in the eye, thanked the creature silently and apologized for taking its life, said a prayer to Jesus and then made a swift cut through the spine. Within minutes he had a stack of filets ready for the skillet.

Big E and Doc fished together most of that weekend and witnessed one of the most amazing phenomena in Mud Daddy history. They were drifting in a large, quiet cove off the main lake in the late morning, barely fishing because the action had ceased. They were lazing about in the john boat, smoking cigars and drinking beers, when E said he wished the lake would show some sign of life. As soon as his words were uttered, a huge bass broke the water about 30 yards ahead of them.

"Damn. You see that?" Doc asked.

Before they could move, the big fish broke the surface again, and this time tail-walked across the water for several yards, its entire body out of the water except for its tail fin, which was flipping furiously and propelling the big bass across the deep blue surface. It was shaking its head violently, like it might have been trying to throw a lure lodged in its jaw. Foam and slashes were everywhere.

When it finally dove beneath the surface, E and Doc looked at each other in amazement.

"Unbelievable."

"What was it doing?"

"No idea. Maybe trying to shake a lure or something." Never saw something like that again – a fish walking on water on command. You spend enough time in the wild kingdom, on bodies of water and in the woods, and you will witness amazing things.

Not all of them pleasant.

When we returned to the campsite on one of Laurel's many islands, we found that the two cases of beer we had anchored in the lake to cool were missing. Gone! Maybe the wash from a boat had dislodged them. More likely they had been spotted and stolen. The perpetrators left a pair of red pliers behind, though, and Slim grabbed them for his tackle box. It was small consolation, but it was something. Even when recreating in the Great Outdoors, ugly reality intrudes from time to time, and this was one of those times: beerlessness. Beer rationing is not recommended for a Mud Daddy. No beer on a long weekend fishing trip can have serious repercussions. People can get surly, touchy, easily offended. And everybody has a knife. You don't want to go there. So we headed into town to find a golf course and beer. The first thing we learned was that the lake was in a dry county, never a good thing. Jesus turned water into wine because his Mom asked him to do it, so what's wrong with these people? The second thing we learned at the convenience store was that if we wanted to avoid a 30-mile trip to Tennessee for beer, we could go two miles down the road, hang a right, pull up to the first house on the right and honk our horn. The clerk stopped short of telling us what would happen next, but we had a pretty good idea. So did the state highway patrolman who was on his way out the door with us. The clerk apparently didn't think he'd mind. Big E looked at the statie and shrugged: Kentucky, go figure.

We followed the directions to the house but didn't have to honk the horn. Maybe because it was a Saturday afternoon, the best time for a cold beer, an old-timer was already waiting. He was sitting on the porch as we pulled up to his trailer and in no hurry to find his feet. But eventually he got up out of his living room chair and ambled to a garage where there was a refrigerator full of Budweiser. Packed, top to bottom. We were amazed. At six bucks a six-pack, the price was steeper than the valley across the road, but we didn't care. A Mud Daddy needed beer!

It was time for golf and off E-man, Drewsie and Slim bounded.

They found it, too, a forgettable goat track that offered hillside views of cows grazing and greens that resembled tees at any other course in America, and, of course, at least one memorable hole. The green on No. 7 remains an artifact of Mud Daddy folklore. Slim, ever the crooner, had made the weekend into a one-song Julio Iglesias festival based on his appreciation for the lush instrumentation on a 1984 Julio release that was later re-released as 1100 Bel Air Place. The song "Moonlight Lady" segues into a chorus of "It Never Rains in Southern California," a pop song popularized by Albert Hammond, and Slim loved it. He couldn't get enough of it, in fact.

"Mooooooonlight Laaaaheeeeeaaady, Shine your light on me. Through zee bright city lights, city lights let them shine on meeeeeee … Zeeaaaay say eeeet never rains eeeen Southern Caleeeefornia . . . Eeeet never rains in Caleeeefornia, so hey, don't they warn yah, eeeet poursssss, oh man eeeet pours."

So Slim crooned Julio while facing down an improbable if not impossible 35-foot putt. He drained it. Then, absolutely delighted, he continued to sing as Drewsie putted his 25-footer. He drained it. E-Dog was next up. He commanded Slim to sing. Slim obligeeeed him: "Eeeeet poursssss, man eeeet pours. …"

E-Dog drained it, too.

Some things on a Mud Daddy you just can't explain.

After we broke camp the next day, the Budweiser having long since been consumed, we toasted one last time the Daughter of Darkness with the final swigs of gin from a hip flask Slim had kept in abeyance.

Just in case.

Pasta Luray Neapolitan

For the price of a pound and a half of good, Italian sausage and the addition of a sliced green pepper added about half an hour before serving, you can Neapolitanize Doc's Famous Pasta Luray recipe.

This is John Erardi's personal wrinkle on this Mud Daddy staple. It's a nice touch, a tribute to his family's roots in Napoli. All you have to do is leave out the ground beef, and while Doc is at the cutting board preparing the rest of the sauce, fry up the Italian sausage, add it to Doc's sauce and let it cook therein for however long you'd like (a half hour is fine; same as the sliced green pepper which can then be served on the side, al dente, as a nice side dish.)

The next day, by the way, you can have Italian sausage hoagies with sauce, or fry up some peppers and onions with the leftover (unsauced) sausage for a kick-ass sandwich that makes a morning on the water without fish a lot easier to bear.

Chapter IX - Muskie Hunting with Pete

Mud Daddy tip: *Anytime you see a fish hawk or heron steadfastly hunting in a bay, from the shore or perched in a shoreline tree, immediately head over to the bird. Your approach will annoy it to no end and cause it to leave, usually with a squawk. That's too bad. You're there because he was there, and he was there because he catches more fish than you do. Fish will be in his vicinity. Count on it. Wild animals are hungry all the time. And when a heron hunts small fish, there's a timeless rule about small fish and big fish that comes into play. You want the big fish. Use a herons or storks or gulls as God-given fish finders. Start casting at the 20-foot depth and drift or simply figure it out. But first find the bird. Then you'll find the fish.*

From the comfort of a suburban living room on a late summer morning, Southern Indiana's Lake Patoka looked like dream water. The icy blue smear on the Rand McNally map suggested that God's little fingernail had gouged a trough from the heartland hills of Hoosier National Forest and, as for fish, well, they simply had to be here. This time we would assuredly catch many. The only question about this water, really, was one of pronunciation: was it PAH-tooo-ka or was it PAH-toe-ka? It was a muskie lake, all the brochures hyped, and that is always an exciting proposition, particularly during those optimistic hours early in a Mud Daddy, when reality has not yet visited this annual festival of food, fun and excess. This would be the year!

The muskellunge, all the books claim, is a fresh-water shark, an enormous pig of a fish that eats Northern Pike for breakfast and large bass for lunch. These monsters have razor-sharp teeth, attack lures with the ferocity of a tiger and are known to chomp wooden Rapalas in half. Old fishermen tell stories of mythical muskies prowling the weed beds and shallows of a deep Midwestern lake. When finally caught, these beasts had one, maybe two lures — antique Daredevils or Pikie Minnows, no doubt – embedded in their long bony jaws, artifacts from fishermen decades past, men who were now food for beetles. The lures were there because the fisherman did not have the presence of mind to use a wire leader – lengths of woven steel that protect the frail monofilament line – from the sharp teeth of the giant. When a muskie is caught, sometimes it speeds to the surface and hurls itself out of the water in an enraged tail-walking spectacle. Flopping there on the surface is a fish that can be the size of a big man's leg.

We had to see that. We would catch a muskie. The fates would be with us this time. That was the optimism that filled the car as Slim, Doc and Big E set out for southern Indiana early on a Thursday morning. We were burning through two precious days of vacation, beloved escapes from the grind of newspaper deadlines.

E-man described journalism at a daily newspaper this way: Elephant keeper's wife and the elephant keeper are at the kitchen table. He's got his shit scooper and broom nearby. He's happy. Outside the window is his happy elephant, getting ready to drop another load. The wife wants her husband to get a new job and is looking at the classified ads in a newspaper. He looks up at his wife and says: "What? And get out of show business?"

On the tape player – no CDs because they weren't yet common in 1989, if they existed at all – we had John Mellencamp, who always did the best that he could do and was somehow on Slim's top five list for the reigning King of rock and roll. This was a debate he raised annually: Who is the king of rock and roll now that Elvis is dead? Mellencamp's "Small Town" was a bittersweet American anthem, and "Authority Song" from his "Uh-Huh" album explained why so many Americans in their worn DeKalb Corn baseball caps and cut-off blue jeans sneered their way through life. "Rain on the Scarecrow" was a bleak and true tale of American greed and its bitter consequences for those stuck on life's blue-collar rung. And "Jack and Diane" has never gotten old.

We were hauling down the interstate at 75 mph, and the lake seemed to be getting no closer, but the slate clouds overhead were. By the time we hit the blue line state highways – always the last two hours of Mud Daddy driving seem to be on twisting state highways or even twistier county roads – the sky was black and the early October air held more than a hint of December.

On Indiana Highway 37 north of I-64 and west of Jeffersonville, Ind., we saw a terrapin trying to cross the road. He was probably in abject terror and stuck on the yellow line.

"Hey, why'd the chicken stop in the middle of the road?" Slim asked.

Vacant looks.

"He wanted to lay it alllllllllll on the line.

"Hahhhhhh!"

Slim was the only one laughing, but he didn't care. He slammed on the brakes and ran back to the terrapin. He grabbed it, not knowing quite what to do with it but certain he had to save it and that it was part of God's plan that this little guy accompany them on a Mud Daddy. So onto the floor of the mini-van it went, down there with the Cheerios and juice boxes and other debris from 1,000 commutes to day care, soccer practice and the like.

The logistics of launching onto big water are always a challenge, and Patoka would keep that tradition intact. The rain that began falling as we were loading the boat soon turned into a downpour. Plastic tarpaulins for tent ground cloths and auxiliary awnings at the soon-to-be occupied campground were pressed into service to cover the supplies and gear on the boat. Bungee cords, a last-minute addition to the quartermaster list, came in handy to hold down those tarps. Under the tarps, too, went the terp. He had a name now: Pete, for the disgraced, gambling baseball player, Pete Rose, who lost his career to guys named Bruno, Mikey and Vinnie.

According to the authorities at the boat rental, our campground area, supposedly overlooking the lake and home to a wilderness picnic table, was more than a mile down the lake from the put-in where the boat bobbed. E-Man and Doc decided to drop the car and bushwhack along shore. Pete made his presence felt in the boat, clawing up the aluminum skin only to slide back after a foot or so. He never quit. He would stop from time to time when a shoe came too close, snapping his lids shut only to tentatively reappear and begin again to trudge in a futile effort to escape. Step, step, step, step, sccccchhhhhhhh, over and over.

When we got under way, the lake's points reached out into the water, but they began to fade in the heavy rain and mist, so Slim

The Mud Daddy Chronicles

churned along the shoreline and began to count: one point passed, two points passed – hmmm how many was it again? Three? Four? Damn, I shoulda written it down. Rain turned to sleet, then back to rain. Slim was wishing he had an umbrella because, although the rain was heavy, the wind was not blowing and an umbrella would have kept him drier than the cheap rain suit he wore. (It would be a lesson he'd employ a decade later on a lake so dead that the marina owner couldn't bear the guilt of selling a lure to E-Man, even though the Big Italian from Syracuse had cash at the ready. The guy refused to sell him the lure! Everyone in the tackle shop had marveled at Slim on that day, piloting the john boat through the storm, smoking a dry cigar under his big golf umbrella. What a power move, Slim thought. What an idiot, everybody else thought.)

Around a bend in the cold, driving rain came yet another point and on it stood a slouching Doc. "This is the campground," he said. No flat tent site, no picnic table, no fire ring. Nothing but tall trees and deep brush. The tent would rise under a grove of oak and hickory, and the fishing … well, didn't fresh rain always bring fresh fish?

At dusk and just before dinner, as a way of dedicating this camp, we took a bag of shag golf balls that E-Man had tossed into the boat, a few tees and his old wooden driver and walked higher up the wooded hill to see which big-hitter could crush a ball out of the woods. There was a window among the branches, and maybe Tiger Woods could sneak a ball through the opening and out into the lake. At worse, E-Man figured, the ricochets ought to make for some nice special effects. We were fueled, at this point, with equal parts Tequila and Old Forrester.

"Whaddya think, Slim? Can I fade this baby through that clearing?"

"You are the original big hitter. Crush it."

Doc, always mystified at the grip this sport had on his fishing pals, was nevertheless ready to whack a few balls himself. He stood safely, he thought, behind E-Man. The effect of a drive from deep in the woods goes something like this: WHACK, BAM, BAM, BAM, WHACK, BAM as the ball bounces from tree to tree in a flight so quick that you can't follow it, especially when it's in the gloaming of the day. It's a very unnerving feeling but, at the same time, absolutely and mysteriously hilarious.

After one of E's monster drives, Doc's eyes widened.

That one whistled by my head!" His voice rang with incredulity.

"Couldn't see it, but it missed me by inches. Sounded like the 'Nam."

The hillside echoed with laughter.

WHACK! BAM, BAM, BAM.

Ball after ball until we were tired and the light was gone and it was too tough to see the ball on the tee. Then Slim remembered something: Pete – the terrapin, was still doing his Electric Glide thing down in the boat: step, step, step, step, sliiiiiiide. Step, step, step, step, sliiiiide. He'd been doing that for hours. Slim brought him up to the camp, and Pete didn't wait long to make a break for it. But that would never do. Pete was scolded. "Pete, you're an ungrateful creature. We saved you from certain death out there on the road, and like it or not you are in for the long haul, here, just like the rest of us."

We gathered sticks about the diameter of a man's thumb and gouged them deep into the dirt. It looked like a miniature bull pen, and into the impromptu pen went Pete. Soon, Pete calmly went at the sticks. He couldn't budge them. He kept trying all through the night, though. Cold, wet and miserable, Doc retired to the tent.

But Big E and Slim remained by the smoldering fire, with E tuning the AM radio for any kind of after-midnight broadcast. E soon found an English translation of top Japanese news events from the day, and his eyebrows went up.

"This holds the potential for strangeness," he muttered.

E's instincts were dead on. Heading the news report? A new species of critter had crawled from the Sea of Japan that day – a 30-pound salamander-sealizard thing, the announcer intoned, his voice riding a current of static. E and Slim stared at one another across the fire in wide-eyed wonder as they pondered the odds of: 1) Stumbling upon an English translation of a Japanese radio broadcast by the light of a dying Mud Daddy campfire. 2) The lead news item is the discovery of a giant Mud Daddesque creature half-a-world away. 3) The discovery occurs while the annual Mud Daddy is in full karmic swing. Slim and E are staggered by the cosmic confluence as the Vortex had once again touched their world. It was wondrously mysterious.

In the morning, Pete was deep in his shell and still in the pen.

By noon that day, he would be gone.

"There's a lesson in Pete's tenacity," Doc said, philosophically. Doc was always looking for lessons, if only to ignore them once he found one.

"What was it Churchill said about when you find yourself going through hell? Keep going, right? Never quit. That's Pete. Outta here."

The morning of fishing dragged into a dismal afternoon. This Mud Daddy was shaping up as a world-class skunking. "When you're going through hell . . ."

Slim then solemnly announced that he was going to catch a muskie. He reeled in and began to rig for the Crowned King of all freshwater fish.

"Sure you are, asshole," came the rejoinders.

By Mud Daddy standards, rigging for muskie is a painstakingly slow process – time when others will still be casting, and, therefore, more likely to land a fish. So it's a risk. Here's how it happens. First, bite the line or clip off the existing lure. Then, fuss around in the tackle box for a wire leader: six inches is fine, but a foot-long or 18-inch steel woven wire leader has more aplomb. Tie it with a double-loop-through-the-swivel-eye fisherman's knot. That takes a while because it never goes right the first time, and the knot has to be a good one.

Give up on the knot for now, and find your bifocals. Once the bifocals are found, go back to the challenge. Eventually tie the knot. Now, find and withdraw the largest Rapala from your tackle box and put it on the seat beside you. Look at it from time to time as you hunt for some large split shot to implant on the line about 18 inches to 24 inches above the lure swivel. If the split shot is not heavy enough, use an elongated sinker that has tiny clips on either end that are supposed to hold it in place on the line. They never hold very well, but crimp them anyhow. Muskie sometimes feed in fairly shallow water, and while a surface running Rapala will do in those cases, a Rapala-sinker combo will ensure that the lure hits proper running depth from the beginning. Clip on the Rapala.

Now the best part. Everybody has been ignoring you through this because it takes a long time, believe it or not, to do all the above, so pendulum the thing in front of a skunked buddy's face when he's not expecting it so it picks up his malevolence. Suggest that the next fish anybody sees will be the biggest fish they've ever seen in their life, as you then wave it out over the water for all to see. Nobody will look at it or you. Doesn't matter. From the center of the boat, where the others are watching it with suspicion and wariness, maybe even leaning back or hanging onto their hat bills because they remember Laurel from the early days, flip out a cast along the weed bed and begin to reel with focus. As if you are actually expecting to catch a fish.

Mind that this entire episode (the announcement of the earnest quest for a muskie, the process of rigging for it and the actual cast) is a manifestation of optimism and hope that is beyond profound. By now it's been two full days of three grown men casting pretty much non-stop and still no fish, not even a bite. To think that somewhere out there along this weed bed in six feet of murky water a muskie waiting to be caught is crazy talk, or maybe a crazy man talking. But the spirit is infectious, and soon E-Man couldn't stand it anymore. He reeled in to clip on a giant orange Rat-L-Trap as he, too, had given up on bass and would now return to his quest for the elusive muskie.

Understand that experience ed fishermen will troll for hour upon hour just for one follow-up, and that it usually takes something like 100 hours of trolling just to catch one of these Titans. So the effort was more Vaudevillian than anything else. None of us had ever caught a muskie. Slim claims he saw one wallow around on top of the water up in Canada when he was a kid. But it was some other guy's boat, and Slim was just on the way back to camp from swimming on a beach that was just 50 yards shy of where this monster was caught.

After the 20th cast, E-Man reeled in and posed a question.

"Hmmmm, was that a hit or just weeds?"

It electrified the boat. Because that is, of course, the eternal question when fishing for muskie, and Doc and Slim had read enough about this fish to immediately peer down to the water with intense focus to see if E's lure was trailing green sludge or if something else of a far more substantial nature was going on here. In other words, did a muskie hit E's lure and back up to make it a straight shot and thus easier to get the smaller fish down the gullet?

And then, slowly, a giant green head materialized directly behind E-Dog's Rat-L-Trap. It was an arm's length from the boat and a wicked thing, too, this fish-face. A head as big as a hound dog's noggin'. A jaw with an under bite of tiny, razor teeth. This fish looked like a log. He hung at the weed line just long enough for all of us to get an eyeful. Then he was gone, back to the murky green depths of an Indiana lake.

Singing Mellencamp spontaneously throughout the weekend ("That's when a sport was a sport, and groovin' was groovin…"), the fierce face of a malicious muskie, a thorough soaking of icy rain, golf ball ricochets, the adventure with Pete, and a granola/apple baked by a campfire: Even without fish, this Mud Daddy was a full one. Doc took home the plaque until a clear winner could emerge a year later. Assuming we all lived to see it.

"In the end, it's not the years in your life that count. It's the life in your years."
Abraham Lincoln

Rankin, Lowery, and Eckberg at Laurel Lake, Kentucky, October 1983 -
Ready to off-load.

Lowery, Erardi, and Eckberg at Laurel Lake, Kentucky, October 1983 -
Heading out for a morning of fishing.

The Mud Daddy Chronicles

Rankin at Laurel Lake, Kentucky, October 1983 - Fishing alone.

Lowery, Erardi, and Rankin at Laurel Lake, Kentucky, October 1983 - Taking a break and talking baseball.

Rankin, Eckberg, Erardi, and Lowery at Laurel Lake, Kentucky, October 1983 - Listening to the World Series by a campfire.

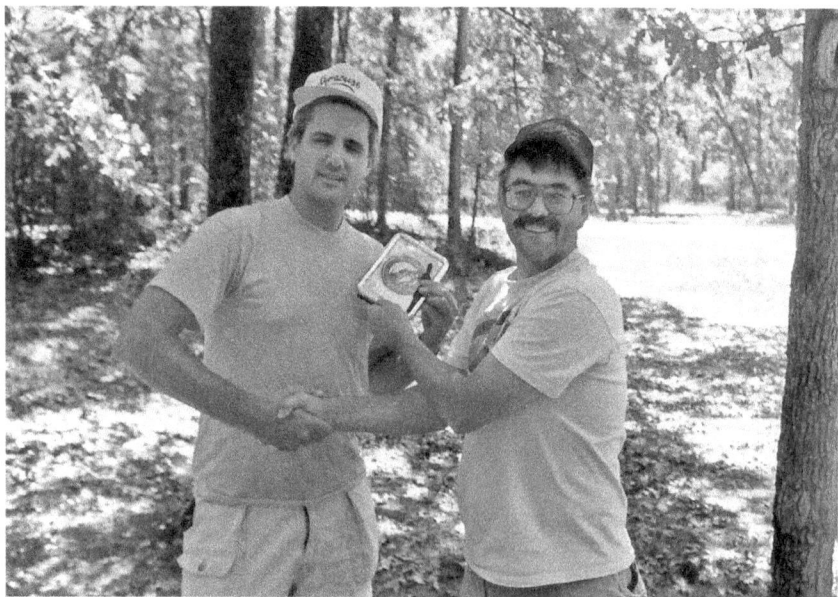

Erardi and Lowery at Lake Rayburn, Texas, September 1990 - Doc surrenders Outstanding Angler Trophy to Big E.

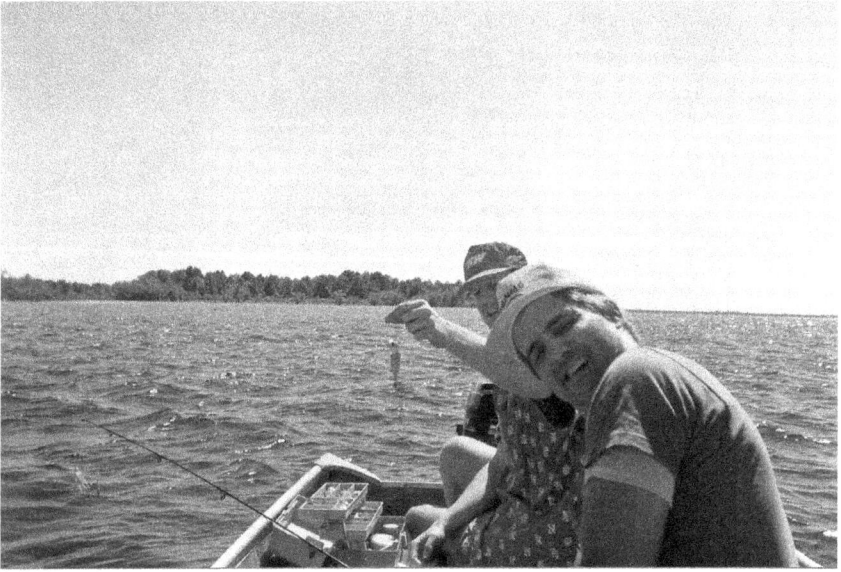

Eckberg and Erardi at Lake Rayburn, Texas, September 1990 - Who has the craziest bait? Looks like Big E.

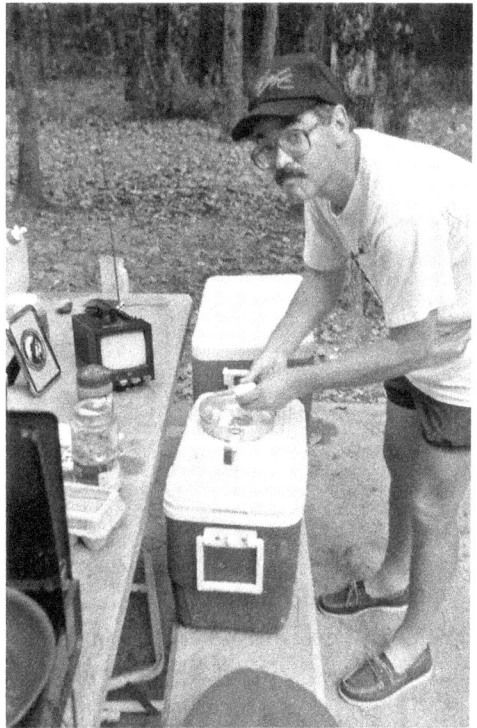

Doc at Lake Rayburn, Texas, September 1990 - Cooking dinner . . . And eyeing the trophy.

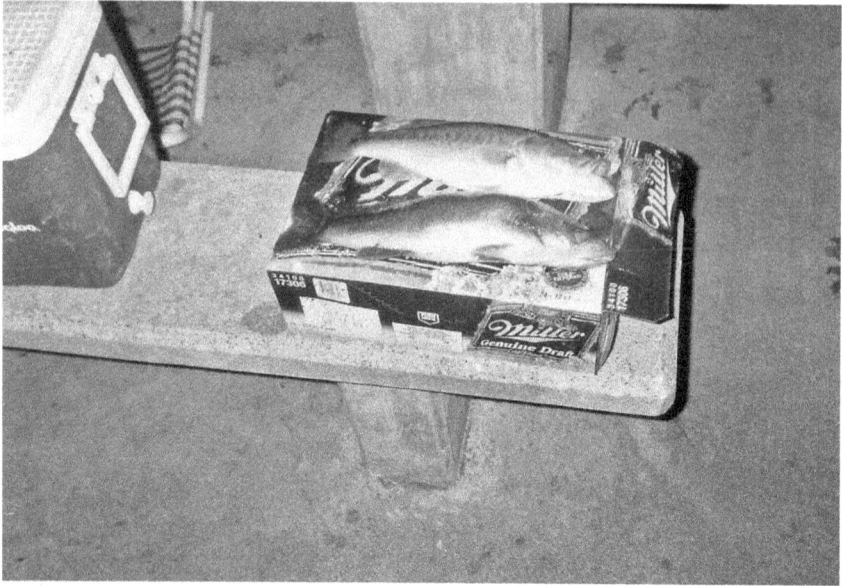

Lake Rayburn, Texas, September 1990 - The day's catch. The night's meal.

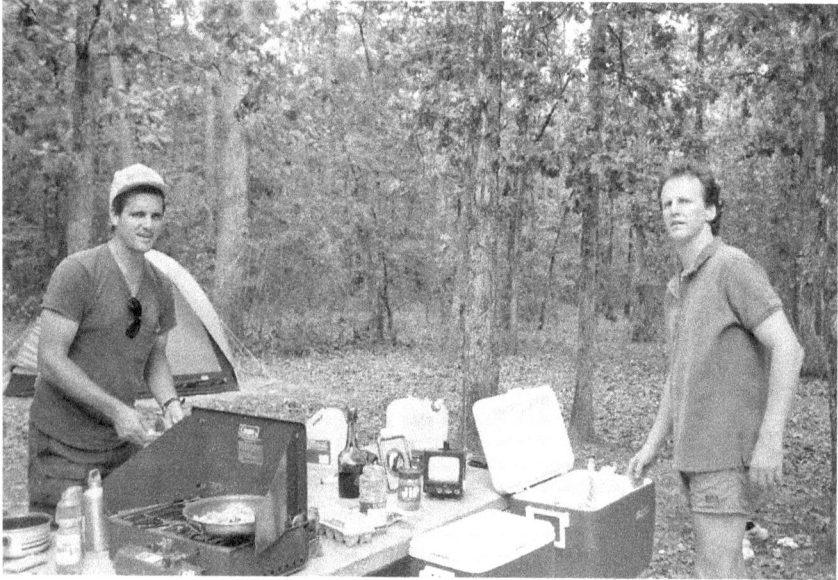

Erardi and Eckberg at Lake Rayburn, Texas, September 1990 - Cooking up a storm. But did that TV even work?

Slim Eckberg at Lake Rayburn, Texas, September 1990 - Eggberg acting out.

Lake Moomaw, Virginia, June 1992 - Sunsetting on a mountain lake.

Lowery and Eckberg at Lake Moomaw, Virginia, June 1992 - Slim at the helm as usual.

Lowery at Lake Moomaw, Virginia, June 1992 - First bass of the weekend.

The Mud Daddy Chronicles

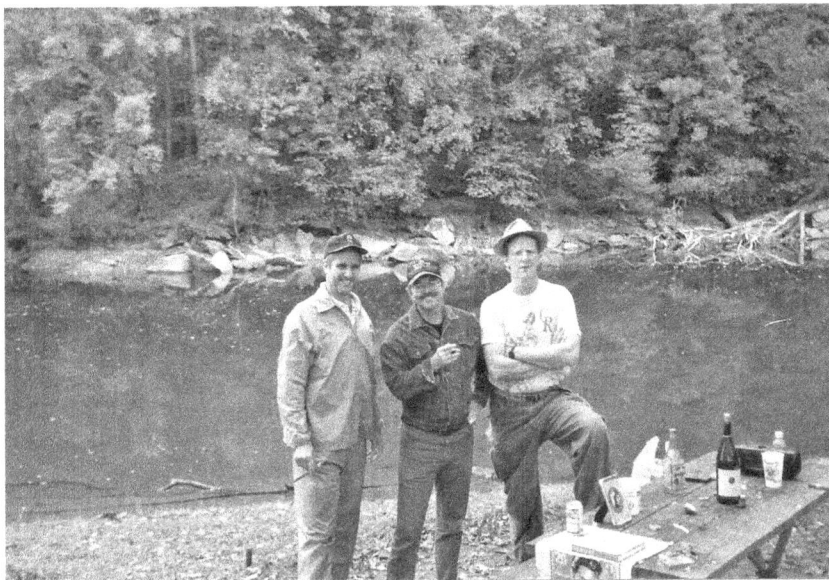

Erardi, Lowery, and Eckberg at Summerville Lake, West Virginia, October 1993 - Homage to the King with Cuervo Gold.

Eckberg and Erardi at Summerville Lake, West Virginia, October 1993 - The rental car after hitting a buck on the drive in.

Rankin and Lowery at Summerville Lake, West Virginia, October 1993 - Two old friends enjoying the day.

Lowery at Lake Travis, Texas, November 1994 - First catch of the day.

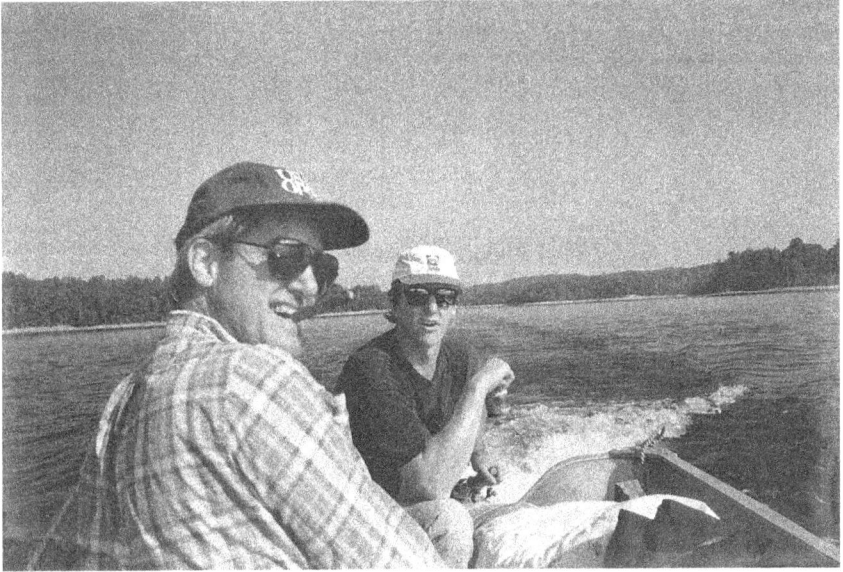
Erardi and Eckberg at Lake Ouchita, Arkansas, October 1996 - Captain Slim and First Mate Big E heading out.

Erardi and Eckberg at Lake Ouchita, Arkansas, October 1996 - Working out of a pontoon boat on a beautiful fall day.

Erardi and Lowery at Pickwick Lake, Tennessee, October 1999 - Rigging up for that big bass.

Lowery at Pickwick Lake, Tennessee, October 1999 - Checking out the producer.

The Mud Daddy Chronicles

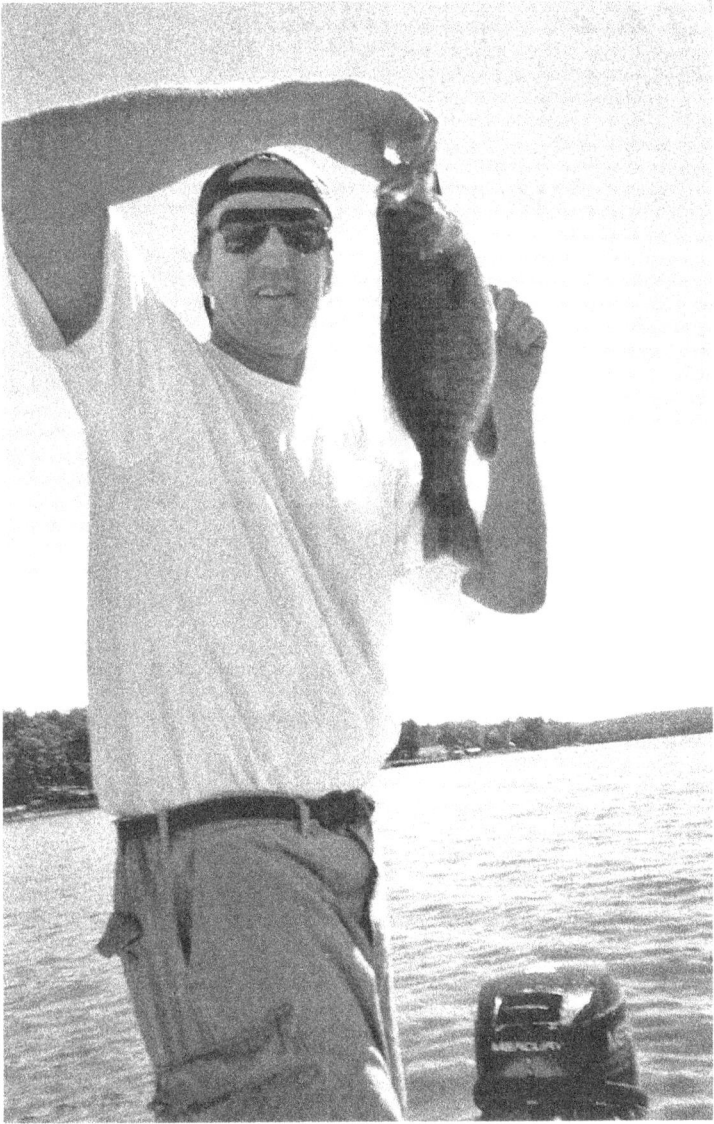

Eckberg at Pickwick Lake, Tennessee, October 1999 - Slim catches the nicest bass of the weekend.

Eckberg at Pickwick Lake,
Tennessee, October 1999 -
Slim wins the trophy with
a nice catch.

Eckberg at Pickwick Lake,
Tennessee, October 1999 -
The champion angler with
his hardware.

Somewhere in the South, October 1999.

Lowery and Erardi at Pickwick Lake, Tennessee, October 1999 - Anchor Beer and stogies. Doesn't get much better.

Chapter X - Modified Limited Overhead Whipcast

Mud Daddy tip: *Most aluminum john boats rented by the weekend do not come with anchors or even rope, for that matter. Well, sometimes they do, but you can't count on it. And you will need an anchor, particularly on big lakes with water movement and wind. Without an anchor, the wind will blow the boat to shore from a prime fishing spot in a matter of minutes. Always bring along at least one anchor and 50 feet or more of rope, though two anchors are usually better. But do not – DO NOT – spend any money for a real anchor from a marine supply store. Instead, make your own in one of these ways: fill a paint bucket 2/3 full of concrete two weeks ahead of the trip and set a loop of coat hanger into the still-wet mash (the bucket handle will not hold.) Another great anchor is a brake hub from a junkyard. Five bucks is a fair price if you can't get it for free. Or rummage around in your garage for a trio of bricks, the kind with holes in them. Four ought to do nicely. But the best anchor by far is one you make on-the-spot. Bring along a basketball net and fill it with rocks, then tie it off. Or cut a fist-sized hole in the top of an empty gallon milk jug and four pencil-sized holes opposite one another at the bottom. Stuff two sticks in an X-shape through the bottom holes then fill the jug with rocks. Of course you'll forget to haul it up at least once – like with Crazy Jim's boat at Pickwick; more later on that one – and it's always a surprise to see the concrete block surface about 30 feet behind the boat as the captain – Slim, in our case – will be fussing and cussing at the throttle because he doesn't understand why the boat isn't going any faster.*

"No, E, like this."

Doc stood in the bow of the john boat, a cigar clenched in his teeth, beer can on the seat beside him. He lifted his rod straight over his head, arms fully extended. He bent back slightly, the tip of the rod arching back with him from the weight of the dangling crankbait. Then, with a quick thrust, he snapped his body forward, his wrists creating a whip-like motion that shot the big lure forward in a speeding arc.

"See?" Doc mumbled through the soggy cigar. "It's like the physics behind a tennis serve. You get the power at the very top."

"I don't think that's much like a tennis serve," Slim commented. "And I know you don't know shit about physics. But we got to give it a name."

Doc looked back, grinning and reeling in a four-ounce Crank bait. "I call it the Modified Limited Overhead Whipcast. Whaddya think?"

"Oh, yeah," crowed Big E. "Gotta love it. Watergate overtones and all."

It was early afternoon on Lake Rayburn in deep East Texas in late September 1990, which is still hard summer in that part of the country. In fact, it was scorching. The fish had quit on us hours ago, but we had beer, beef jerky, pepperoni, cheese, cigars and more beer. We were well-provisioned and we weren't going in. Instead, we went into full Mud Daddy mode by having a casting contest. Who could cast the farthest with the most accuracy – and with the most style? Big E always had a cannon of a rod in his case, which actually looks like a cannon, and big crank baits he could throw for what seemed like a hundred yards. He ran away with the distance award.

Doc and Slim competed for accuracy, with little agreement about who was tossing the most strikes. But when Doc came up with the Modified Limited Overhead Whipcast, the style competition was over. The three of us practiced it, laughing at ourselves as we whipped the stupidest, ugliest, silliest, strangest baits we could find at imaginary "hot spots" on the huge lake. We actually thought it might be working as a casting technique. But that probably was the effect of the sun and the beer.

We were fishing – or more accurately, casting – our way to another spot when another boat approached and a game warden hailed us. "Man, this day is shaping up to be a real Mud Daddy," Slim observed sourly as the lawman's boat came alongside. Imagine what we had looked like to him from across the lake. Not good.

Like most everyone, we all have had mostly minor and mostly

unpleasant histories with law enforcement. Slim and Doc had actually seen jail bars from the inside during periods of youthful indiscretion. Small potatoes, really, but it leaves a certain taste. Big-E had several incidents concerning automobiles he doesn't like to talk about. We all agree that when guys in uniform come around, it is rarely good news for any of us.

"You boys doing any good today?" the warden asked, with that phony, good-old-boy tone common to men with badges in the South. He was as transparent as spring water.

"None at all," Slim replied, flashing a grin, no teeth, like he was approaching a Silverback gorilla in the wild and going for eye-contact, but not too much. Slim had faith that eye contact would bring him empathy and perhaps the treasured "I'll-let-you-go-this-time" warning. He does the talking in almost every situation and turned up the wattage on his smile to wry. But still no teeth. Teeth, even in a smile, triggers that fight/flight response and cops run from nobody. We are mammals and have mammalian instincts. Never smile and show your teeth when trying to buffalo somebody….that was Slim's rule. "We caught zip. Come on, tell the truth. There's no fish in this lake, right?"

The warden chuckled absentmindedly, then went ominous. "Mind if I see your licenses?" Slim and Big-E handed them over. Doc had a little more trouble.

Doc was, at that moment, sprawled in the bottom of the aluminum boat at an awkward angle, head on his hands along the gunwale. It took a moment for him to claw his way out of his ready-to-puke position, the water-cop eyeing him suspiciously all the while. With some difficulty he handed over his resident's license.

"Not feeling too good are you?" the warden asked archly.

"Too much cigar smoke," Doc answered honestly, slowly lowering his head back onto his hands and covering his eyes with the bill of his cap.

"Well, you boys are OK," the Mountie said as he handed Slim and E their licenses. Then, looking at the green-gilled Doc, "But yours is expired."

Uh-oh. Trouble coming. It was inevitable, wasn't it? One of us was going to get busted for something.

"What?" Doc yelped, struggling to sit up. "I just bought it last month."

The cop explained that in Texas, annual licenses expire at the end of August. You have to get a new one in September. It was a crazy wrinkle of law, since changed, thankfully. "But since you weren't actually fishing, I'll let it go," the cop said. "But don't be fishing out here until you get a new one."

"Thanks," Doc sighed. "I appreciate it."

The warden left, and we were sputtering our way around the big water looking for the hydrilla – underwater plants that reach the surface and form a bed of greenery – because that's where everybody said the big fish were holding. Thinking he'd ducked the law and lightning doesn't hit the same place twice, Doc immediately started fishing. Soon, dark clouds appeared and the wind picked up dramatically. With heavy weather upon us, we headed across open water at one of the widest parts of the lake, trying to beat the storm and get ourselves back to the marina before the situation got treacherous. Wrong move. Shortly after we started across, the motor coughed and died and we were instantly at the mercy of a gusting wind on big water. It was, after all, a Mud Daddy.

"Shit," Doc groaned. "People die on this lake every year just this way. Storm swamps their boats and they're gone."

Stinging rain pelted us as the wind shoved our helpless craft towards the shoreline. White caps were everywhere as we bobbed like a cork on the water, the round-bottomed boat tipping precariously with each wave. By the time we ran aground we were soaked and shivering, but relieved at being alive.

What now?

"We could wait for help to come by, if it comes by," Doc said. "But would anyone see or hear us?"

"We could bushwhack to the marina and tell 'em what happened," offered Slim.

"Do both," E said.

Doc and Slim decided to hang out on shore and try to hail a passing boat for a tow back. E would hike through the brush to try to find the marina and return with another boat. As E pushed his way into the woods, Slim and Doc, with nervous laughs, wondered if they'd ever see him again.

After an hour had passed, Slim and Doc were seriously worried. Did E get hurt? Did he stumble into the lake somewhere? Or was he just wandering around lost in this huge National Forest? Was the big man crashing through the woods, thrashing among the trees and underbrush like a wounded bear, lost, angry and confused? Or was he at the marina drinking beer, talking sports and laughing with the locals? The storm had moved on, but there was no sign of E-Daddy. After an eternity or two, Slim hailed a passing bass boat and got a tow back to the marina. As they were dragging in, wet and tired and somewhat humiliated by the circumstances, Big-E was gunning another john boat away from the dock.

"What do we do now?" he asked when he saw us in tow. "I just rented this boat for half a day."

"What the hell," Slim barked, his mood instantly lightened. "Let's fish."

We found the hydrilla and went at it with rubber worms, top water crank baits and rubber lizards rigged Texas style, with a sliding bullet sinker hard against the rubber bait. Though it was too late in the season for rubber lizards, it was Slim's only top-water lure, so he threw one colorful wriggler after another onto the weed pads. Nothing. A splash now and again but not much else. Meanwhile, Doc and Big E were slaying largemouth bass with top-water crank baits they jerked across the surface at the edge of the hydrilla patches. It was like nothing seen before on a Mud Daddy. Big E hauled in a three-pounder, then a two-and-a-half pounder. On and on it went.

E-Man tossed a silver-blue torpedo he'd purchased at the marina then ripped it back. He always asks marina managers what is working best and buys two. It's a "trust-in-the-kindness-of-strangers" sort of thing, and sometimes it works. Slim and Doc are way more skeptical about marina managers' suggestions and rarely act on them. But this time E's trusting nature paid off.

Doc's Bass Assassin was getting good action, too. It moved across the weeds like J-Lo at a South Beach night club. But Doc was having trouble. His style that afternoon had a cartoonish element. Think Mickey and Goofy fishing in a tiny boat. (Donald Duck would be somewhere complaining – that's always Slim. Like Donald, few folks actually listen to his lamentations.) Doc would reel, get a hit and pull back too fast, ripping the lure out of the bass's mouth before the hook was set. This is what all guys do when they haven't caught a fish in awhile.

"You're killing me, Doc," Slim cried in exasperation. "You've missed more bass than I've caught in two years. Open the bail and count to three or something before you try to set the hook, will you? You're driving me nuts."

"Hey, Slimbagger," E said impatiently. "We're competing here.

Don't be giving Le Docteur any help in any way shape or form. Let him keep missing 'em. If he wants to pull out too soon, that's his business. Maybe that's his style. So button it."

Doc slowed down his punch and began to boat a few nice bass. None the size of E-Man's haul, however.

The day was complete. We'd had an encounter with the law, nearly capsized, floated to shore, developed and experimented with a strange and fascinating casting technique, and lucked our way into some primo bass along the way. Living large, we were. We fished the hydrilla until the late summer sun sank below the Texas horizon. The day was done, and another Mud Daddy was ending. We turned the boat and headed back, with only the lambent lights of the marina to guide us home.

Antipasto Plate

Whenever possible, have an antipasto plate before your main meal. It eases those pangs that come on when you've been on the water too long and dinner is still an hour away. Antipasto is an Erardi special. He is master of the wilderness antipasto, and the following recipe has been a continuing pleasure for decades. Use a little greenery if you like, but the true antipastos have none. Sometimes, we have a touch of green salad with it, most of the time, not. This is for post-fishing noshing, when the fish aren't biting but the fishermen are.

Ingredients:

Sliced up pickled eggs from your pickled egg jar.

Thinly sliced marinated onion from your pickled egg jar.

Salami sliced up in thin strips from your sandwich stash.

Artichokes (in oil in jar, we prefer, but we did non-oil in can in '04 and like it, too).

Provolone cheese sliced into thin strips from your sandwich stash.

Olives. A mixture of Greek and Italian from a deli jar but black Spanish in a can are welcome, as well.

Italian bread ripped into chunks (toasted in thin slices if it's so dry you worry about chipping a tooth).

Nothing beats saltines, either.

Sop up the oil with the bread or crackers. Cold beer from the can to cut down on dish washing.

Chapter XI - Cheating Death Again

Mud Daddy tip: *This one looks strange from shore but is very effective when the boat motor does not run slow enough to give the lure an attractive and realistic action. Instead of trolling at idle speed going forward, put the engine in reverse and troll backwards. Sending the stern into the waves instead of the bow will slow the speed of the boat immensely, thereby bringing a lazy action to the lures now arrayed out the bow. Also, do not cast to get the lure out into the water when trolling. Your line may get fouled around the lure hooks on a cast, and nothing is as frustrating as spending a half-hour trolling, then reeling in only to find that the lure was fouled for the entire time that it was in the water. Think, too, about trolling with the anchor at a five-foot-mark to ensure a slow speed.*

The pattern was established. We had been doing this for a decade now and knew what to expect: The fishing could be mediocre or worse, but none of it would matter because we would have a great time anyway. In addition, there would be unusual acts of God, unexplainable vortexual events and strange encounters with wildlife.

That fall we found ourselves in a sweet cabin on a hilltop overlooking Lake Ouachita outside Hot Springs, Arkansas. We had a television that was locked onto the League Championship Series (the Braves and Twins would win), and in a fit of exuberance at our good fortune, we rented a pontoon boat rather than the usual low-rent john boats. The outpost was owned by Tommy Trantner, and after meeting him we knew a full-moon vortex would shine upon us this trip. Trantner, we learned, had been an all-conference defensive back at the University of Arkansas in the 1960s. His wife looked like she belonged with him, too. The former Razorback cheerleader was still a raven-haired beauty. In keeping with his hellbent-for-action outlook as a DB, Trantner apparently did nothing halfway. Later that weekend we spotted him in scuba gear spear fishing for big bass.

"Where y'all from?" he asked us. When Doc said Austin, Trantner's eyes narrowed and he gave Doc a critical once-over.

"You go to UT?"

"No, Ohio State."

It's a good thing because otherwise we might not have been allowed to rent a boat. Texas and Arkansas were playing in the Southwest Conference for one of the last times that season. Their rivalry was a storied one. With the Austin connection sufficiently explained, we took the pontoon out in high spirits. Nothing different in that – we always set out in high spirits, only to have reality send us crashing back to earth. Right away, the "Zara Spooks" hot lure we were promised "couldn't miss" didn't do much. When we motored up to a small arm off the main lake, though, each of us landed an odd fish.

"What you got there, Doc? A muskie?" Slim asked when Doc pulled the first one into the boat.

"Can't be. Too small, isn't it? And not much fight in it."

Then Big E landed another, slightly larger one. It went about a pound and a half.

"What else could it be? Think there are muskie in here? It's too hot here, isn't it?" asked E.

Slim pulled one in before the fishing shut down totally. We shrugged and headed out. Tommy told us later that what we caught were chain pickerel, not muskies by a long shot. We didn't care. A chain pickerel was still a fish! We had caught fish! And we ate fish that night – at Tommy's restaurant. His fish, no doubt.

During the ball game on TV, Big E reproduced his now-famous chart, and we each bet on which inning a certain event would occur. There were a few bunts and double steals on the chart, but mostly it was the unusual: first to spit (top of the first), first error, first crotch-grab (bottom of the first), mouthing the F-word, throwing a helmet into the dugout, punching the water cooler (seldom and not this game). Not an intellectual exercise, exactly, but damn fun. Baseball is pretty boring most of the time. Better in the abstract, as E always said, quoting MLB writer Chris Haft. But with Big E's chart, every producer's quick cut, every new camera angle could mean money and laughs.

After a night of cigars, beer and baseball, the weather went sour on us. A cold front moved in and the temperature dropped from nice to cold. Fishing on Saturday morning was weak, so Slim and Big E took off before noon for a round of golf at the Hot Springs Country Club, which wasn't in the country and if it was a club, its membership had to be suspect. Slim and E were accustomed to courses of resort quality. This one, though historic, needed fairway sprinklers in the worst way. Somebody raking a trap every now and then would have been nice, too. Doc agreed to wait for them until four o'clock, after which he was free to take the boat. There wouldn't be a repeat of the near disaster at Wautauga years before, when the golfers stayed too long and had to navigate a big lake in the darkest night with nothing but a weak-beamed flashlight.

Years later, it is still a matter of dispute whether Doc left early or the golfers were late – again. To this day Doc swears that he shoved off right at 4 as per the agreement. Slim and E insist they were pulling into camp just before 4 and saw Doc already moving out to the main lake, the big pontoon cutting a V through the water only seconds before heading around a point and motoring out of sight. Some things in life can never be resolved. An hour later, an unhappy Slim and the E-Man cruised up to Doc's pontoon in a newly rented john boat.

"Why didn't you wait for us, asshole? You're going to pay for this john boat, by the way," Slim said.

"I did wait. And the hell I am," Doc shot back.

"Bullshit. We were there right at four. You pulled out early. We saw the V cutting the water as the boat rounded the bend." Doc shrugged and mouthed "No way."

Fishing was typically bad, and as the sun dropped behind the hills, Doc turned the pontoon back toward the marina. Still pissed, Slim and E kept at it, vowing to catch the fish Doc had missed to keep him from winning the Enquirer Outstanding Angler Award. They didn't catch anything either. But the twilight was not uneventful.

Doc motored back to the marina, as the sun's dying rays painted the calm water in a Maxfield Parrish light, with the trees on distant hills like countless thumb smudges of tangerine, raspberry and lime. The water was smooth and the light otherworldly. Doc saw what appeared to be a bush in the water ahead. It looked like it was moving, but the light was dim in the shadows cast by the hills. He kept staring. It was moving. Doc pushed the lumbering pontoon forward to get a better look. It wasn't a shrub, but the spectacular rack of a large stag swimming across the main channel. Doc pulled up alongside, until he could look the buck in the eye.

"There was no fear in his eyes," Doc later told the others. "Just resolve. He wasn't scared a bit. I could have reached down and touched him."

"You should have jumped on his back and ridden him to shore," Slim commented. "Then slit his throat at the shoreline. We could have had venison tenderloin tonight."

"When the stag pulled himself out of the water he galloped straight to the top of the hill. Only then did he look back at me," Doc recalled. There was magnificence in that animal. And the buck knew it. He could swim several hundred yards of open lake, bound up a steep hill and still have attitude and energy to burn. You try it sometime, he seemed to be saying. Then he vanished into the brush.

Slim and E had their own adventure to recount. Slim had tied on a Pikie Minnow, an antique lure with glass-bead eyes and an alluring wiggle. It was his late father's lure and only used on the calmest of waters and in the most serene conditions. He could throw it that evening because the big lake was as smooth as a mirror with the setting sun turning the water orange and then crimson as the sky stayed blue before finally turning navy to purple. It was an ancient light. He and E lingered in the john boat too long it turned out, and by the time they started back, the sky had gone completely black and the moon was up.

Because Slim was sometimes cursed with competence, he was the captain and therefore had to keep track of where they were and how to get back to where they wanted to be. He gunned the heavy metal bullet down the lake through the night, not really knowing if he was in the right channel to Trantner's place but pretty certain – well, sort of certain – that he was going the right way, cursing the fishing, cursing the darkness and, of course, cursing Doc for making the whole mess happen in the first place by leaving before 4. E and Slim cut across the water and figured they would be home watching a World Series game in only minutes. Still, why are the banks on both sides beginning to narrow? Things didn't look quite right.

"You think this is right, E?" Slim yelled over the roar of the motor, the uncertainty in his voice giving away to acknowledgement that it definitely wasn't right.

The Mud Daddy Chronicles

"Hell, I don't know, Slimbagger. I can't see a damn thing."

"This doesn't feel right," Slim said. "Let's check it out." He eased up on the throttle and brought the speeding boat to a full halt. The flashlight beam went forward into the gloom beyond the bow.

Slim exhaled loudly. "Holyshit!"

The boat was roaring into a dead end. There were stumps everywhere – small trees poking up above the water line – and only a few yards beyond that was the end of the channel. It had been the wrong arm of the lake all along, and if they hadn't stopped when they did they would have plowed right into the stick-ups at full throttle in a few seconds. Slim could picture it: thrown from the boat, impaled on some stickup, leaking to death right there in the lake, a bluegill nibbling at his ear in the morning, a catfish chewing on his toes. He shook off the image.

"Time to check the map," Slim said.

He slapped his hip pocket. Gone, left on the pontoon boat. That frigging Doc, Slim muttered. Lost on the big water at night with no map. No good could come of that. Would they have to spend the entire chilly night on the john boat? Or would they wander the lake for hours in the surrounding blackness until running out of gas and THEN retire to the shore to huddle in cold misery? Miles away on the far side of the lake a few faint lights glittered and that was it, that was all they could see. Lost on a strange lake, their watched their prospects fall with the temperature.

Suddenly E snapped to: "I got a map." Unbelievable. He did have a map! Slim remembered it now. At the dock the day before, he had tossed E an extra map and told him to hang on to it. And, thanks to his time at the Naval Academy, E did just what he was told. Within the hour they were back in the cabin, checking out the baseball game.

The next day, the fishing would be solemn and slow and with minutes ticking down to the 10 a.m. deadline, each rummaged through his tackle box for a "go-to" lure for the last go-to of the year. And then, with time running out, Slim hooked a nice smallie on a combo: white silver spoon the size of his thumb tipped with a split-tail pork rind.

The plaque was his for another year.

Packing to leave Tommy Trantner's, we watched John McLaughlin's discussion group on a Sunday morning PBS talk show. McLaughlin, talking about the Gulf War, meant to invoke the name of

U.S. Gen. Norman Schwarzkopf but instead said Schwartzwalder, the legendary Syracuse University football coach. Ben Schwartzwalder was a paratrooper during the Normandy invasion in World War II and a hero to Syracuse homeboy Big E. Back in Cincinnati, the E-Man wrote McLaughlin in care of the show and tried to explain the name mix-up. It must have been one of the strangest letters the newscaster ever received. "Every year there has been a Syracuse connection on the Mud Daddy, whether it be Syracuse upsetting Penn State or an inadvertent slip such as yours," E wrote to McLaughlin, who wasn't known to smile all that much

"Obviously, there was nothing you could have done to avoid it. Since we were watching you, it was one of those cosmic things which simply had to happen."

It must have been a letter that confused McLaughlin terribly.

Mrs. Hawkins' Greens

Like it or not, everybody has to have their veggies, even on a Mud Daddy. But that doesn't mean the vegetables have to suck. We've learned you can have some good green food if you give it just a little thought. Here's one of our favorite vegetable dishes. It is most tasty. If you are camping in the great outdoors, you can prepare this dish ahead of time in the great indoors and warm it up for dinner.

4 batches of Collard greens or Swiss chard

3 Tbs any kind of oil

1 tsp sugar

1 tsp red pepper

1 hambone or smoked beef bone

1/2 onion, quartered

Optional red, green, yellow pepper

Put smoked beef or hambone in one quart of water in crock pot with ingredients and cook for four hours on high or eight hours on low. If not using crock pot, boil hambone or smoked beef for one hour, then slowly simmer all the other ingredients for two hours. Salt and pepper to taste.

Chapter XII - We Fought The Law and The Law Won

Mud Daddy tip: *Buy a retractable wire clip – the kind used for office ID badges – at any office supply shop. Attach a fingernail clipper and use it on trips for clipping line or trimming tippets, closing lead sinkers and ending the battle with an ugly backlash. It also pins nicely to jackets or baseball caps or piasano hats. Slim likes to wear it as a pin on his Costa Rican peasant hat, using it to hold up one side, ala Aussie Bush hat. When the fishing's really slow, you can twist the hat around to resemble Festus on Gunsmoke. While wearing the hat in this fashion, feel free to offer a Festus imitation at any point: "Marshall Dillon, Marshall Dillon, ya gotta come quick..." is a good one.*
    Or: "Why Miss Kitty, you sure are a mighty fine ..."

Every Mud Daddy is a measure of our manhood. Often these tests consist of enduring awful weather while fishing your heart out anyway. Or bearing up under the intense frustration of fishing for hours without a nibble, morning after morning, day after day under a blazing sun, or in the midst of a downpour in a boat with nothing but an unrelenting aluminum bench to sit on. The lakes, like us, have usually seen better days: Sprawl, acid rain, pollution from farm run-off, coal slurry or yellow boy, that slimy, yellow runoff from abandoned mines – the list goes on and on.

The 20th Century was not kind to fish, and without fish, there have been plenty of times on these trips when we had to take matters into our own hands to create memories and carry on traditions. That's what happened at the '92 Mud Daddy at Lake Moomaw in the Virginia Mountains. For more than a decade the Mud Daddy had been a fall experience. But, as we had learned the hard way, fishing is iffy in changeable weather on the cusp of winter. Slim had been lobbying for a spring or summer event for a few years, so this year's Mud Daddy was a June outing.

By the early Nineties, it was clear that the years were mounting and middle age was upon us, like it or not. The Mud Daddy was getting tougher to pull together. Doc and Slim had two kids each. Doc's boys were in elementary school and running him ragged with trips to baseball and hockey practice. Slim's son was a first grader and his daughter, Rachel, a toddler. Bob "Raging Bull" Rankin, a sometimer on these trips, had a son in elementary school in the Washington, D.C. area, and he was going through the same routine with youth sports, school activities and sleepovers across town. Big-E's son was younger, but that meant round trips to daycare, the doctor and juggling schedules with his wife, Barbara.

Big E was covering the Cincinnati Reds at the time and couldn't get away for the '92 trip, but the Bull committed and Slim and Doc simply refused to miss a Mud Daddy. It had been going on too long. Doc flew from Austin to D.C. for a night on the town in the nation's capital with Bull, aka Junkyard Dog. The plan was for them to drive to Covington, Va., early on a Friday morning in Bull's timeless Firebird, which just happened to have a massive new sound system. Slim drove in from Cincinnati solo, and we met at a bait shop/dry land marina in the middle of nowhere. How we managed to find each other in the pre-cell phone era is still a mystery.

Appropriately, hassles with the boat began right away.

He was no older than 40, looked like he needed a good meal of steak and taters and had a bad case of I-don't-give-a-shit-about-you-guys.

"We got no record of that."

"But I called you," Slim complained. "You said it would be no problem."

The boat guy muttered something unintelligible and shuffled around, eventually finding us a john boat and hauling us and it down to the lake. We were on the water by mid-morning, only to be immediately drenched by a torrential downpour, a soaking that Doc said was right out of the Mekong Delta, circa 1969.

We sailed on in the john boat packed to the gunwales with us and our camping gear, our feet splayed over the load, the water lapping at the aluminum skin. Suddenly, from out of the gloom above, several bolts of lightning snapped, exploding on the hills around us. We made a hasty turn to shore and hunkered down against the load to offer a smaller target. We beached the boat and piled out like Marines under fire, getting away from the metal boat and up the shore as fast as possible. Slim always remembered his father's warning: lightning hits high points and the highest point on a lake, well, that'd be you, wouldn't it? We trekked up a hill to shiver beneath some scrawny pines as the cold rain pelted down and the sky cracked and thundered all around us.

But it was just as terrifying on the hill beneath the trees, and an air of fatalistic remorse filled our morning, which never happens in the first hour on the first day of a Mud Daddy. By the second day when the fishing really sucks, yeah, of course – but never on the first day.

What if this is it, we wondered. What if we get hit by lightning and die right here? Had we lived our lives to the fullest? Could we have been kinder, more understanding? Had we given our children anything solid to cling to for their journey forward? Had we given to them enough of our time and attention? And our wives? Had we cared enough? What would St. Peter say about our livelihoods? Would he charge us with mendacity or bearing false witness upon false witness day after day after day?

Did you ever stop lying, Slim?

That's what St. Peter would ask. We'd only be able to look down at our shoes and shrug. Could we say we tried our best? Every day? Day after day?

Thunder exploded directly overhead. The reality of our somewhat desperate situation led to an inevitable Mud Daddy conclusion: A man can step over the rainbow at any moment of any day – stroke, heart attack, head-on – and this ridiculously loud and threatening thunderstorm was a chilling reminder that life should be lived to the fullest. As the thunder roared, we found ourselves drenched, shivering and silently lamenting our mortality on a steep hillside in Virginia.

Doc and Slim had thin rain shells, but the Bull, a true junkyard dog, was only in a T-Shirt.

"You got a jacket?" Slim asked.

"In the boat," Bull shuddered, nodding at the john boat rocking in the water below as lightning sizzled then cracked through the rain to hit the tree tops above us again and again and again. This was an acid rain storm, Slim said. They hold five times as much lightning because the water is slightly acidic and conducts energy easier and quicker. Bull and Doc looked at Slim. What bullshit is he talking now? It's wayyyyy too early in the trip for Slim's pseudo science.

We could see it as a fishing break, so the rain and thunder were just something we'd have to endure. Bull had been through tough times in the 1980s – a failed stint as an expatriate novelist in France, kept from his dream job as an editorial writer at the Philadelphia Inquirer by a strike, his home in the D.C. suburbs burglarized. But he'd had his successes, too: a Pulitzer Prize with the Miami Herald and a job with Knight-Ridder in Washington, the nation's power center. There was no doubt what he'd miss if he never climbed down from that hill – his 8-year-old son, Ben, the light of his life.

"Let's go get that jacket," offered Doc.

Bull looked at Slim and Doc, their rain shells completely soaked through, providing neither warmth nor protection from the pelting rain or falling temperatures. They were as wet and cold as Bull, and shivering just as fiercely.

"No, thanks," Bull replied. "I'll take my hypothermia straight."

Slim had his laments about an early exit from the world, as well. Not just Matthew and Rachel but his wife, Carol. Both his parents were gone now, and so his immediate family and a handful of close friends meant everything to him. Career had come in second place – it was never much of a driver. Maybe I should have been more ambitious, he thought as the curtain of rain soaked him. Recriminations abounded. Had he been all he could have been as a father. Would Matt remember Sting's "Field of Barley" and think of his Dad? Would Rachel one day hear ol' Jerry Lee singing "Every Day I Have to Cry Some" and think of her father? Would they remember exotic family vacations to Costa Rica, Vieques, the Four Corners? Would Carol think about him when she was singing and remember how Slim would sometimes ask: Is that an angel I hear?

Doc thought about Jason, 8, and Evan, 5, and wondered what he'd miss if he didn't return. Any no-hitters? Fourth-quarter interceptions and runbacks under the brilliant lights of a Friday night in Texas? Would they be great students? Good athletes? Chess nerds? Musicians? Artists? Jason was a great guitarist and Evan already showed that he had a big heart and kind ways. Their young lives had just begun to form and could go in any direction. And Doc thought about his mother, Mabel, who'd raised him and his younger sister and brother alone after their father deserted.

"You got that thousand-yard stare going, Doc," Slim said. "Whatcha thinking about?"

"Saying good-bye to my mom. She's gonna be pissed if I don't make it out of here."

Slim countered. "Shit, I'm not dying from a lightning bolt or widow-maker branch falling from the sky on some damn hillside in Virginia, I'll tell you that much. That just isn't going to happen."

Then the rain eased and the thunder grew distant and so did our remorse. We stopped quaking and walked back down to the boat, grinning like monkeys because we had survived. The storm had reinforced our commitment to make the most of this weekend, because you just never know what's around the next curve and heading straight for you.

"I propose we have a beer," offered Slim.

"Hell, yeah," came the second to that motion.

With Slim piloting, we rounded a point and saw that a family had staked out a nice area on a peninsula in the rustic campground. Rather than bother them, we motored across the small bay, walked up a steep hill and tossed a ton of gear on a grassy area beneath the trees. It was fairly flat and seemed to be a pleasant enough spot, with a back bay view of a giant hill. The rain returned and so we double-timed the tent erection. After getting the tent up and toasting the lake and our ability to survive anything that God and Mother Nature could throw at us, we headed out to the water, the rain gone again.

Doc and Bull caught a couple of smallmouth quite soon and had high hopes for this mountain lake and the Mud Daddy days to come. (Grubs rigged Texas tight was the thing.) Shelves of limestone pocked the mountain walls leading to sheer drop-offs. And there were old roadbeds that were there before the valley was flooded to create Moomaw. Not much was up in the Appalachians on the Virginia-West Virginia line, which is why they could dam the Jackson River and flood the natural basin created by three separate mountains. But there had been a few roads across the valley, and underwater roadbeds are always good for holding fish. We had maps. We'd figure it out. We trolled over and cast at humps, little knobs on the bottom of the lake, but the fishing went quiet too soon and we headed back to camp to make preparations for dinner. The other family across the bay went about their business, and we didn't think anything more of them, figuring we were far enough away not to bother them.

Dylan and the Red Hot Chili Pepper roared from our boom

The Mud Daddy Chronicles

box. We had extra batteries and good cigars. There were cases of beer, a quart of bourbon, a fifth of tequila and several bottles of red and white wine scattered around the campsite. Pretty much anything a man on vacation could want. We'd never drink it all, but it was there to taste if we wanted some. We stayed up late that night, smoking cigars and rapping about life and politics, cars and music, women and children, the burdens of daily journalism, the importance of Hunter S. Thompson and why a man had to believe in his craft.

"Clinton got a chance?" Slim asked Bull, throwing back a shot of tequila, "or is Bush unbeatable?"

"Perot gives Clinton a shot," Bull said.

"He came through Atlanta in '88," Doc interjected. Doc was city editor at the Journal-Constitution when the Democratic National Convention landed in Atlanta that year. "Jesse Jackson caused the biggest stir in the newsroom. Clinton has a way with folks, though. But I got a bad vibe right away. Too ambitious, too self-centered. Don't trust him."

"I danced with Bill once," Slim said.

"Wha ..."

"Yeah, he was governor of Arkansas and visiting Cincinnati for the national governor's conference. It was the last night. He was swinging with two, maybe three beautiful women in the middle of the dance floor at Coney Island – Moonlight Gardens – and an editor had been bugging me all week to interview him. Whenever an editor wants something really bad like that, I tend to finally oblige. So, I shimmied out onto the floor doing the Subway, you know, fist up, pointing the way with your bent elbow like you're hanging onto a subway grip ..."

"You're making this up," Doc said.

"Nope, every word is true. I got out to him and he leaned in. The women were knock-outs, I'm telling you. And they were looking at me like, 'Get outta here!' So I lean in and shout at the guy that I'm a reporter for the Enquirer. You wouldn't believe how tall he is. Then I ask, 'Who's your favorite group?' I couldn't think of anything else to ask. I mean, whaddaya say? I leaned back and did a little funky boogaloo with one of his babes. She looked back at me like she'd just stepped in dog shit. Then Bill leaned in and shouted back, "The Beach Boys!" I nodded and turned away, Scooby-Doing off the dance floor. Then, I feel a tug on my elbow!

"It's Bill, his face is all red now, he looks sort of desperate, and he shouts, 'No, I mean the Beatles. The Beatles!' Even then, even there on the dance floor, that guy was figuring political odds. He dances pretty good, too."

Bull was facing intense pressure every day at Knight Ridder's Washington bureau. He covered the government of the most powerful nation on earth and continually sparred with elected officials, bureaucrats, editors and, of course, other reporters. Fighting was in his nature and debate was his weapon of choice. He was good at it, too, which doesn't win him many friends. Competing with the Washington Post and New York Times to find out if Alan Greenspan was going to raise the interest rates or not was harrowing. Bull would call 20 people a day trying to get something – anything – that would give him an edge. Sometimes it worked. More often it didn't. Like every reporter, he'd sit and stare at the silent phone, trying to will it to ring with a tip. The worst words in the English language, he said, were, "Did you see what the Times just moved on the wire?"

"Is Dr. T covering the campaign?" Slim asked Bull, referring to Hunter Thompson, who had been a touchstone for all of us as young newspapermen.

"Don't think so. Get "The Great Shark Hunt" though, if you don't have it yet. Some of his best stuff is in there. Nobody writes like him."

"Or plays guitar like Jimi Hendrix," Doc added. "Two originals. Don't ever try to copy the originators. Can't be done."

Doc was managing editor in Austin and working under a crushing burden of endless tasks and responsibilities. Every day was a battle to get enough space for the news stories, to keep the budget under control, to manage 200 cranky reporters and editors. Sometimes he saw the problems coming, sometimes he didn't. Like the question over which bathroom the staffer undergoing the not-quite-complete sex change operation was supposed to use. The women didn't want him with his male equipment in their sanctuary, and the men didn't want to share a rest room with someone wearing a skirt. True story.

Slim was a local news business columnist, always struggling to come up with something interesting to say – something that wouldn't offend his bosses at the Enquirer or the plutocracy that ran the town. It was three days a week of opening the big vein. So Slim wrote about worm wholesalers, kids on golf courses who sold golf balls, the guy who thought his kitty toilet would replace kitty litter, a flute repairman, a wacky guy (who turned into a great pal) who restored a 1953 Allard Grand Prix race car. He wrote about zoning disputes that would age a healthy man 20 years in the 20 minutes it took to write them up.

Dead people are sprinkled everywhere in a newspaper – and sometimes haunt the sleepless nights of the reporters who must write the obits. One of Slim's obits that year for a noted Cincinnati lawyer left out by design the simple fact that the guy was a CIA hitman who would disappear for days at a time and often woke up in a cold sweat from a recurring dream of garroting a man in a Bulgarian telephone booth. How do you put that in an obit? Where's it fit? The dead man's son told the story and then said that he and his brothers always wondered where their father went when he disappeared. He added that his father went to church every day of his life to pray at noon.

As committed newspapermen, we considered this our daily burden. Thus, the prodigious amounts of liquid provisions once a year.

"What's the best Dylan album?"

"Blood on the Tracks."

"No way. 'Freewheeling.' "

"How about 'Highway 61 Revisited' – 'Where you want the killing done? Out on Highway 61 …'"

"Blonde on Blonde?"

"I'm sticking with 'Self Portrait.' " Hoots all around.

" 'Slow Train Coming' and 'Shot of Love' are way underrated. Not appreciated. Dylan had Robbie Shakespeare and Sly Dunbar of Black Uhuru backing him. How cool was that?"

"Where's 'Slow Train'? Put it in the box. Crank it up."

Staying with the evening longer than we should have, we set out too late the next morning, but everyone caught something, And with the storm now a memory, we had the beauty of sheer cliffs rising from the water, a deep blue sky, rolling mountains of pine and hardwood climbing to the clouds above a lake empty of other boats. Perfect.

After a break in the fishing, Bull decided to stay in camp. So Doc and Slim headed back out and ended up hooking a few smallmouth, though nothing worth taking back for dinner. We weren't going to kill these magnificent bronzebacks for an appetizer. When you kill a living thing, even a fish, it ought to be for a reason. It ought to matter. We've had too much experience with Karma not to believe in it. We had food. Three large steaks awaited in the cooler. We were at Moomaw to catch fish, but we stayed within the local law and only kept them for dinner when they were large enough and plentiful enough. Otherwise we would catch and release, when we caught at all. The earth's fish are in little danger from an annual Mud Daddy.

After an afternoon with few fish, it was time to plow back and celebrate with an early Happy Hour. As Slim rounded the point at mid-afternoon and headed back to camp, it was obvious that big trouble had descended on this Mud Daddy. Water cops were everywhere. Rangers in uniform manned boats with blue lights and more stern looking dudes with bad attitudes were kicking around the campsite on the hillside above.

"This doesn't leave me with a warm feeling," Slim said.

Slim tried his small-talk big grin strategy with the ranger by the shore.

"Morning officer, love the lake here. Planned this trip for a year, and we are having a great time. Hey, what's going on? Is there a problem?"

"You bet you have a problem. Family across the way couldn't sleep until after midnight because of the ruckus you boys were making last night," the ranger said. "You need to get on up the hill."

Our beloved campsite was over-run with rangers, and one guy, apparently in charge, was a dead ringer for former Surgeon General C. Everett Koop, he of no-smoking fame. Bull had a sick look on his face.

"Apparently, this is an illegal campsite," Bull said, an edge of indignation in his voice.

"This is a disgrace," barked C. Everett Koop, kicking at some empty wine bottles. "This is not a legal camping area, and alcohol is prohibited. What do you think you're doing? You kept the family camping across the way up all night with your music and your loud talk."

Slim stepped forward and graciously apologized.

"Well, officer, it's my fault. I thought as long as we were on federal land in a national forest, we could camp just about anywhere as long as we were 500 feet back from the water's edge. That's what they told us back in Cincinnati. We are awful sorry about that family. It sure won't happen again."

"You bet it won't," snarled Koop, "because you are going to tear down this campsite right now."

At this point Slim knew aw-shucks had failed, as it sometimes will. But he offered a palms up gesture of supplication, as if to say, "No no, sir, you can't be serious?"

Bull spoke up, indignation rising in his voice.

"Look, we didn't know we couldn't pitch here. And what's the problem? We all have responsible jobs. We're under a lot of pressure, and we just want to have some fun. What's so wrong with that? Isn't this America? David fought in 'Nam so we could do this. What have we really done wrong? Nothing!"

"All this alcohol …" C. Everett Koop began.

Bull cut him off.

"Most of it un-drunk, you'll notice. We expected some other people who didn't show. We're just some guys trying to fish and camp and have a good time. We're hard-working Americans who want to taste the wilderness once a year. We're responsible people. Give us a break, will you?"

Instead of a break, C. Everett whipped out his pad, gave us a ticket and ordered the site cleaned up and the three of us out of there.

"Right now."

"Thanks for nothing," Bull growled.

"So what do we do? Where's the campground you want us in?" Slim asked.

"I'll show you," C. Everett replied dryly. He took Slim in the boat across the lake, about a half-mile away, to a dismal primitive campground with pit toilets still ankle-deep in water from the previous day's deluge. Slim eyed the mud, the pit toilet with water pooling outside the door and the bleak array of primitive campsites before him. It was not the beautiful, wooded hillside he was about to leave, and the outrage rose in Slim.

"What about cholera?"

It was long past time to screw around with C. Everett.

"Cholera?" C. Everett seemed taken aback.

"Yeah, cholera. You know, the Third World. And dysentery, puking and shitting from bad water for weeks on end? Are we gonna get it?"

He pointed at the latrine and the water seeping from beneath its walls. "Are we gonna get cholera? Or maybe cryptosporidiosis? You ever have any cryptosporidiosis around here from camping in places like this?

"Bet that would bring a lawsuit for sure for medical and punitive damages. How do you know we're not gonna all get sick from this shitty place?"

C. Everett gazed back with the dumb look of a cow in a Virginia pasture, hat cocked back like a camp cook in a black and white western. Then he began to focus on a distant peak and it was about then that Slim knew it was pointless, that this Mud Daddy was headed in a seriously wrong direction. On the boat ride back Slim kept at him with questions that were ignored. Slim kept them coming anyhow.

"What about those rangers back in the camp. That many guys on duty for a Saturday?

"How many of 'em are on over-time? Who gets overtime in your organization anyhow? Which brother-in-law? And who decides who gets it and who doesn't? Public money. Anybody from the press ever look into that?

"You know, I was thinking. I wonder what a couple of bad reviews of the fishing in this lake would do for tourism? We're writers. Oh yeah, we told you that, didn't we? You ever hear of Sports Afield? That one fellow up there is a freelance writer for Sports Afield. I write travel stories for The Cincinnati Enquirer? I guess we told you that..."

C. Everett went stoic, and since it felt like picking wings off a fly, Slim backed off and looked into the distance at the mountains and green lake shimmering in the sun like the glaze on pottery from the 19th century. It was so pretty that it was hurting to have to leave.

C. Everett and his band of unmerry men soon pulled out. But one of the rangers stayed behind to see that we did as we were told. He didn't say much, and in fact looked a little sheepish as we gathered up our mess (a Mud Daddy never ends with a messy campsite but it can sure get messy at times) and hauled it all down to the boat. The lone ranger had to field some more cholera-oriented questions, but he shrugged them off without comment. Then we shifted tactics.

"Ever have to pitch a tent like this in the cold rain, and in the dark like we did? And then have take it down because some idiot's in charge?"

The lone ranger looked at us, turned and walked back down the slope to his boat. Apparently he was done with us, too.

Back out on the lake, our defiance turned into open rebellion.

"We're not going in," Doc fumed. "We're going to fish and then we're going to find someplace to camp."

"I'm with you, man," Bull said firmly.

Slim started humming the old Bobby Fuller number "I Fought the Law and the Law Won." Soon he was singing it like the Clash, then even edgier: "Ahhhhh breaking rocks in the hot sun, Aw fought the law and the law won. AW FOUGHT THE LAW AND THE LAW WONNNNNNN!"

The Mud Daddy was back in gear. But we had a hell-hound on our trail – the lone ranger. We headed to an RV campground miles away at chuga-chuga trolling speed, the water cop trailing us the entire way. It took forever, but we didn't care. The gunwales were barely above the water line when we pulled onto the shore of the campground and climbed out like we were looking for a site – we had no intention of camping there. It was just a feint to fool the lone ranger.

We trudged through a nice, almost-full campground filled with families in big RVs and little trailers strung with party lights. Mothers viewed us with suspicion and pulled their children to them. Fathers offered a little nod and a mumbled "H'lo." We looked like serial killers, so who could blame them. Eyes trailed us wherever we went.

When we returned to the boat, the deputy was gone, and so we headed back out onto the water with renewed vigor and the elation of full rebellion. At dusk, we slid the boat into some reeds near where we had camped the previous night, hiding it pretty well in the dark. We repaired to a dip in the land to fry our steaks and drink beer in the dark. We couldn't pitch the tent without being seen, so we spread it out on the ground behind a berm and slept under the stars.

Late that night, we heard a boat approach and a spotlight beam swept the far shore. It worked across the trees toward our makeshift camp. We kept low and were tense, like escaping convicts in those prison movies, avoiding the beam. The light swept through again, then was gone. Later, we heard a boat again and it repeated the searchlight sequence. The light swept over us, back and forth. No one breathed. Fortunately, no one came ashore. Still, sleep did not come easily, and at dawn, we packed up the gear and got back on the lake like we were early risers, trying to steal part of another day of fishing from a rapidly vanishing summer.

The day's ending came soon enough. We cast our way back to the put-in to wait for the half-drunk old geezer from the marina to come for his boat. Doc and Slim pitched in to pay the ticket, which had been issued to Bull. He'd put the most mouth on C. Everett. It came to $125 total. Doc got the Enquirer Outstanding Angler award, Bull got the left-over booze and Slim got a Lewis Grizzard tape for his ride back to Ohio.

"How'd the fishing go?" the old man asked at the marina.

"Doesn't matter," Doc told him. "It was a Mud Daddy."

Fritatta Mundatta

From the very beginning, the final breakfast of a Mud Daddy has relied on this frittata recipe. It's the perfect way to use the leftovers from previous meals to create a sumptuous breakfast. This is THE key to Mud Daddy living. You use what you have but hold some back. You'll want to use something – or everything – for a later repast. Because the Fritatta Mundatta maker will tend to be the guy who works with the peppers and onions during the feasts leading up to the morning of the Mud Daddy wrap, he will subconsciously keep his eye on how much of the peppers, onions, pepperoni and eggs are being used. He needs to make sure there is enough left over for the foundation of the Frittata Mundatta.

Big E almost always is the frittata chef, and as such has become an expert at this dish. Splash a liberal layer of heart-healthy vegetable oil (we usually do corn or safflower or peanut or olive or most any oil, actually) into the bottom of the frying pan and warm it up on medium-low heat. Cup the egg shells into your eye sockets and ask somebody to pass you a plate. Wait to hear the laugh when they finally look at you. Back at the pan, toss in your chopped green peppers (about a half a bell pepper is fine; if you brought red and/or yellow bell along with your green, so much the better). Once these are soft, add your chopped onion (you don't need a lot, about one medium-sized onion; more if you like onion) and get these softened up, too. (Onions always cook quicker than peppers, which is why we add the onions second, but maybe you already knew that.) By the way, you can't overcook this stuff – as long as you don't turn it black – so if you like it caramelized, go for it.

Add your diced, sliced or chopped (however you like it) pepperoni and warm it up. Add beaten egg mixture (we like to put some milk into our egg mixture, but no more than half an egg shell's worth for every two eggs) and cook it up and serve. The beauty of the frittata is that you can put almost anything left-over into it: mushrooms, scallions, pepperoni (although not a lot of these, because they are stronger flavored than the rest of your ingredients and might dominate) and tomatoes (use the rindy parts, not the seeds and juice because they will make your frittata runny) and any sort of sandwich meat you might have brought along, such as salami or boiled ham. If you have potatoes left over – and room on your stove for an extra pan – fry up some taters, as these make a nice ketchup-splashed accoutrement for your Frittata Mundatta. Garnish options: We usually have some sort of bottled salsa left over, so this can be served on the side, for the Tex-Mex freaks in your party. Also, for the fresh freaks (which we tend toward) a garnish of chopped tomatoes mixed with a mellow cheese (such as provolone or mozzarella) and a smidgen of your green-topped scallions are a nice touch. This all can be enjoyed with hearty glasses of O.J. (you won't have consumed much of it previously, trust us) or, if your frittata moment occurs toward mid-morning, an ice-cold beer (if there's any left, which there shouldn't be.)

Chapter XIII - The Deer Hunters

Mud Daddy tip: *When traveling into the heartland, always wear a baseball-style cap into gas stations, roadside restaurants and marinas, preferably one with something written on it. (There are only two kinds of people in the world: People from West Virginia and people who wish they were from West Virginia). If you don't have a cap because you forgot to bring it, by all means suck it up and buy one at the closest truck stop. Wearing a ball cap will make you appear like a local and buy you some small degree of credibility, at least until you open your mouth.*

In October 1993, we camped along a lovely gurgling feeder stream pouring from a West Virginia mountain into Summersville Lake, which was formed by the damming of the Gauley River. The water was supposed to be astonishingly clear, the Bahamas of the East. Suffice it to say we were surprised to find it the color of a cedar table – dirty but deep. We had settled in after a frustrating day of not catching fish and were enjoying the cool night, listening to Sinatra and Elvis on the boombox, when headlights shattered the dark as a truck came through the camping area and parked. Doc, the only one in the campsite familiar with weaponry, muttered under his breath that he wished he had brought along the Army-issued .45-automatic he'd spirited out of 'Nam, because we were sitting ducks. Doc has always had a dark side.

Three men tumbled out and went immediately to the back of the truck. There was a metal clang followed by the loving howl and baying of three hound-dogs. The dogs bounded from the truck bed without hesitation and tore across the little mountain stream that fed Summersville Lake, barely acknowledging us as they took to the woods with single-mindedness to track down whatever unfortunate varmint's scent those dogs happened to stumble across. By any measure, coon hounds are not God's smartest creatures, but they have expert noses and do the one thing they do quite well.

We pulled our baseball caps lower, looked at the three newcomers, also in caps, and then they were gone, too. This crew was presumably out for a night of coon hunting or deer jacking, and it was our great fortune to witness a timeless American ritual that was equal parts get-away-from-the-wife and outdoor adventure – exactly what we were doing. The dogs' baying and yelping echoed through the cool night air for awhile, seldom an actual bark and never a bother. The friendliest of the gentlemen had muttered hello just before sloshing through the stream on a rock crossing, and we watched the erratic beam of his huge flashlight dance across the dark hills, wavering in the distance until it disappeared.

"Did they have guns?" asked the Raging Bull, not one anxious for armed confrontation. Especially when he is unarmed.

"Didn't see any," Doc replied.

"Come on, this is the heart of America. Everybody has a gun in these parts. Man, people brush their teeth with a gun on the bathroom counter. Bet on it. They had guns."

And it was, after all, hunting season. For many in that part of the world, hunting season is as much an economic necessity as a faux pioneer abstraction or casual pastime. A fellow who had a family back in the hollows hunted whenever he felt like it, and who could blame him? A deer was dinner on the hoof, a big-eyed, wandering hunk of freezer meat that would feed his family for at least a month with a nice supply of tenderloin, sausages, jerky and venison stew, not to mention another head to put on the wall. Like Mellencamp once said: some guys, they got it so good.

Were they coon hunting? Not damn likely. If they were hunting deer after dark illegally, it was all right by us, as we'd already had a disturbing number of deer encounters on this escape.

Our first run-in came about 24 hours before on the drive east from Northern Kentucky. We were barreling at 70 mph down Kentucky Route 8 shortly after midnight when our headlights illuminated an enormous stag leaping through the median of the road and then it was upon us.

"Oh, shit," exhaled Big E, who was driving the rental car. He's had some bad experiences while driving rental cars. He doesn't like to go into detail about it though.

"Don't do it," breathed Slim. "Don't. Do. It."

Before wide-eyed E could slow the car below 60, the buck slammed into that rented Buick at full force. It exploded onto the hood, mucus and lung matter spraying the windshield, then bounced up over the roof and into the night. The airbag engaged and blew E-Man's cigar out of his mouth. We came to a screeching stop on the edge of the empty highway, with a short-circuited horn now howling into the night and E-Man's cigar burning in the airbag, emitting acrid fumes. Stunned and shaken, we got out to survey the damage. The deer was nowhere to be seen. And we didn't go looking for it. Somebody started chucking empties into the field. We were on a Mud Daddy. The cops would soon be on us. That much we knew.

"There's no steam coming from the radiator," Doc shouted over the horn. "If it's okay, we're golden. Trip still on!"

We were in luck. The driver's side door had been crimped on impact and wouldn't open very far, and the front bumper and grill were ruined, but that was it. The engine was still running, the steering wheel seemed okay and the suspension was sound.

"What the hell do we do about this air bag," laughed E, pointing to the limp bag drooping over the steering wheel.

Time for a jury-rig. Slim, the master jury-rigger, stepped up. He'd always rather fix something in a goofy way than in a by-the-book way. He stuffed the air bag back as much as he could and then tied the rest of it down to the steering wheel with criss-crossed rope from the camping gear. It worked well enough, and we were on our way again, horn blaring.

We howled on through the night, following the Ohio River on through Kentucky and into West Virginia. The annoying horn soon died, as we figured it would. On the drive we talked about luck, Karma and fate, reminding each other of stories we'd heard about bucks crashing through windshields and killing the occupants in its last dying rampage, a bloody storm of hooves and antlers and glass. It happened all the time, we knew. As journalists, each of us had covered the night cops beat, and in the fall, car-deer collisions were commonplace. That we had survived a life-threatening episode before the Mud Daddy had officially begun inspired a twisted confidence, and even more than usual we were pumped for whatever destiny brought our way.

The camping that night was rough. Just before dawn at a

The Mud Daddy Chronicles

remote campsite somewhere west of the lake, we tumbled from the car, pitched a tent and crawled into it, exhausted. When we awoke, we saw that the marina was just over the hill. A few hours later we arrived at the marina to meet the Bull. When we drove up, there he was: a jaunty soul, leaning against his gunmetal gray Firebird, smoking a cigar. The parking lot was rocking with the soulful sound of Curtis Mayfield. Bull took one look at the rental car and grinned.

"What the hell did you do?" he asked.

"Hit a damn buck last night coming in," Doc answered.

"You shoulda' gone to look for it and tied it to the hood," Bull said.

"Yeah," said Doc, clasping his longtime friend's hand. "And take an antler in the throat from a dying stag. 'Course that's what we shoulda done."

We got squared away with the boats, loaded the gear and headed out with Doc and Bull in one boat and Slim and Big E in the other, casting as soon as we could, throwing at various points off the main lake. Immediately, Doc and the Bull shouted from across the water: "Get over here! Get over here! Check this out! You gotta see this!"

In the clear lake beneath where their first casts landed was a staggering apparition: the carcass of a deer. It apparently had plunged off the precipice above and broken its neck on the rocks below.

"Something must have been chasing it. Maybe a pack of dogs," Doc ventured.

We were not keen on seeing yet another dead deer. In fact, we'd had enough of it.

"What's up with these deer?" Slim shouted to the heavens above. "We get the point. Life is short. Every day is a blessing. We know that death haunts every minute."

"But would you knock it off with the deer?"

And now here we were again, hours later in camp, encountering men and dogs in the dead of night. Coon hunting was recreation. Deer poaching was work, and they went about it in earnest. Cigars in hand and sipping whiskey from Dixie cups, we watched the flashlights flicker while Smokey Robinson moaned about the tracks of his tears.

"Hey E," somebody asked after the hunters were gone, the baying of their hounds growing ever more distant, "are you still singing or is that those dogs?"

"I'm singing."

"Well, stop for a minute and tell me what happened to the handle?"

"What handle would that be?"

"The handle to the bucket that most people use to carry a tune."

The hounds were more on key than Big E, and that was clear to everybody, including, mysteriously, E himself. Not that he cared. He sang because he was happy, and that was all that mattered.

The next morning the fishing came early and within an hour, Doc made an astute observation: "Have you guys noticed that the fish don't bite much when the water is the color of a red dirt road?"

When the fishing is impossibly bad, we tell stories. Some of them are true.

For Doc, the big passage in his life was stumbling around in high school and somehow winning a scholarship to a boarding school. He says the experience built character. Slim says it was a futile effort to build character. Doc's strongest memory of those times is playing third base during a shining moment in mid-60s history. Doc wore a blue blazer to class and drove a nice '54 Ford convertible that had red leather seats. He was looking good and life was pretty good until that game at Woodberry Forest.

In the late innings, with runners on first and second and two out, the batter poked a pop-up up behind third. Doc still recalls the entire sequence vividly, and at night it sometimes revisits him in slow motion: the ball drifting up and up, higher and higher, impossibly high, in fact, the sounds of the runners' feet pounding as they rounded the bases, one after another. The ball's slow then suddenly fast descent. Then, impossibly, the ball hit the heel of his glove and bounced to the ground. Runs scored. Woodberry took the lead and held it. Doc was banished to right field on the spot. Humiliated. He was Ralph Branca giving up the homer to Bobby Thomson; Bill Buckner letting the easy grounder roll between his legs.

Decades later, the whole scene was still fresh in his memory. He even remembered what he had for dinner that night: fried chicken, green peas and milk. Trying to erase that memory, or make up for the transgression in some way, might have had something to do with Doc joining the Army a few years later at the height of the Vietnam conflict. He's not sure.

E-Man's highlight memory, on the other hand, was a good one. In the fall of his junior year in high school, he watched from the stands as his team's graduating punter, Don Luke, launched sweet-spiraling kicks high into the night. E recalled Syracuse University punter Doc Bullard doing the same a half-dozen years earlier. E thought, "I bet I can do that." And so, in the summer before his senior year, Big E taught himself to boom 40-yarders in a high arc that upon landing always seemed to bounce forward and out of bounds inside the other team's 10-yard line. Coach wanted E to play backup tight end, but E knew better. Tight end meant having to block. Backup tight end meant passes over the middle from a quarterback who might stretch his receiver out high, which usually meant getting slammed in the lower back by a hungry middle linebacker, who would view a gangly and slow tight end as his ticket to All-League honors.

"Punting is just fine with me," E replied.

When his team, Christian Brothers Academy, a huge underdog, upset its undefeated and despised archrival, Henninger High School, CBA head coach Pete Vercillo bounded up the bus steps and passionately gazed down the aisle at his bedraggled but victorious squad. Guys were nursing cuts, scrapes and bruised hips. Their uniforms were mud-stained. Some were blood-stained. Shoulders were out of whack. All were worn out. Surveying the scene from the first row of the bus, the coach spied E-Dog in his spotless uniform. "Helluva game, Erardi!" E had kept the opponent buried in its own territory with his booming punts, one of them a 61-yarder, another a coffin-corner job that the Rockne-like Vercillo had asked E to put inside the five-yard line late in the fourth quarter. E responded with a sharp spiral that bounced once and went out of bounds inside the one.

"I knew right then and there that I had the best position in all of sport," E said. It earned him an offer of an appointment to the U.S. Military Academy. But he already had been offered an appointment to the U.S. Naval Academy for baseball, and so he told the West Pointers he was Annapolis-bound.

Taking a puff off his cigar and blowing a smoke ring at the night sky, Slim recounted one of his defining moments of sport:

"I was a sophomore, teeing off in the high school state golf tournament, somehow the fourth man on the varsity team. It was the regionals – the first round on the first day – and the first hole was a 595 yard par 5. There were dozens of other golfers watching as they waited their turn at the tee. I took a mighty swing because I had been putting on the green for an eagle three before on this hole, and since I was a big hitter, huge off the tee, I knew I could do it again. But this time I whiffed the club across the top of the ball, barely touching it but touching it just enough to send it slowly hopping across the tee and then halfway down the tee incline, where it stopped in the ankle-high rough. For my second shot, still on the tee and on a steep downhill grade, still under the unforgiving gaze of dozens of other golfers and coaches, I had to hit an eight iron on that par 5. And I prayed that I wouldn't chunk it. Finally, I was away from the crowd and off onto the course. You know, that memory will follow me to my grave. It was awful."

Slim didn't want to end his tale of his sophomore year on a negative note.

"Of course, there was the glorious evening when I was 14, and me and my brother, Dale, discovered that the trunk key from our stepmother's hot little five-speed 1965 Corvair also started our other brother's 1960 Corvair. Keith had left the house that evening, jangling his keys at us, knowing we could not 'borrow' his rebuilt Corvair. On a whim, we tried the trunk key. When the older Corvair fired up, we loaded the car with friends and drove through the Buckeye night, as far as 79 cents would take us, which was a decent distance in those days when gas sold for 29 cents a gallon. Wotta world."

Bull told of the night when he went cruising with his older brother, Richard, basically looking for trouble. Bull was a thoughtful, studious sort. Richard was a hell-raiser of some repute. So Bull, 14 at the time, relished the opportunity to hang out with his crazy older brother and see what it really was all about out there in the big city on a Saturday night. At a North Richmond drive-in, Richard, not surprisingly, mouthed off to some guys from a rival high school. It was agreed they would meet at a nearby parking lot to settle differences the way teenagers did in the '60s: just fists, no guns or knives. Bull – scared and worried, his manhood challenged – preferred to stay in the car. But when Richard got out to meet in combat, Bull went with him. It didn't last long. Richard went down with a punch to the nose and Bull rushed to help him. That was it.

"After that," Bull explained, "I thought I'd pursue a life of the mind."

The 1993 Mud Daddy ended in a familiar vein. Slim was reduced to stalking the elusive pumpkinseed Bluegill with a fly rod and No. 14 Adams – though a Wooly-Booger brought one stream smallmouth to hand. But with no witnesses, the others would have none of it. Doc flipped tiny rooster tail spinners to lakeside shrubs and took home the beloved Mud Daddy Enquirer Outstanding Angler plaque on the strength of three fish, enough to deny the award to Slim. It didn't help, either, that Doc strutted like a prize rooster. When you're the Enquirer Outstanding Angler, you're expected to be insufferable. And on this score Doc never disappoints.

Laurel River Lake Baked Apple Delite I

Here's a nice little dessert for those late night munchies. Easy to make, too.

Peel and core apples (or, if hardcore, just core).

Complain about having to do all the work.

Fill cavity of cored apple with crumbled pecan twists bought from gas station at last stop.

Put tab of butter into each. Douse with dose of sugar.

Wrap in foil.

Bake in campfire (or oven) at 325 degrees for 15-20 minutes.

Allow to cool before eating. That's the hardest part. Serve with glob of ice cream, if you have a cabin and the ice cream came in with supplies. Purloined coffee creamers, preferably half-and-half, from above mentioned hotel chains will work nicely out in the woods. Cream cheese or slice of cheddar goes well, too.

Chapter XIV - Rolling Stones and Sugar Mamas

Mud Daddy tip: *Mine the free breakfast bar at most chain hotels while en route to campground. After you finish your breakfast, make another trip to help yourself to cream cheese containers, sugar packets, creamers, bagels, white bread, maple syrup, corn flakes and cereal to-go – as much as you can purloin while keeping it from being smashed and leaking in your pockets. You can't take too many jams, either. Wear cargo pants. Fold napkins around fragile items. And remember that hotel chains are hospitality companies and want you to leave happy. And if, as you leave, you do not have at least 12 cream cheese containers, 30 sugar packets, 18 creamers, three bagels, eight piece of white bread and nine maple syrup containers, realize you are short-changing the trip.*

Even at $75 a pop, we figured the tickets to the Rolling Stones' Voodoo Lounge Tour were probably bad ones back in 1994. Nobody sees the Stones in a great seat for that price, or maybe for any price, unless they are a celebrity or royalty or Eurotrash. We didn't fit any of those categories, but we were compelled to see just how bad these tickets really were and hear the best rock-and-roll band of all time in the process. Since this was a Mud Daddy, albeit a two-man Mud Daddy with Erardi and Rankin AWOL, and because Mud Daddy trips are mostly about the doing and being and not necessarily the fishing, we cut short our time on the water at Lake Travis in Central Texas to go to the show in the giant Alamodome in San Antonio, about an hour or so from Austin.

Doc had promised that the fishing on Lake Travis would be extraordinary, and about that much he was right. It was extraordinarily bad. The lake was a marvelous body of water, close to the skirts of the Austin metropolitan area and only partially developed with split-level mansions and escape homes at that time. Doc had fished the lake the month before with one of his pals, who knew all the right holes and proved it by dragging bass after bass from the water all day long.

"How could the fishing be anything but stunning?" Doc asked, as he and Slim watched Doc's buddy's almost-new ski boat get fork-lifted from storage and gingerly eased into the water.

"We're fishing in this?" Slim asked, marveling at the boat with its built-in tape player, trolling motor and – will wonders never cease – fish finder. It was like being the Bell Boy at a Ritz who had to make one last room-service run, only to find himself in an empty room with a panoramic view, grilled lobster and a perfectly chilled bottle of Dom Perignon.

"There must be some mistake," Slim said.

He would soon find that there was at least one mistake in this stunning tableau. The fishing. Doc had forgotten about the Mud Daddy factor. But the fishing ended with Doc boating a nice smallmouth on a top-water Rapala, always a beautiful thing to behold. He returned it to the water, and we abandoned the boat and lake with the Stones still ahead.

Long drives are chances to reconnect and discover startling elements about lives and worlds. Doc noted midway through the run to San Antonio that he had made this drive far too often and usually in the dead of the night. He was in a carpool, the driver/authority figure who took suburban kids to ice hockey practice and games in San Antonio at 5 a.m. That meant picking up the carload of kids about 3 a.m. in Austin. Plenty was wrong with this picture: ice rinks and youth hockey in the heart of hot, hot Texas didn't seem to make any sense at all. Setting an alarm clock to do Dad Drive Time in the middle of the night brought the second mental jam: no-way-this-can't-be-true-you're-making-it-up. But it was true. Excessive? That depends on the perspective. Doc was cool with it.

"Sports don't necessarily keep your kids out of trouble," he explained. "But it makes 'em too tired or too preoccupied for the really bad stuff. At least I hope so."

Of course the Stones were great. How far back were the seats? Stretch out your arm and hold out your hand. Find a white dot on a fingernail. That was Mick Jagger. Find another white dot on another nearby finger. That was Keith Richards. Charlie Watts was invisible behind his drum set. By the time the music reached us, it was muddy mush. Still, it was the Stones making this muddy mush, and the stage was stunning, with a giant Cobra and other Macy's Parade-style balloons towering over the stage: Elvis, a HooDoo Man and an African-American woman with diabetes and Twinkie issues.

The band kicked off with "Not Fade Away" then rolled through "Sweet Virginia," "Who Do You Love," "Start Me Up" and "Jumpin' Jack Flash." Then the balloons started dancing and wiggling around. We got our money's worth. The experience would not fade away.

Everyone should see the Stones at least once in his life. And if a flagging fishing trip needs to be cut short to do it, well, there will always be another day on the water and another fish to catch. But one of these years the Stones will be no more. Time is definitely not on their side.

The next day, Doc had built in a little repast for the ride back to the Austin airport, where Slim was to catch his flight to Cincinnati. We stopped by a club called Sugar's for some refreshment and to watch the performing artists. But when we lifted the first beers to our lips, POP, the electricity went out. Minutes clicked by. No music. No performance art. Only the stale smell of a bar. Staff opened the doors to let in the harsh afternoon light, and the girls, bless their hearts, sat around in the altogether waiting for the music to start up again. Finally, they couldn't take it anymore.

It might be the only time in strip-club history that dancers actually put on their clothes during a show. The juice was still off when we left for the airport.

"I can't believe what you did," Doc said to Slim, shaking his head. "I mean, your bad mojo shutting down the electricity."

"That was you, Doc, not me."

We looked as far as we could see down the street in one direction: the lights were out. In the other direction, the traffic lights worked perfectly. The power outage occurred at that moment in Austin from Sugar's on out.

And it happened because, well, it was a Mud Daddy.

Syracuse L'Orange

A Mud Daddy is not complete without two things: dessert and a Syracuse connection. For us, there is always something Syracusian – Doc catches a flight to Cincinnati that continues on to Syracuse; or the Orangemen are playing on TV; or the Orange basketball team whips Texas and wins the national championship. The dessert 'Syracuse L'Orange' pays tribute to that longstanding Syracuse connection, to Big E's hometown. It's easy to make, too. Cut an orange in half, invert each half and chew or pull out the fruit and pulp for breakfast. Save the half-dome peel. That night, as dinner is cooking, create a mush of oatmeal, granola, sweet yellow raisins, nuts and anything else, including donut crumbs, cookie crumbs or smashed-up little dessert cakes from the Stop-N-Rob – cakes that you bought on the way in but didn't know why you were buying them. Make a nice, small, fist-sized wad of sweet gook. Flavor with whiskey – not too much – to get the right moisture content. It should be gooey. Put in a tablespoon of jam, preferably raspberry, if you have some and feel like it.

Stuff the ball of sweetened gook into one of the saved orange halves, then close it up with the other half of orange. Thread three or four fishing hooks through three places to hold the top and bottom halves together, then place into the coals of the fire. (This can also work with grapefruit.) Carefully turn after 10 minutes of baking, depending upon the heat of the fire. The orange or grapefruit skin won't burn up. (Wrap in aluminum foil, if you must.) Upon opening, re-douse with a splash of Woodford Reserve whiskey before serving. Don't burn your fingers. It hurts to burn your fingers. After finishing your portion, find Mars in the summer sky. (Maybe research this before you leave so you know where to point.) If, like us, you don't have much of a clue, find the sky's only orange star (some think it's red but it's not) point at it with your fork and say: "Mars." Nobody will know the difference.

Chapter XV - Lost Weekend

Mud Daddy tip: *Leave a No. 16 hare's ear nymph in the Velcro tag on a jacket sleeve of your favorite autumn jacket to remind you on some chilly March Saturday morning of running errands that a fishing trip in the sun awaits you in the fall. To everybody else, it will look like a big smudge of lint. Not to you, though. It is a talisman. And when you notice it from time to time, it will surely bring a memory and a smile.*

Every fisherman has been skunked. No matter how good you are, how experienced, how much pro equipment you have, the day comes when you don't get a bite. We've obviously had our share of those days, which are worse for us because we fish so infrequently and because the annual Mud Daddy means so much. But we've learned to roll with it. The following is an anatomy of a skunking, and how even during a skunking, a Mud Daddy offers a variety of experiences and memories, most of them probably annoying – but hey, it's still a memory.

We agreed in 1995 to return to Laurel River Lake, Kentucky, the scene of two previous Mud Daddies and a lake at which we had always had at least some fishing success. It's a beautiful body of water, with numerous islands for camping and not too much pressure at that time of the year.

This Mud Daddy began in typical fashion. Slim met Doc at the Cincinnati airport, and as soon as they shook hands, the baggage carousel died.

"Look what you did," Slim said, nodding at the frozen carousel and pissed-off travelers. "Your karmic baggage and bad vibes shut down the place."

"It's your fault," Doc protested. "Remember in Austin last year, at Sugar's when that vortex that follows you around shut down electricity for 40 blocks?"

"Well, it doesn't look good for fishing, does it? One, or both of us, has some powerful negative mojo going on about now."

But there was beer and Cincinnati chili. We hit the bars all night, heard some good bands and caught up on the past 12 months of our lives. About 4:30 in the morning, after taking a light nap, we went to pick up E-Man for the late September trip down to Kaywacky. After driving the length of the Commonwealth, we hit the marina, where it took about 30 minutes to transfer all the gear down a long, steep ramp to the john boat. The lake was sparkling and appeared as inviting as ever: deep jade with a silver sheen, a shimmering reflection of blue sky dancing on small waves. But nothing around us looked familiar. It was not the same marina from previous trips, and the landmarks we were familiar with weren't to be seen.

We boated to an island and made camp at a lovely spot under tall trees on a hill above the lake, with fallen trunks for back rests, tables and chairs, and toasted another Mud Daddy. Our lives had changed considerably over the years, but we had managed to keep the fishing trip together. The Mud Daddy remained sacred. The next morning, no one got a bite, not even a nibble. We packed it in and returned to camp for lunch and a spirited round of Trivial Pursuit, which we called Trivial Prosciutto in honor of the E-Man's heritage. Late afternoon and early evening fishing would be better, Slim predicted. E and Doc nodded in agreement.

The evening was spent listening to a high school football game on the radio, Van Morrison's "A Night in San Francisco" on tape and fretting about the poor fishing. Someone left the tent door wide open all night, and the Saturday sun greeted us with a tent full of spiders and bites all over our faces, necks and arms. Nice way to begin the day.

Sunday was an electric morning, as bright and blue as they come. But the fish weren't going for anything. We fished holes that looked familiar, cast over the points off the islands, threw baits at the ledges below rock walls. Nothing doing.

"What the hell is going on?" Big-E wondered.

"Bad Karma," offered Doc. "Real bad Karma."

What happens by the end of a second full day of a skunking is a kind of mental breakdown. The frustration combined with the knowledge that you've waited a year for an adventure that has crumbled and is slipping through your fingers is too much for a fragile mind to bear. Desperation sets in, and angry words are soon exchanged. Blame is cast and friendships fray. Then, like clouds on a sunny day, all that passes, everyone finds the humor in the situation and makes the most of the time they have left together. Getting skunked is like enduring the five stages of death: denial, anger, bargaining, depression and acceptance.

In the last hours of the skunk, we went through all our tackle, looking for the craziest things we could throw. If the fish were going to mess with us, by God, we would mess with them! Big E tied on an enormous Lazy Ike he used exclusively for Great Lakes fishing. (He's from upstate New York, remember). Slim held up a Day-Glo chartreuse buzz bait with a pink, split-tail slab of rubber speared onto the treble hook. He made it on the spot and named it, too. "I call this 'The Slayer,' " he crowed.

Doc pulled out the largest Cordell Redfin he could find, a bait usually cast into a mess of Striped Bass or Chesapeake Bay Blues. "This is 'The Producer,' " he explained. "It's designed to piss them off so much they want to kill it."

So it went for the remains of the day. We threw plastic frogs; rubber worms with red, blue and gold flecks; dry flies; wet flies; pork rind; cheese; Vienna Sausages tight on the bottom – and some things we didn't know what they were. We dunked stuff in garlic oil. We sprayed lures and wobble lips with Panama Jack and WD-40. We cast things we never knew we had, things we didn't remember buying, things no self-respecting manufacturer would even consider making, much less selling to the public – but there the lure was, in the bottom of the tackle box. We cast red plastic and green rubber. Black jigs on yellow worms.

"Look," Doc laughed, as the boat edged along the shore. "This ought to work, don't you think?"

He had hooked up a black rubber mouse, the size of a large fig. It dangled there in the sunset like a joke. "Hell, why not?"

Nothing. Nada. Zip!

We had returned to the marina at lunch to ask what was up with the fishing. The warm weather, we were told, had forced the fish deep, and they would stay on the bottom of the lake until the weather cooled off. We had to go down and get them, the man said, and he had the perfect thing for that.

The Mud Daddy Chronicles

From the wall of lures he pulled off a wire contraption that looked a lot like that thing Bob Dylan wore around his neck to hold his harmonica whenever flowers on the hillside were blooming crazy. It didn't look like a bait. It was a Bottom-Walker, the man explained. You hook a worm onto it, drop it to the bottom of the lake and as you jiggle the line, the contraption moves along the bottom like it's walking.

"That's it!" cried Slim.

We bought three.

When all else had failed, when nothing was left at the bottom of the tackle box, when the last plastic bait had been put on backward in a desperate-yet-futile attempt to attract at least one curious nibble, we went with Bottom-Walkers and night crawlers.

"Is this rigged right?" Big E wondered as he held the wire aloft. We shrugged. Maybe. In the dying rays of the last Mud Daddy sunset of the year, we worked our bottom-walkers as best we could.

"How do you know if it's on the bottom?" Doc asked. "How do you know what's going on down there? How do you know if it's walking, not tangled up in the line, not snagged on a stump, not . . ."

"I'm gonna make mine do a Michael Jackson moonwalk."

"Yeah. Like with those original Mad Toms in Virginia."

If the bottom-walkers were strolling along the bed of Laurel River Lake, we didn't know it. If the fish were laughing at us, we didn't know it. If the marina manager was laughing at us, we didn't know it. And we didn't care. He deserved a good laugh at our expense. We figured he was already telling the story over beers at his local bar – how he conned three rubes into buying the last three bottom-walkers at the marina.

That's the way it goes during a full-on skunk. But it wasn't miserable. The weather was great and the lake was beautiful. We listened to one of the last Reds games of the season on the radio, played good music, wrestled with Trivial Pursuit and spoke about the things we loved – families, sports, writing, books, music, and yes, fishing.

Sometimes events are memorable for what doesn't happen.

Trolling

Trolling is the oldest and surest way to locate fish on an unknown lake – unless you have a fish finder, which we don't. You cover a lot of water while trolling, since it usually involves cruising past points, where holding fish can be found. After a strike, we return to that area and begin to cast. On a Mud Daddy, we toss out big bottom dragging baits and troll as slowly as possible to the dock. In many ways, it's pure leisure, but you're still fishing. There are multiple lines in the water, but everyone is leaning back, smoking cigars and relaxing in that pure way that only anglers can relax. This can, of course, end with lines inextricably tangled, expensive lures lost to logs and rocks on the bottom and some inventive swearing, but that is the price that a fisherman must pay to find fish.

On a Mud Daddy troll, there are usually six lines out, so the odds for trouble are high. Sometimes a guy will back off to one line to avoid the hassle of a snarl. And fish do get caught. Doc side-hooked a striped bass on one occasion. And Slim swears that he always catches fish this way.

What usually happens then is this: because the fish is now hooked sideways, Doc always gets extremely agitated because he thinks he has a huge fish. He reels hard and fast. But because it's coming in sideways, the rod is bent double. And then a dinky fish arrives at the boat. Sideways. That's how it happens with Doc.

The Mud Daddy debate on the merits of trolling is a timeless one, revisited often and usually with loud voices. Slim, perhaps feeling the ancient tug of a Swedish ancestor trolling off the Stones of Faroe, insists upon trolling. He once nailed a three-pound smallmouth at Pickwick Lake in Alabama this way. He's even caught catfish trolling. (Doc claims the one he hooked on the James River arm of Table Rock Lake in Missouri was even larger, though that wasn't on a Mud Daddy.) Doc is a doubter and sees trolling as giving up on the lake. E-Man likes to troll but is okay with casting, too. E looks for no foe or fight. He enjoys life – like a big fish.

"One always looks neat in a hat made from meat."
Mark Twain

Chapter XVI - Taters of Ouachita

The velocity was astounding. In an instant, the potato hit the wall and became mist and then nothingness. Slim knew he had to have one. A potato fired from a white PVC contraption at a party at the historic Viking Club above the Ohio River on that Fourth of July changed his life. Slim knew it would be perfect for a Mud Daddy, a diversion for the slow times when the fishing was a footnote to shenanigans and bullshitting around the fire. Or maybe it would be nice to fire off a few vegetables while waiting for the water to boil, which always takes forever. A potato cannon also functions in a Mud Daddy sort of way because when broken down into its component parts it can double as a rod case, as a rod fits nicely in the barrel.

Within days of his introduction to the cannon, Slim was at the Big Box Hardware Store, a man's mall on the suburban outskirts of Cincinnati, going down his check list: glue; four-foot long, 2 ½" PVC tube; four-inch end cap; four-inch screw fitting with the screw insert; three three-inch sections of four-inch tube to be glued to the end cap; screw insert fitting and the four-inch T unit; as well as a reducer to hook up the chamber to the 2 ½ inch four-foot long barrel. Add a female fitting for a garden hose replacement, a tiny screw clamp (like for a radiator hose) and the barbeque lighter (round shaft only). Slim also bought a couple of end caps with screw-type insets for either end of the barrel so it could double as the aforementioned rod case.

The unveiling and first shot came months later, in the fall of 1998 on our return visit to Lake Ouachita in Arkansas. First came the assemblage of the ordnance, then a potato was ram-rodded down the barrel with the butt end of a fishing rod. After the back chamber was unscrewed and pumped full of butane, about five seconds worth,

Slim screwed the cap back on, aimed it, pushed the barbeque lighter button and WHAMMMM! The potato slammed into a nearby tree with terrific velocity.

Oh-man-oh-man-oh-man.

We launched spuds far out into the lake, perhaps 200 yards or more, in a great curving trajectory of speed and sound. Strangely enough, E had brought along a baseball bat. After several shots of the cannon – and shots of whiskey – he waved the bat around, declaring that he might like to stand in against a tater. Everyone agreed it was a great idea until a higher power intervened with a coherent thought.

"I was thinking," E said, "a half-pound 'tater at that speed would probably kill a man, or at least permanently scramble his brains."

"Hey E," Doc intoned. "In your case, how could we tell if your brains were scrambled?"

"Discretion is the better part of valor," E declared before dropping his Louisville Slugger of ancient white ash – a relic of his long-bygone amateur era – into the dust and needles of our island.

"To tell you the truth, I just don't trust Slimbagger's aim. I'd rather face a drunk Nolan Ryan than Slim sober with a potato gun," E said. "And Slim ain't sober."

He hadn't forgotten his near-fatal run-in with the fates on the inaugural Mud Daddy, when his bad Karma and a tumble into the river bed nearly cost him a leg. He could see the headline now: Crescent Springs, Ky., Fisherman Decapitated by High, Hard Tater.

It was more than he could handle.

Previously, Slim and E had made a long-drive pilgrimage through the night to Little Rock from Cincinnati, where they had tee-times at a local public course.

"I've heard of 8:30 a.m. tee-times," E-Man would mutter in a comment forever bronzed in Mud Daddy lore. "But in Arkansas?"

E pulled out the win that morning because Slim's collar tightened on the final set of greens. After 18 holes, the two picked up Doc at the Little Rock airport, and it was on to the lake and a secluded island for three days of fishing.

Fishing optimism rules in the first hours of a Mud Daddy. Until reality sets in. We soon realize that the fish, as always, will be scarcer than Baptists in a liquor store. And there are other inevitable challenges. On this trip, Slim forgot the big pot to boil the spaghetti noodles.

"A minor setback," said Slim, and besides, he said, it wasn't his fault. There was so much to remember . . .

A more significant setback would come later and lead to another important Mud Daddy insight: When pumping up the pressure on a Coleman camp stove that is already lit, if your hand suddenly feels wet, it's probably not water.

"Hmm, what's going on," thought Slim at dinnertime as he rubbed his fingers together and smelled them.

Why are my fingers wet?

VAROOM! The stove was no longer a heating element but now a raging conflagration at Slim's feet. Slim immediately kicked at it, knocking it over onto its side, still burning.

Doc and E stood by, mouths agape, watching the drama unfold as if in slow motion and thinking thoughts like: "Hmmm, was that a good idea, tipping it over like that?" "Is this thing going to explode?" "How does one put out a burning camp stove anyhow?" "If it blows, will we all be injured?" "Slim will get the worst of it, but how bad?" "Minor burns on face and hands?" "Scarred for life?" "Is this going to ruin the trip?"

Those thoughts were composed in about a half-second.

Did somebody flail with a towel? Did somebody empty a milk jug? Kick dirt? All of the above? Just how the fire went out exactly – and whose heroics saved the day – is the subject of great and heated debate to this day. Sadly, or fortunately, the truth has been obscured by the fog of time and 101 proof.

Still, we needed that stove because we were on a distant island, so Slim went at it in the dark with a flashlight and his fishing reel repair kit – that would be one small pair of adjustable pliers – and dismantled it methodically before putting it back together again, only this time ensuring that the regulator nut was tight around some sort of paper gasket/washer that he fashioned on the spot.

Want to know what faith is?

Relighting a one-burner camp stove that Slim has just "fixed."

Doc and E stood back at a safe distance to watch. They would have none of it. Slim was up close and personal with his stove now, doing the priming, the pumping and, finally, the lighting.

And what d'ya know! It worked. We had to boil noodles in a frying pan filled with water, but it worked well enough.

After the dinner dishes were given a gravel wash and dried, Slim left his foam pad to meander over to the stony bar for an Akron sour refill. As he did so, up came a breeze that quickly turned into a wicked wind. As Slim watched, his foam pad curled into a cylinder, and as if it had a mind of its own, lifted up into the air and then rolled away down the hill. The pad was now headed toward the water at a breakneck speed with Slim running down the hill after it, drink in hand, in a desperate chase. His comfort was on the line, and he knew it. Never slowing at the shoreline, the foam danced from shore and rolled out onto the water and then rolled away into the night, riding atop the waves. Slim watched it go. At the campfire, the fellows roared with laughter. Doc and E's happy faces were bronze above the orange light of the fading campfire. Slim would have an uncomfortable weekend of sleeping on the ground.

The next morning, we found the lake had turned a sorry brown, like a tired cup of coffee with cream. With the chances of hooking fish remote, Slim was looking for any possible edge. Breaking out his flyrod, he cast a No. 14 Adams up tight to the shore under a crummy little bush. Strike! Slim hauled back on the rod and set the hook, then proceeded to fight and land the tiniest bluegill caught in Mud Daddy history. It fit into the palm of his hand and not lengthwise, either. Slime was proud. He took a picture of the fish in his hand. Slim was just happy he wasn't skunked.

"That's not a fish. That's a minnow."

Undeterred by the jeers, Slim impaled the bluegill on a hook tied to about 15 feet of line and then tied the line to a milk jug, like a giant bobber topside with a lead-weighted bottom bouncer hanging below, leaving the tiny bluegill helpless and forlorn in the lake's depths. Sad, but that's life at that end of the food chain, Slim figured. He put the rig into a bay with a steep drop-off, and resolved to check his jug-rig the next morning.

"Big fish coming," he said.

The rosy fingers of dawn clawed across the sky the next morning, and before we headed out into the foggy main channel for a few more hours of fishing, we motored over to the little inlet to have a look at Slim's jug. It wasn't there.

"Hmm. Strange. Oh well, must have drifted off," Slim said.

Nobody thought much more about it until we pulled out of the bay and headed toward the middle of the lake. There, off the starboard bow about 30 yards out, was the jug! And it was moving in circles!

"Holy shit!" Slim cried, gunning the motor and heading for it. Turtle, giant bass, the Lock Ness Monster? Something big was on the other end of that line! Slim couldn't wait to get to that jug. The Mud Daddy plaque would be his – and maybe a record-setting fish, too.

"Somebody grab that sucker! Oh yeah! It's Jaws! It's Moby Dick!"

We were all thinking the same thing. This triumph of patchwork tackle-rigging and dogged fortitude would earn Slim the title of Mud Daddy Angler of the Year. No, make that Mud Daddy Angler of the Millennium! World record holder for milk jug fishing! Whatever the title, we knew that after this, fishing and life with Slim, already a challenge under the best of circumstances, would be insufferable. If we just hadn't given him so much grief over that minnow!

Everyone in the boat was just as excited as Slim was to find out what was dragging the friggin' jug in circles. With Slim at the helm, he nosed up to the jug on Doc's side – Slim's first mistake.

"Grab it, Doc!" Slim barked.

Second mistake.

Doc bent over the gunwale, made an awkward grab and missed, almost falling in.

"Man, Doc! There's something huge down there. Grab it would 'ja!"

Turning towards Slim, Doc removed the cigar from his mouth so as not to be misunderstood.

"Screw you, Eckberg! Steer the boat so's I can reach it, ya big dumb ass Swede."

"Argghhhh," Slim replied like a pirate of yore.

Slim made a little jink with the motor, slowed the boat, hit reverse, twisted, then moved forward and bumped the motor a touch to bring the bow up to the jug one more time.

"Grab it, Doc!"

"Shut up!"

Doc, his cigar purposefully clenched between his teeth, made a stab at the jug, connected and hauled it into the boat with a loud grunt.

"Yeah, baby, yeah! That's what I'm talking about!" Slim cried.

The line in the water pulsed in and out and side to side in slow, determined thrusts. Off-balance and having a hard time holding on to the jug, Doc instinctively clasped it to his chest.

"Careful, Doc! Play it. PLAY IT!" There was alarm in Slim's voice.

As he struggled with the jug, the line taught and quivering, Doc muttered something largely unintelligible but it sort of sounded like:

"You asshole! I've got a milk jug for a rod and reel!"

And then suddenly, as quickly as it began, the struggle ended. The taught line went limp.

"Doc!"

Doc pulled back on the jug a few times. Nothing. Just the line and a jug. We stared at the opaque surface, imagining what might have been. A long audible groan emanated from the back of the boat. Slim was disheartened and ready for another Akron Sour. After that, we made a few desultory casts out there in the middle of the lake, but nobody's heart was really in it. We'd hooked the fish of the day, of the year, of the forever. And lost it.

There were some low-key recriminations, mild by Mud Daddy standards.

"You tried to horse it in. You should have played it."

"Yeah, well next time give me a rod and reel with fishing line, not some low-rent Arkansas special."

But neither Slim's nor Doc's heart was in the repartee.

We reeled in heading for camp, and eventually home, our heads full of "if onlys," and "what ifs." Back at camp we packed up and said our good-byes until next year.

"Yep. That's why they call it 'fishing' and not 'catching' "

Slim took home the plaque for the smallest fish ever caught on a Mud Daddy.

Lady Luck – no doubt feeling sorry for our ineptitude – smiled on us anyway. On the way back to the marina the motor began to choke. Slim looked at the gas can. The needle was on empty. He gunned it and the last of the fumes punched us forward, just enough to coast into the marina. We cheered as we bumped the dock. Slim and E headed east and found time for a twilight round of golf outside of Memphis, a mystical round that led to an inexplicable 440-yard drive for E on one of the holes on the back nine. No cart path or sprinkler head bounce. All carry. Monumental. The pain would not soon end for Doc, though. A thunderstorm turned the sky black and delayed his plane's departure for more than an hour. Rerouted to Houston, he was soon trapped in an airport that looked like the Fall of Saigon. He snagged the last rental car, drove through the rest of the night to Austin and finally made it home at dawn – about the same time E and Slim made it back to Ohio.

Oh yeah, we're good. Can't wait until next year.

The Mud Daddy Chronicles

Baja Tennessee Bluegill

Bluegill filets
Juice from one or two limes
Three shots of Tequila
One egg
¼ cup milk
1 cup Italian-seasoned bread crumbs

Take filets and marinate in lime juice for one hour, then add tequila for another half hour. Drink a shot or two of Tequila in the meantime and yell at a football game on TV as if the players and coaches can hear you. Remove filets, dust with bread crumbs, run through egg/milk mixture, then dust again with crumbs. Fry in fairly hot frying pan that has equal parts oil and butter. Make it crispy brown.

"Also I wanted the whiskey for itself, because I loved the taste of it and because, being as happy as I could be, it made me feel even better."
Green Hills of Africa by **Ernest Hemingway**

Chapter XVII - Radiology Ranger and All the Intangibles

In 1999 we had agreed on a Mud Daddy weekend at Pickwick, a lake bordered by Tennessee, Alabama and Mississippi. Doc had some vacation to burn, so he decided to do some camping and fishing in Oklahoma and Missouri before heading down to Tennessee. It was late September and the weather was great – sunny days, cool nights. There was baseball on the radio on the weekdays and football on the weekends. Doc hit some pretty good fishing spots, too, on Broken Bow reservoir and Lake Tenkiller in Oklahoma. On Monday, he was pulling into the Bull Shoals area of Missouri to spend some time fishing up there before heading for Memphis. It was a perfect early fall day, and the leaves were just beginning to show their colors against a cobalt sky. He was winding through the hills around lunchtime, searching for something to listen to on the radio. Nothing came in strong enough to hold for long. Finally, he dialed in a baseball game out of St. Louis.

"Maybe this will interest me for a few hours," he thought as he wandered through the colorful Ozarks. It was one of the last games of the year, and the Cardinals were in Cincinnati to play the Reds, who still had a chance to make the playoffs. Doc thought that was pretty funny. But the game wasn't going the Reds' way. The Cardinals quickly jumped on top and looked destined to stay there. McGwire hit his 61st homer in the fourth inning. Ah, the miracle of steroids.

The Reds were five runs down in the 6th inning and Doc was about to lose interest when Dmitri Young hit a two-run shot to get the Reds within three. Could the Reds possibly claw their way back into the game and keep their playoff hopes alive?

In the 7th, the Reds got another two-run homer, this one from

Eddie Taubensee to give them a 7-6 lead. The Reds scored two more in the eighth to win 9-6. As Doc was cheering with the announcers, a fact hit him like a hammer and he had to pull over. They were there.

Slim and Big E were AT THAT GAME and he was listening to it. That's why it happened the way it did. He would have bet a month's pay on it.

When they met up at the campsite a few days later, there was the usual round of greetings. Then Doc said, "Were you guys at the Reds game Monday? When they came back to beat the Cardinals?"

"Oh yeah," said Slim. "Businessman's special. I slipped down there for lunch and bought a scalped ticket. What a game."

"I was listening on the radio when they made the big come back. And I figured – hell, I KNEW – you guys were there. Were you there, too, E?"

"In the press box. I wasn't covering it, but I slid in to catch the last half to maybe find something to write about. Couldn't believe that ending. And you were listening, huh? Weird."

"Weird, hell. That's why it happened the way it did. The Vortex. The Mud Daddy had already begun because we were all three involved in it."

"The Vortex, again," Slim said, laughing. "At the Reds game. Who'd believe it?"

It was the end of the 20th Century, and we wanted to catch fish before Y2K brought the world to its knees. We knew Pickwick had the potential for great fishing. The Tennessee River meandered in an enormous U, from northeastern Tennessee on south into Alabama then north again back into Tennessee and Kentucky, before finally draining into Kentucky Lake and the Ohio River. But Slim had another reason to explore the region. It was the land of Madoc, the Welsh prince who brought five ships of Englishmen to what he said would be a New World. The year? 1170. And together they sailed into history. Slim knew about Madoc because he had written a story about traces of him and a tribe of blue-eyed Indians for the Enquirer years before. Slim wondered if there might be a mystic pull to these parts, and whether anybody in 1999 could still get a sense of Madoc and his time in the New World.

Rapping on about Madoc on the drive south, Slim let it flow, meandering through the subject like the Tennessee River itself.

"Somewhere on a ridge above the Tennessee River are two ancient foundations that are perfect matches for castles in England.

They've been dated to about the 12th Century. Nobody has ever been able to explain that."

Slim talked of the Filson Papers, written by Cincinnati pioneer John Filson. The papers inventoried all the stories that settlers told about a strange tribe of blue-eyed Indians living in the Ohio Valley several centuries before Christopher Columbus and his crew grabbed all the credit for "finding" America.

"You know," Slim continued, "one night on a flatboat, Daniel Boone told Filson how the old chiefs would sometimes gather to talk about their grandfather's, grandfather's, grandfather's grandfather's time and of a great battle at the falls of the Ohio, now Louisville. The red-skinned Indians surprised the fair-skinned, blue-eyed Indians one fateful day and killed them all – everybody but one boatload of stragglers that they exiled to the upper reaches of the Missouri River. They became the Mandan Indians, a tribe that had some pretty odd customs. They came into pow-wows under three albino buffalo skins pinned to crosses, and instead of canoes, they traversed waters in animal skin barks, like the Irishmen of old.

"Filson had other stories, too. Once, an Indian came to the Pittsburgh fort from out of the wilderness and spoke Gaelic. Another time, two Presbyterian ministers were captured by Indians in the wild mountains of North Carolina and were about to be put to death. When they began to pray in Gaelic, the Indians stopped the ceremony, started to talk to them and some rushed off. They soon returned with a bundle of skins and inside was a parchment scroll. The preachers couldn't read the scroll, even though both could read and write Latin. In any event, the Indians let the two go.

"And why couldn't they read the scroll?" Slim asked, mostly to ensure that E was still listening.

"I'll bite. Why?" E replied.

"Because when Madoc set sail, as shipping records from Bristol, England, indicate, he would have sailed with a Bible that was written in Greek. The Bible was not translated into Latin until the early 13th Century. The preachers had been looking at Madoc's Bible – nearly 600 years after it was brought to the continent – but it was in Greek and they couldn't read it!"

E was driving on this late-night run and was fascinated.

"You making this up, Slim?"

It's a question that Slim is frequently asked on Mud Daddies.

"It's true, man. I've researched it. I know it's true."

Stories and Mud Daddies – they go together like fish and water.

On that first night, when we approached the lake area at about 1:30 a.m., Slim and E shuddered to see the letters on a sign for a Ramada Hotel:

"Welcome Regional Bass Champions"

We were cooked – again – because they sure as hell weren't talking about us. The sign meant the lake would be cluttered with bass boats and fishermen all weekend long. What we didn't yet realize was that a couple of hundred bass boats on a lake with hard-to-catch smallmouth bass might be a blessing in disguise.

Doc, as usual, had a supreme campsite prepped and a fire going. We talked. About family, work and sports. Doc had been listening to a Braves game on the radio, maybe the last of the season, while making camp. Slim and E were listening to the same game on the drive in. We laughed about the announcers talking about a player who had "all the intangibles."

"What's that mean," asked Slim. "Is it better than having all the tangibles?" We laughed some more, had another drink, then hit the sleeping bags. It was cold. When we awoke a few hours later, it was just dawn, and there we were, wide awake in the wilderness and witnesses to the howl of 250-horsepower outboards roaring out of the nearby marina, five at a time and at full throttle. It was like camping on the infield at the Indy 500. "Welcome Regional Bass Champions" took on a brand new significance as the trio of wanna-be bass champions stood in the great dawning of yet another Mud Daddy..

"Some wilderness experience," groused Doc.

"Here's how I break it down," Slim said. "Two hundred boats, more or less, five ripping out of there every few minutes. This could go on for hours. Might as well get started ourselves."

Marinas and johnboats are always a treat. You have to slug your way through the language barrier – they speak Southern, we speak Yankee, so there's lots of "Excuse me?" or, "Pardon me, what did you say?" Or, if you grew up in Cincinnati, "Please?" Then one must undergo the humiliating, two-minute training seminar on how the motor worked while a few good old boys stood nearby, watching. Apparently there wasn't anything more entertaining or amusing than a trio of presumed buffoons, their meager gear loaded into a dinky boat, sitting like dunces during a lecture on the obvious.

"Now, this little switch on the side here has to be straight up, in the 'On' position before the motor will crank," the old boy drawled. "You see what I'm talking about?"

"Sure," Slim said. "Like I said, we've been using these boats and motors for years."

"Well, I understand this ain't your first rodeo and all (spits), but these motors are expensive. And I don't want neither you nor me to have to be buying a new one cause I didn't explain how it works properly (spits) and you didn't pay attention. You see?"

(Spits)

Slim sighed deeply, tipped up the brim of his cap and succumbed. He wasn't going to speed up the lesson by complaining. He smiled, pretended to get into the spirit of moment, and said, "Right. What's next?"

It's a high-pressure position to back any johnboat out of a marina under the watchful eye of all those guys with their Really Big, Really Nice Boats, then chug-chug away – and do it with aplomb. We have developed a comedy routine that usually gets the locals on our side. Slim is good at that. He backs a boat up until it's headed straight at about a zillion dollars' worth of floating fiberglass – some fellow's watery pride and joy – only to turn and announce loudly, "Wonder how much it'd cost my homeowner's if I backed right up into that bad boy over there?"

Slim was in back, Big E in the middle and Doc pushed off. Slim gave the nearest Bass Boater a big grin. "We'll try not to make too big a wake getting out of here."

The Good Old Boys chuckle and adjust their hats. Then Slim usually gets to the point just before pulling away, his voice loud over the idle.

"So let me ask you this: Are they holding off the points or in the shallows?" he asks. We don't expect real fishing tips from guys there for the competition. But angling questions are icebreakers, and they let everyone know we are more serious than we look.

"Oh, little bit of both."

"What're they hitting? Crankbaits? Plastic worms?"

"I'd try one, then t'other."

"Hey, thanks for the tips. We can sure put those to good use."

Puttering away from the marina, Slim offers a gesture. Not a wave exactly, not one of those city gestures like somebody is unscrewing an invisible light bulb. Nope, Slim just snaps his finger and points at the sky. They always smile and wave or nod back. Brothers in angling and all that. They wouldn't give us a real tip if we were holding their mothers hostage. But they can't totally disrespect guys who love to fish, even goofy looking, ill-equipped Yankees in Akron U baseball caps with the strange kangaroo Zip logo.

Once on the water, we always have the question, "Where to first?" Slim is a fan of early trolling, particularly over submerged road beds and from point of land to point of land along one bank of the main channel. And so, since he's captain, this is usually what we do first – until the whining from the others becomes unbearable. This time Slim's plan worked, but only for Slim.

Fish on, he said. Moments later, a smallmouth exploded from the water in the distance. It was way back. Slim reeled furiously and held the rod high with each leap. Reaching down, he killed the motor, still playing the fish, and after another two leaps, the tired, two-pound bass was at the boat. Later, Slim came back with a foot-long catfish, trolling again from point-to-point. His secret was a customized crank. (Take your typical silver-toned River Runt or any lure with a modest lip, chop off the top of a tube bait, then pull the tail skirt over the back treble. No bass alive can long resist the sharp wiggle of a hula skirt. Most men have trouble with that one, too.)

These shores were not the picturesque mountains of West Virginia, as vast stretches of water blurred into the distance, a low horizon that was the green carpet of Tennessee and ran back from the shoreline in hilly humps. Here, too, the main channel held giant barges that moved in slow motion and trailed rolling wakes. The constant pull of the channel made hard work of holding a position for any length of time. Our jury-rigged anchor – a plastic milk bottle filled with gravel – could not hold us against the current and heavy wakes.

We found an old roadbed on the map, and it held a great number of fish: smallmouth, bluegill, even striped bass. Everyone caught fish there. It was fall, the burnished Tennessee hills were splashed with umber and yellow, and the sunny afternoon was blissfully quiet. The sense of peace and satisfaction was profound. This was soul feeding – what we had waited a year for, and it was worth every minute. The marina manager wouldn't allow us to keep the boat at the campsite overnight – rules, you know. As we headed to the campsite to get dinner going, Slim had what he called a brain hurricane, which is always far better than a mere brainstorm.

"Why not head over to the weigh-in at the bass tournament and work the points until just before dark?" Slim asked.

After each day's competition, authorities weigh each catch, and the bass are released back into the water right there at the scales. It's a perfect case of fish in a barrel, and Slim was not going to pass it up.

"Now you're talking, Slim," Big E replied. "Full Akron! Let the bassmasters bring the fish to us."

"That is just too low-rent," Doc declared. "I refuse to stoop to those levels."

"Well, then – later," said Slim, as he and E headed out of the bay and back across the main body for the mile-or-more run to the marina.

On the way over to the weigh-in, the lake surface shimmered with great dark patches of minnows that seemed to burn black and then flame in the dying rays of sunset. Dozens of these giant pockets moved atop the water, a rolling smudge of thousands of fingerling shad swimming and barely leaping into the air, flashing in the fading day. Sometimes a larger wrinkle moved through the firmament. A big fish was feeding. Maybe one released from the weigh-in just around the point, thought Slim. Slim cruised over to one patch, killed the motor, and he and E cast into the glittering carpet, a golden Rapala for Slim and a Rat-L-Trap for Big-E. Then came the silent and strong tug of a big bass. Slim caught and released two smallmouth in that last half-hour of sunset. At the weigh-in itself, we moved along the shore, casting tube baits to root pockets, but that was a total bust.

Back at camp, Doc had a visit by a campground assistant manager, who was collecting trash. Doc tried to hide his nervousness.

Alcohol was forbidden at the campground, and we had the customary prodigious amounts of Mud Daddy booze in various spots. Most, but not all, out of sight. The ranger seemed not to notice or care as he chattered away. After tossing the trash bag into the bed of the pickup, the man in his late 20s finally paused and looked into the distance beyond Doc. It's never good when authority figures get that 1,000-yard stare.

Uh, oh, thought Doc. Here it comes. Busted by the booze patrol again. And there's no empty hotel room for dozens of miles thanks to those Bassmasters.

"I'm thinking about a career change," the junior ranger said solemnly. Doc breathed a sigh of relief.

"I've been thinking about radiology. What do you think? Would that be a good move?"

Radiology? Doc thought. He wants to become a radiologist? Is that what he's asking me – about 10 years of schooling and interning? From park ranger to radiologist? Well, you gotta have dreams. Who knows, it might work out for the guy.

So Doc gave the only answer possible for such a personal and improbable question, offered with all the solemnity Doc could muster.

"You go for it, man. Go for it!"

On the last day, Doc told Slim and E that they really should take a side trip to Shiloh Battlefield in Tennessee on the way back to Ohio. "There's a lot of boys buried there from the Ohio Company," Doc explained. "You might have relatives there, Slim. And you ought to see how they treated those rebel soldiers, still in trenches. No names. No markers. The Union fallen all have names and markers. The winners write the history, don't they? The Union wanted to send a message to the Confederacy. This is what happens when you go against the government."

That was when the realization hit Slim: If he did have relatives dumped into that hallowed ground, they were surely on the rebel side. While it was true that he was born in Akron, Ohio, his roots ran to the South, which probably explained his gabbiness. His mother, Sarah Nell, came to Akron as an infant in the 1920s. Her parents, Milton and Lucille, were from Northern Alabama, only miles away from Shiloh, and surely both branches on her side of the family, the Oaks and the Wises, spilled blood on that fateful April morning.

Slim's ancestors would be in the trenches, not under the well-kept, orderly headstones. Blood of his blood – still in trenches!

Back in Cincinnati, Slim called his neighbor Joe Yearwood about something or another, told him of the weekend of fine bass fishing and ended with the story of the trenches at Shiloh.

"You're not going to believe this," Joe said. "I'll be right over."

He was at the door in minutes with a letter telling of his great-grandfather and how that soldier of the South held a dying brother in his arms in the Spring rain of Shiloh then had to abandon him to die when retreat was ordered. One brother left another to die in that soft spring rain.

Those boys had names. It's time to give them headstones, too.

Award-Winning Twinkie Tiramisu

This dessert has a powerful impact on a fishing trip and represents American dessert excess at its best because it's based on the Twinkie, a tasty creation anytime anyhow and a Mud Daddy staple. Don't count calories. Don't count carbs. Don't short yourself on seconds, either. You'll never have a better tasting, quick-fix dessert.

        1 box of Twinkies
        1 container of sweetened cream cheese fruit dip
        1 half-pint coffee-flavored yogurt
        1 half-pint lemon-flavored yogurt
        1 can pressurized whip cream
        (At least) 3 individual serving-sized pieces of chocolate
        1 package powdered hot chocolate mix
        Some instant coffee (or 2 tbs of leftover coffee)
        1 sheet non-stick aluminum foil
        Maker's Mark whiskey to taste

Slice the Twinkies lengthwise (toughest part of the process). Put a layer of Twinkies — first layer should be top part down — six in a row onto a large sheet of nonstick aluminum foil. Then spread a thin layer of equal parts coffee-flavored yogurt and cream-cheese fruit dip — infuse with some left-over coffee (but don't use too much because it will get watery. Leave out altogether if unsure). Sprinkle powder from chocolate mix and/or shave chocolate. Put down another layer of Twinkie, then a layer of the coffee-yogurt frosting and chocolate and so on until the Twinkie layers are gone, building the cake into a loaf shape. Coat sides with a combination of cream cheese fruit dip cut with lemon yogurt. Paint the top with whipped cream and add a lower rim of whipped cream where the cake meets the foil. Shave one whole piece of chocolate onto the whipped cream. If you're Slim, you top the creation with an origami fish folded from the square aluminum wrapper from around the chocolate pieces. Drizzle individual slabs with Maker's Mark. Savor.

Chapter XVIII - Millennium Mud

Mud Daddy tip: *Bring an umbrella. Not one of those dinky dime store umbrellas, either. Bring a giant golf umbrella, a huge, ugly number as big as all outdoors – just like the game of golf. Autumn rains in the Midwest can be more monsoon than summer sprinkle, and nothing ruins a weekend fishing trip like a flat out deluge. You can just about count on at least one downpour per weekend in the fall. But if you have a golf umbrella, you can fish in relative comfort and certainly troll in comfort. Couple raingear with an umbrella, and you have the total package. You can even smoke a cigar during a steady downpour. Sure, you get some looks from locals unaccustomed to seeing a fisherman beneath a big green-and-white golf umbrella that maybe advertises a bank that's four states away. But that's okay. Your cigar is still burning. Let 'em stare. You got it made. You're on a Mud Daddy – and they are not!*

The Big Chief towered over Lake Wappapello from his perch, a bare-chested plaster giant in buckskin breeches and eagle-feather headdress. He had one hand raised to the sky, giving Gaia a high-five, and the world answered with stunning sunsets and stirring quarter moons that moved across his namesake waters. At maybe 35-feet tall, Big Chief was no mockery of a native people. Instead, he was a proud monument to the first North American fishermen, who put bait on bone hooks to fish these waters eons ago, long before rods and reels and glitter-paint speed boats crowded the bays and filled the day with noise.

Big chief had been rescued from a back lot where he had been banished, probably by PC do-gooders, and after some time in exile, he was resurrected when the owner of the marina stumbled upon the fallen leader. Big Chief was erected on a pedestal 10 feet high with a large wooden deck at his feet. His countenance touched all who came to buy a bucket of minnows or a tub of slacker worms, or to rent an aluminum john boat and spend a weekend casting for bass.

Guys like us.

Doc drove in from Austin to Little Rock, Arkansas, and picked up the Bull at the airport. They spent an evening having drinks at all the places that Bill Clinton had made famous with his poor man's libido, an engine that drove him into the arms of lounge singers with big hair.

"The Capitol Bar is good, and The Excelsior had a bit of ambience," explained Doc, ever the drinking establishment connoisseur. Clinton would have enjoyed the soft lighting and dark wood, the cut-glass cabinets and top-shelf drinks. And to a sweet young thing charmed by the governor's sweet voice and caring eyes, well, it must have been something of an aphrodisiac: "Honey, I have a room across the street. You want to go up and talk some more?"

"That's where it all happened," Doc said. "I could just see it!"

Bull had a close connection to Clinton, having covered the White House for the Knight-Ridder news service, tagging along on trips to Poland, Russia and Japan with the Leader of the Free World. But the highlight of his tenure as White House correspondent was being thrown out of the Oval Office. The Big Dog didn't like the Junkyard Dog's questions about the Whitewater land development scheme. It was the early '90s, and that story was moving so fast you needed the Hubble telescope to keep it in sight. Bull wasn't supposed to ask about that, so when he did an irate Clinton terminated the interview instantly.

As journalists, we knew that Bull's exit was pretty much the predictable and, in a twisted sort of way, perfect conclusion to any hostile interview. All it needed was a perfect ending with a presidential minion escorting Bull to the door uttering under his breath, "You will NEVER get another interview! Never!"

"The spirit of the Mud Daddy reaches all the way to Pennsylvania Avenue, Bull."

"You are the man!"

We toasted his moxie and laughed into the night.

Slim had pulled an all-nighter. Driving from Cincinnati, Slim had to pull a solo all-nighter in his quest for Everyman's American dream – a lake full of hungry bass. He was saved from on-the-road ennui by a tribute album, a fabulous CD of various artists doing their versions of Doc Pomus songs. You haven't truly experienced music until you've heard Lou Reed's version of "Save the Last Dance for Me." Or Dion's sizzling and soulful rendition of that sappy old Fabian hit, "Turn Me Loose." Dion and his hot band blow it away, too, on "Written on a Subway Wall." Doc Pomus would have been thrilled.

The landscape surrounding Lake Wappapello was more than hill but not quite mountain. When we got on the water, with its countless coves and bays and a wrinkled shoreline, its color was a by-now-familiar coffee-brown. Fishing a lake clouded with muddy water because of a regular autumnal temperature inversion requires skill, wisdom and the right gear. We had none of that. But we were, if nothing else, tenacious. And we were motivated. We suspected that this would not be a weekend thick with fish but a man can dream.

Most anglers had given up on the lake weeks before, trading in their fishing gear for rifles and slug-loaded shotguns to take to the brush in search of skittish white-tail deer. In the Midwest, that means seating yourself in a tree stand like an armed stoic to wait for an eight-point buck to emerge from the bush and briar. It is a notoriously dull way to pass the time, unless you doze off and fall from the tree. But some people love it. As male Americans, we understood the ancient and irresistible pull of deep woods solitude and fire power, but we preferred the frustration of bad fishing to the tedium of hunting – even good hunting. Plus, we were worried about mixing guns with Mud Daddies. After all, nobody has ever died from a wayward cast – yet. (E, in a Molson-laced haze, once suggested that "we should go rent some shotguns and go hunting." E probably figured his and Doc's training on M-16s were prima facie proof that the trio could be trusted. But Slim, wisely and in an uncharacteristic display of restraint, suggested instead more Molsons.)

So we slugged our way back and forth across the lake, from dead stump to rock shoal; from sandy shore to water-covered former roadbed; from deadfall tree to lonesome, blustery point; from deepwater drop-off to waist-deep weed bed. Nothing. Nothing anywhere, except for the occasional avid bass fisherman, who was not out hunting as he should but was instead blasting past our shoreline in a glorious burgundy boat, complete with fish finder and trolling motor and about 19,000 horsepower.

"What good is a fish finder when there are no fish to find?" Doc wondered aloud in a tone filled with derision.

"Jesse says keep hope alive. Ya gotta keep hope alive."

We all agreed, and so we kept casting and reeling.

"Damn, that sure was a nice boat!"

Hope combined with grace are qualities in a fisherman that should not be casually dismissed. But the signs were ominous from the beginning. And poor Bull. He never had a chance. He went to check out the lake from the back of the cabin and there he stood, drink in hand, admiring the view, when he noticed some critter nosing up the hill. Something, a force greater than himself, compelled him to stand and stare, Bull later admitted. It was a skunk, going about his skunky business, and then it paused and looked up to where Bull stood, transfixed. Their eyes met, and the spell was cast. Bull knew it. The skunk knew it, too. The fishing would be hopeless for the Bull after this exchange. He could rage as much as he wanted to about it. He could kick and scream and curse and whine. It wouldn't matter. He was doomed to a fishless weekend.

Mud Daddy spot tip: *Avoid skunks whenever possible. And never, EVER, look them in the eye! If you even think that something moving nearby might be a skunk, turn and walk away as swiftly as you can. Avoid the skunk. Always.*

Though the fishing was bleak for all, nobody even once considered sitting it out. We could have kicked back to bullshit all day on the wraparound deck overlooking the water, smoking cigars and tasting bottomless cups of Maker's Mark, Old Forrester and Jameson's. That was a temptation, but never a real option. We could have avoided the acute disappointment of yet another fishless Mud Daddy, but there is no quit in a true fisherman, and we had come to fish. After our fishless fate was clear and the first day long gone and done, Doc and Slim paid a late-night visit to Big Chief, ball caps in hand, to seek forgiveness for the sins of our forefathers and to ask politely for just a bit of luck on his lake tomorrow. Above the stoic, unmoving face of Big Chief, the firmament spilled from hill to hill and blazed in magnificence about his feathered head.

Maybe it did some good. Lake Wappapello was dead, but the map showed another nearby lake called Clearwater. After this turgid mess, a body of water with "clear" in the name sure sounded enticing

We knew the fish below were manifestations of grace, and grace was always worth seeking, even in the sweaty tedium of a bad day in an uncomfortable little boat with two surly pals. And so we sought grace. And in so doing we kept hope alive. Once at Clearwater, Doc caught two small, washed-out bass, so the skunk was off him. Slim grabbed a pair, too, and that evened it up.

But with regard to the Enquirer Outstanding Angler Award, there was always Slim and his fly rod – a chilling prospect on the last day of any Mud Daddy, as Slim has caught many fish with it, some so small that a man's middle finger, shown to Slim by his fishing buddies, was usually longer.

Slim fell to his fly rod, waving and whipping the thick line through the air so the No. 14 Adams could land as gently as a butterfly with bunions on the calm water about a foot from a bush on shore. It would only take one, maybe two, tiny fish to claim the Enquirer Outstanding Angler award this year, and Slim was sure a hungry Bluegill would be there in the shadows of the shallows. Time was running out on the weekend, but sure enough, two miniature bluegills later, Slim became the first-ever Mud Daddy three-peat winner.

Was it a pointless trip? Not hardly. No Mud Daddy is pointless, although they are often less than great fishing. As we got ready to pull out of the parking area in the final wrap to our annual weekend, Doc celebrated Slim's rare three-peat by playing the theme from Rocky as loud as his sleek black Thunderbird's stereo would allow, offering a heartfelt thumbs-up to the winner.

Gravel flying, Slim roared away – gone for another year.

Tishomingo Sweet Potato Bread Pudding

For many younger American men, white bread is a delicious and exotic treat that is banned from the household. Whole wheat has intruded into our lives, along with awareness of cholesterol and transfat, so old-school white bread has an appeal on a fishing trip that is simply irresistible. We dedicate this recipe to the wonders of white bread.

1 leftover cooked sweet potato (preferably uneaten from a dinner on the way to the lake)

2 eggs

½ cup milk

10 or more sugar packets

Four slices of bread.

Stir up/beat the eggs, milk, sugar and finally mash in the sweet potato. You will have a gloppy orange mixture. Spread butter onto a piece of bread and place bread butter side down in a frying pan over low heat. Put a heaping tablespoon of mixture on top. Add another layer of bread, another glob of stuff, another piece of bread and so on until the gloppy stuff is gone. Cap with a piece of buttered bread, butter-side up. Fashion a foil lid and wait. When the bread on the bottom is thoroughly brown (low heat, remember, low heat), then carefully flop it over and continue to cook. Most times pudding desserts are done when a toothpick comes out, but all we know is this stuff is done when it looks done.

More Stuff You Won't Hear on a Mud Daddy

- Do you know how many carbs are in that?
- Is the patio furniture going to be outside until New Year's Day again this year?
- When are you going to mow the lawn?
- Are you trying to see how long grass can grow?
- How many more times are you going to go golfing this year?
- You're not going to smoke that in here, are you?
- This tofu burger tastes pretty good, doesn't it?
- There's not another football game on after this one, is there?
- You're not going to watch it, are you?
- Stop flipping channels on that remote so fast.
- Why do you always stop channel-surfing when you come to a woman with big breasts?
- You'll have these dishes done when I come back from my manicure, right?
- How do these jeans look on me?
- Isn't this soooo cute (darling...lovely)?
- Do these shorts make my butt look big?

Big Chief at Lake Wappapello, Missouri, September 2000 - The Big Chief greets a misty morning.

Doc and Rankin at Lake Wappapello, Missouri, September 2000 - Fishing is so bad no one has a line out.

Eckberg at Leesville Lake, Ohio, September 2001 - Golf umbrella, stogie, beer. All the rain gear a man needs.

Eckberg at Leesville Lake, Ohio, September 2001 - Rods in hand, shoes and socks on the roof.

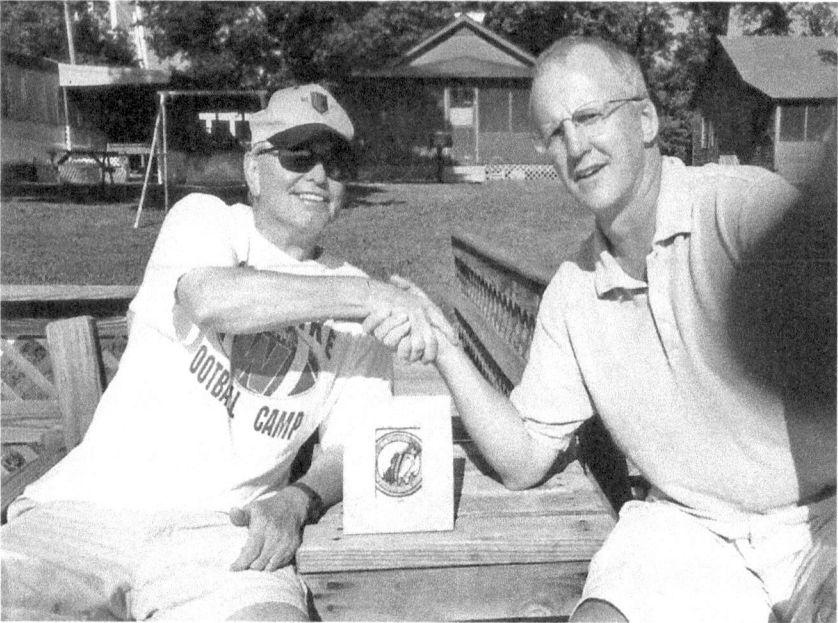

Lowery and Eckberg at Reelfoot Lake, Tennessee, September 2002 - Slim surrenders Outstanding Angler Trophy to Doc.

Reelfoot Lake, Tennessee, September 2002 - Stumps, snakes, and crappie.

The Mud Daddy Chronicles

Tiptonville, Tennessee, September 2002 - Carl 'Blue Sued Shoes' Perkins.

Erardi and Lowery at Reelfoot Lake, Tennessee, September 2002 - Fishing hard and looking good.

Eckberg at Norfolk Lake, Arkansas, October 2003 - Captain Slim in a jaunty bush hat.

Erardi and Lowery at Norfolk Lake, Arkansas, October 2003 - Lowery surenders Outstanding Angler Trophy to Big E.

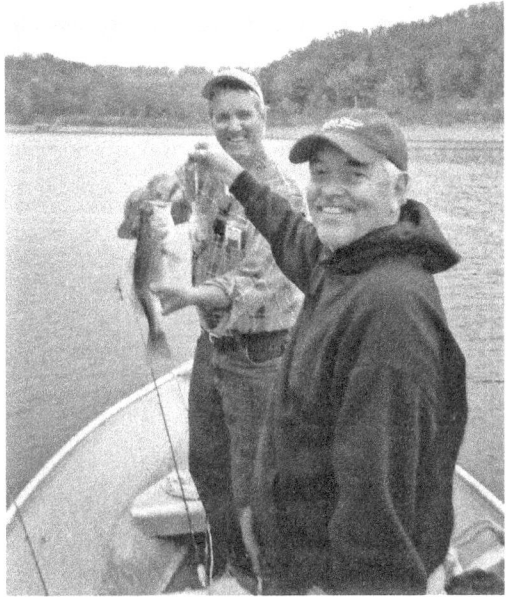

Erardi and Lowery at Norfolk Lake, Arkansas, October 2003 - Doc holds the bluegill he took out of the mouth of the bass Big E caught barehanded. The old first baseman from Murray State still had it!

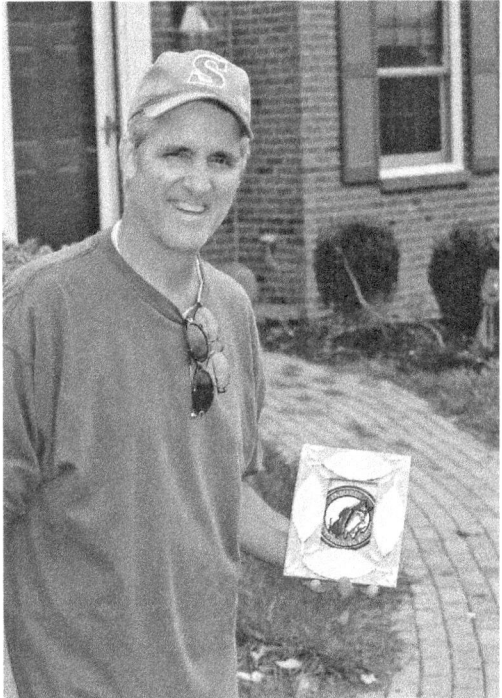

Erardi, October 2003 - Showing off the trophy at his Old Kentucky home.

E-man at Muddy Pond, Laurel Lake, Kentucky, November 2004 - The Battle of Muddy Pond was a fierce contest.

Eckberg and Erardi at Pickwick Lake, Mississippi, September 2005 - Captain Slim making sure he doesn't tear that motor up.

The Mud Daddy Chronicles

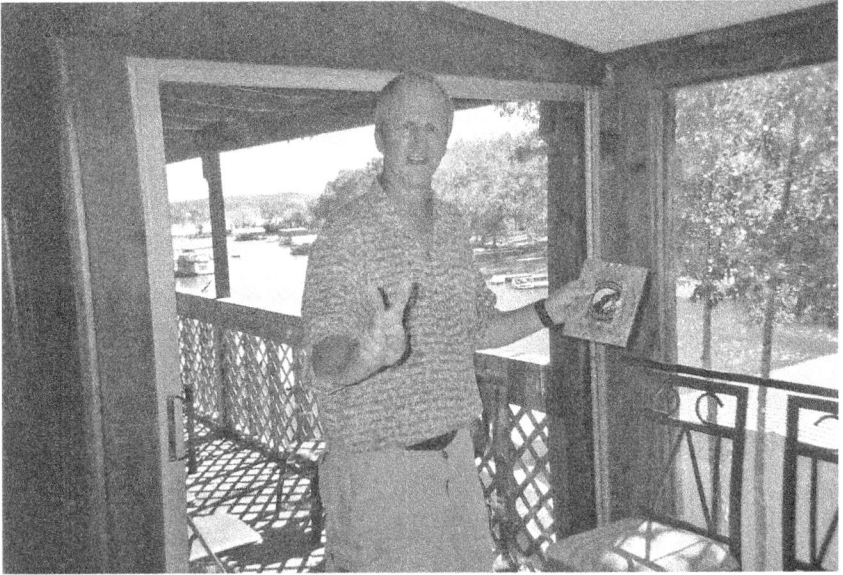

Eckberg at Pickwick Lake, Mississippi, September 2005 - Slim celebrates his repeat win as Outstanding Angler.

Lowery, Erardi, and Eckberg at Pickwick Lake, Mississippi, September 2005 - Ready to head back to the daily grind.

A nice one brings E the lead.

Potato launch during Happy Hour.

Chief Wappa high fives the universe.

Which point was our campsite again?

The Mud Daddy Award in the Tennessee sun.

Austin American-Statesman

Friday
Nov. 1
Dia de Los Muertos

Now this guy has been on a mud
DADDY!

FIRST, we were too stupid to realize the
time changed Sat. night. So we lost an
hour of fishing time and I spent an extra
unnecessary hour in the Little Rock Airport.

Then a storm hit Dallas and we sat
on the plane, at the Terminal for 3 hours.
When we landed in Dallas I sat on the
plane, on the Tarmac 1 hour. Got into the
Terminal at Midnight — it was like the
Fall of Saigon in there. 140 flights had
been cancelled or delayed — people stacked
up, sleeping on the floor, screaming.

I caught a shuttle and got the last
Rental Car in Dallas — luxury Buick for
$140 and drove through the night. Got
home at 5 AM. Went to work at 10.

What a fucking nightmare.

I miss my framed Trophy. Enjoy it
while you can. Pix to come eventually.

David Lowery

Rx

Chapter XIX - Husky Muskie Homeboy Roots Tour

They called themselves the Husky Muskies, and when we saw the blurb promoting their upcoming fishing event on their online newsletter, the news was met with less than unbridled enthusiasm. The Husky Muskies planned to fish Leesville Lake in north-central Ohio for their end-of-season grand finale – the very same Leesville Lake where the 2001 Mud Daddy was to be held and it was too late for us to change our trip because cosmic forces were at work.

On the same day that Slim decided to go to Leesville, Doc happened to be fishing in Arkansas when he saw something floating down the James River arm toward him. It was a cap. An Ohio State Buckeye cap – where Doc went to school. At about that same moment, hundreds of miles away, E-dog, not knowing Doc was fishing, was calling his pal, Doc, in Austin to see if there was anything to this Texas star Adam Dunn, who'd just been drafted by the Reds. Slim was simultaneously picking Leesville Lake in Ohio. So the die was cast. There was no way we were not going to fish in Ohio with those omens. And besides, Husky Muskies or not, Doc had bought his airplane tickets for Ohio and Slim had analyzed Muskies caught over a five-year period to find the Ohio lake that offered up the best chance of catching one of these monsters. We had little choice but to share our lake with the Ohio Chapter H.M's. But we didn't have to like it.

We had seen some of the fishing tournament phenomenon before on Pickwick Lake in Tennessee, so we understood the downside. It was like being told that your weekend cottage retreat was right next door to a Westin Resort. A Shock-and-Awe Armada of $20,000 boats would be skimming across the water in deafening waves, ripping through an otherwise peaceful autumn morning right outside our tent flap.

We knew it would be like having an interstate highway or maybe a busy municipal airport right outside your tent flap: Avid fishermen would certainly be turning every secluded alcove into a noxious swamp of boats, not to mention making the wait interminable at the local steakhouse if we decided to eat out. This trip appeared to be a disaster, and it hadn't even started. And yet, looking on the bright side, (which a Mud Daddy participant must always, always do, lest he lose faith in the goodness of the human spirit, become depressed and smoke a pistol) a grand classic like the Ohio Husky Muskie Fish-off, a winner-take-all event, on Leesville Lake also suggested that decent fishing was to be had there. Brighter still, in 2001 Leesville held the Ohio record for muskie landed. We're talking monsters, too. Look at your right leg. That's how big a muskie can get. None of us had ever caught one, but we'd seen the pictures and seen the real thing one time on Patoka Lake in Indiana. We were not discouraged about the odds of us landing one, either. The fishing books said it usually takes 1,000 hours of trolling to catch one. That's a lot of beer and sloppy ham sandwiches to consume in the meantime. Still, Slim, ever the optimist, went to the trouble to create a muskie-landing rig out of a pair of old blue jeans and four former tent poles. Just in case. A net was useless because most muskies are just too big to fit in it.

Because we aren't great fishermen, we try to copy better anglers' approaches and choose our lures from whatever we can glean from these Men-With-Too-Much-Money, guys who scowl beneath their branded fishing caps while piloting glitter-paint boats at breakneck speed through the main body of the lake. They had electric trolling motors and fish finders and all manner of lures and rod and reels at-the-ready.

We typically used a clangy, cheesy and often leaky john boat with maybe six rods and reels among us, at least two of those always in some state of Gordian snarl.

"You know," said Slim on the drive from Cincinnati to Leesville, launching into one of his patented riffs. "Jesse Jackson best summed up the spirit of a Mud Daddy, and he didn't even know he was talking about it. Think about it. We quote Jesse all the time: 'Keep hope alive.' Oh, and this: 'Stay outta the Bushes.'"

"It's the 'stay outta the Bushes' that used to trip me up. How's that relate to a Mud Daddy? Well, you don't want to cast into the bushes because you'll lose a lure. It's that simple."

Slim was right, but Jesse didn't address what you do when there is no hope to keep alive, which explains why every Mud Daddy is an absurd exercise in optimism. This year we had good cause for good spirits, too. At the first bar we stopped at for a celebratory cold malted beverage, The Head First in downtown Cincinnati, big-hearted owner Jeff saw the three of us, reached into his cigar stash and flipped three $5 stogies across the bar to us. He didn't know we were bound for big water and an annual fishing trip. What a way to start a fishing trip! Free cigars! Unbelievable. Finally, a reason to be hopeful on a Mud Daddy. We found an omen of optimism in a downtown bar.

"This is the year that we will catch fish after fish after fish!" crowed Slim.

"This is the year that will be recorded with multiple poses on disposable cameras!" roared Doc.

"This is the year that our luck WILL change," cried Big E.

This is the year! This is the year! We tell ourselves that en route, and on the docks, and on the water, and around the campfires. "This is the year!" has been our mantra on lakes from one end of the Midwest to the other. We've told ourselves that year after year after year — until the years became decades and the decades became eras. d it, too. We've never stopped believing it.

Now every Mud Daddy requires a trip to a big box sporting goods store to stock up on the artificial lures that are sure to "bring in the big one." These are fun trips. The retail world of fishing lures, equipment, baits, clothes and 10,000 gadgets you don't need – but, oddly, you want – is beyond appealing.S Giant stores have special aisles devoted to muskie lures, as the reclusive muskie will not, apparently, go after a lure that does not cost at least $23.95. Lures costing that much might not bring a follow-up, as promised on the splendid packaging, but they will for certain clobber a hard-earned paycheck. And there's always this to consider: Why buy one gold Rapala when you can buy five? The fishing might be fast and furious. You never know. And what about metallic-blue Rat-L-Traps? Salmon hues with cranberry highlights on big old Rebels? Plum on ambergris salted tube baits? Periwinkle, with just a touch of smoky gray on snarling crankbaits?

No SoHo NYC interior designer with his bolts of chintz and paint swatches of pearl has anything on these lure creators.

Then there is the matter of hooks. Would a three-hook version be best? Can I find a four-hook one? Should the lure for this trip be a giant spoon, the size of a woman's flip-flop, with a hammered curve as big as a soup ladle? There were enough costly lures and gear on the walls and bins to lead a man to open a home equity account and buy a bunch just in case.

Trips to the big box sporting goods store should almost always be made solo, because a jaunt with kids inevitably brings up the question that fishing dads dread:

"Can I come? I want to go on a Mud Daddy!"

After all, these little people with their grubby fingers and candy-coated mouths are sentient beings, too. They can feel the excitement as the time for the trip approaches, and they want some of the action. A whole weekend with no chores? No bedtime? As many doughnuts as you can stuff in your gullet? Anytime you want?

"Do you take chocolate bars, Dad?"

"Yes, as many as we want."

Unbelievable.

"Pop"

"Case of soda."

They ask again with big, pleading eyes, and who can blame them?

"Can I go, too?"

The answer is always the same, though.

"No, I'm sorry."

Maybe sugar-coat it with a, "This is Daddy's trip."

The price of these muskie lures would surely limit our supply – a timeless equation, that! Slim picked a big flat black slab of wood with a little aluminum lip on the front and back. It was a lure that all the books said was the lure de rigueur when casting for these freshwater sharks. He drilled out the back lip and put a tiny silver spoon there for extra action then drilled through its undersize and glued in some lead. When he was done, it resembled a half-assed science fair project, but Slim didn't care. Doc and E went for huge spoons with red beads on the shank and evil black eyes. These spoons glittered with malevolence and seemed to weigh about two pounds.

The literature also suggested that at the end of each retrieve, the angler was to make giant figure 8's in the water with the lure, waving the rod all around in a downward loopy motion, tip well into the water. If a muskie has followed up to the boat, this final, taunting gesture will be certain to spur a violent strike. Muskies, apparently, do not handle taunting very well, probably because they are the biggest, baddest things in the lake and know it. The literature, of course, was written by somebody who had never been on a Mud Daddy. Fishing for muskie means endless trolling, (Remember the 1,000 hours? That's six straight weeks of trolling, twenty-four hours a day!) Here's how you fish for muskie. Rig your 20-pound test line with a steel leader at least 12 inches long, clip on the biggest lure in the tackle box, set your motor for trolling speed and let the lure drift out behind you for at least 75 yards before clicking the reel bail shut. Then forget about the lure, the rod and any chance of catching a fish, grab a question from the Trivial Pursuit box and challenge Doc or E.

We arrived at the cabin, settled in and headed for the marina. We loaded the boat and began to pull away from the dock when the woman in charge of the marina came outside and spoke above the drone of the motor.

"What's she saying?" Slim asked.

"Turn it off. Turn it off I can't hear either," Doc said.

Slim killed the motor and the gray-haired woman repeated herself but this time she had her hands on her hips.

"I said – are you all just gonna leave it like that," she announced, then turned and nodded back at the mini-van. We looked beyond her to our van.

Three doors and the back hatch were wide open.

At least the music wasn't on, Slim would later proclaim.

It was early evening on our first day on the water at Leesville Reservoir, and we were tired, wet, cold, frustrated and bummed from no fish, the perfect time for a good, hot meal at a local steakhouse. Cleaned up and somewhere southeast of Canton, we pulled into a likely looking roadhouse that had a full parking lot, always a good sign, but strangely enough, no wait. The hostess, tall and wearing little makeup, was striking,. Her shiny auburn hair reaching down almost to the small of her back. She gave us a knowing smile, and with a confident air greeted us warmly, "How are you fellas doing tonight? Right this way, gentlemen."

We followed her through the noisy throng to a far-flung booth feeling like celebrities, such was her presence. After some pleasantries, she looked at each of us and said, "Enjoy your meal and have a wonderful evening." Comfortably situated we glanced around at our surroundings to admire the funky décor: fake flowers on wall sconces, early American lighting, people in their polyester finery. And then we turned our gaze to the wall above our table.

Mounted above the booth was an old newspaper in a frame. Journalists all, we gave it a glance – and then gave it a trio of full, head-jerking second takes. It was an old copy of The Cincinnati Enquirer, where the three of us had done time together on the Metro desk. Our home newspaper, the source of endless carping, complaining, hard work and boundless pride, and the namesake of the Enquirer Outstanding Angler award! How did a newspaper from a city more than four hours south end up on this wall? And out of all the possible booths and tables, how did we come to be seated directly beneath it? Had to be the vortex. One of the Lord's little practical jokes.

Muskie fishing here was also a joke, a parade of excess, and the next day we joined it under gray Buckeye skies and a steady rain – Slim, as always, at the helm. How is it he became captain? Nobody knows. Maybe he was the first to jump into the back of the boat lo those many years ago. Or maybe, because his dad helped build anti-submarine missiles, Slim, with some standing, felt he had an affinity for propulsion, guidance and payload systems, i.e. the boat and motor. Or, truth be told, maybe it's because he can talk like a pirate better than anybody else in the boat.

Regardless, Slim, with a cigar in his mouth, held the tiller with one hand and, because it was raining, an enormous green-and-white golf umbrella with the other, well aware of the looks from the other boaters and quite pleased with himself.

"Aaaarg, me maties!"

Everyone fishing at Leesville that weekend was trolling. There were only about 150 boats on the water, but it seemed like a thousand because they never paused, never stopped. And these boys were serious about their trolling. They rigged at least six rods per boat in a fan-shaped array, with the lines trailing out behind them in a very pleasing geometric pattern. Put your thumbs together and fan out both hands at arms' length. That's what it looked like. And they mostly worked one 300-yard long narrows, all crammed in there, trolling to the end of the narrows, then turning in a big sweeping arc to go back over the same water again. One after another they trolled the narrows, all lined up with perhaps 60 yards between them, sort of like a drive-through line at a really big Arby's. One screw-up, one double line snarl, and surely the whole system would collapse into a fury of idled boats, annoyed reeling, sinking lures snagging other lines and plenty of profanity uttered through clenched teeth. We soon left that grim caravan.

Now just about any high school football game broadcast on the radio will do on a Mud Daddy. Often we don't know who is playing, and we don't care. We love the announcer's clichés, the bone-head plays, the startling accounts of superb athleticism. We've listened intently as the Arkadelphia Badgers defeated the Lake Hamilton Wolves in a nail-biter. We tuned in when the Hardin County Tigers lost a homecoming heartbreaker. Many times we've talked about attending one of these local contests, to soak in the local color firsthand. But only once has it actually happened.

On the 2001 Homeboy Roots Tour, we found we had the time and inclination to actually take in a game. The newspaper bought from a stand outside the small restaurant near Leesville Lake noted the time and place of that night's game in East Canton, which was close enough. Slim's Homeboy MoJo was pumping that night. Of any game within reach, we spent that Friday night in the autumn chill watching Slim's high school alma mater, the Manchester Panthers play East Canton. What were the odds of that happening, as his hometown was 40 miles away? Vortex you say?

The Panthers had a running back who would not be denied, and he was behind a giant offensive line, so they clobbered that poor East Canton team.

In the crowd at East Canton were two of Slim's classmates, Denny Snyder and Gene Schiendewolf, now the school athletic director. Slim got him through unified geometry. They did time together in study halls and on the basketball court, where Schiendewolf was All-League and pretty much unstoppable.

"What are you doing here at an away game?" asked Denny when he recognized Slim. It had been some 30 years since they'd last crossed paths.

"Good question," answered Slim. He started to explain. "Uh … There's this thing I go on every year … called the Mud Daddy?"

He looked at Denny. Denny was still slogging merrily through life in the town he grew up in, and 30 years after graduation remained an avid booster of the Manchester Panthers, his high-school football team. And what was wrong with that? Not a damn thing. Slim looked at him with more than a little envy, in fact. Denny had a big kid of his own now, out there pushing East Canton around. But a Mud Daddy and The Vortex? An annual outing that had become an annual obsession? How to explain it all to Denny?

Finally, Slim summed it up: "Strange shit happens, I guess."

Denny, an old chess club pal, nodded.

"Indeed it does. Indeed it does."

Both turned back to the game. Manchester had the ball and was driving hard. East Canton had a tragic football team, and Manchester's massive players glowed with the patina of the local champs. Standing there, Slim wondered whether Denny had a clue as to what he was talking about. An annual fishing trip that was so much more? Impossible fishing for a mystic muskie? Tater guns? The Vortex?

"He acted like he understood," Slim said later. "But how could he, really?"

By Saturday evening we couldn't help ourselves. Resist though we might, ultimately, we gave in to a base impulse. We had to go find the weigh-in center for the Ohio Chapter of the Husky Muskies and check the results.

Here is the math. Number of boats: about 90, we learned, with an average of 12 hours on the water each. That was about 1,000 man-hours of fishing. But multiply that times six lines per boat and it leaps to 6,000 hours. Now, how many muskie do you think were landed on that weekend of cold rain and gray skies? How many did you say? 35? 22? 11? Nope. Three. That's it, just three fish caught and weighed. We didn't bother to find out how big they were. It was too discouraging. When Sunday morning rolled around with the disheartening inevitability of another Mud Daddy having come and gone, we packed and then returned to the water for two more hours of fishing, though we all knew that this last exercise would probably not involve fish, and if perchance it did, certainly not a muskie. We were right again.

At one of the lake's marinas, E-Man and Slim came upon a member of the Buckeye Chapter of the Husky Muskies. He bounded up the steps to the little luncheonette, which was closed, with unbridled enthusiasm. His baseball cap had verve, was slightly crooked and pitched back on his head. He was smiling and full of hope, even as his weekend of fishing drew to a close and the morning had dawned cold and dreary.

"You with the tournament?" he asked.

"No," we replied, "We're just on a little fishing trip."

"Have any luck?" he asked.

"Not much. And you?"

He paused, still smiling, and then started to nod exuberantly.

"Yeah! Oh, yeah! Not here, though. Last week I was over by Mansfield at that tournament. Fished all weekend, and you know what? I got a follow-up!

"A follow-up!"

He beamed as he informed us of this fish he'd seen for a brief moment as it followed his lure to the boat. Here's some more math, mixed with a little sociology: two full weekends on the water, maybe 40 hours of fishing multiplied times, say, three trolling lines in the water gives you 120 man-hours on the water, and the guy gets one follow-up? That's it? A frigging follow-up? Surely he was ready for a new hobby: woodcraft, NASCAR, hunting for Indian arrowheads, skeet, knitting – anything. He looked at us, then to the closed shop and reached to light a cigarette.

"You know," he said, his smile now full of proud pleasure. "I think I'm starting to get the hang of this muskie fishing."

Leesville Sloppy Ham Sandwiches

Not wanting to waste a minute of fishing time, we often eat lunch on the water. These waterborne repasts are catch-as-catch-can affairs involving potato chips, cheddar cheese, pepperoni sticks, chocolate and other such fare. But occasionally we do have lunch at the campsite or cabin — when the downpour has lasted for five hours since dawn and we simply can't take it anymore. These lunches can be fine affairs. Below is a recipe for sloppy ham sandwiches we created at Leesville Lake in Ohio. Fishing in a steady rain, and witness to the Husky Muskies' boat parade with not a single bite among us, drove us to the cabin for lunch. This helped to allay the morning's misery. A sandwich like this will surely lift a hungry man's spirits — rain or shine.

> 1 1/2 to 2 pounds chip-chop lunchmeat ham
>
> 1 can or less (use your own judgment; you can't rely on us for everything) of Seven-Up, Sprite or Mountain Dew
>
> 1/2 cup ketchup
>
> 1 or 2 tbsp Grey Poupon mustard or purloined regular mustard
>
> 1 Tbsp Worcestershire sauce (announce loudly, "Whasis here sauce?")
>
> Juice of a half lime
>
> Splash of tequila

Put it all in a big old frying pan on low to medium heat, stir and let it cook uncovered for a while. Mix it around from time to time. Then maybe cover it and cook and stir some more. Do it for a good while. Bet somebody a buck that the next play is a pass over the middle. Give him odds. To serve, glop it on hamburger buns or bread or even left-over spaghetti noodles. The day will be saved, especially if your team wins and you rake in some side-bet bank.

Chapter XX - The Isadore Dunking

The Vortex is stronger and more prominent on some Mud Daddies than others, but few have been Vortex-free altogether. On several Mud Daddies that appeared to be Vortexless, things happened that escaped our attention at the time. But The Vortex has a way of coming back around, making itself felt years later. Some Vortex incidents are funny, others simply strange; but at times they are awesome and eerie. The one Vortex that truly chilled our blood happened on Reelfoot Lake in far western Tennessee in 2002.

The Mud Daddy began auspiciously. Hurricane Isadore had roared straight up the Mississippi River in late September, dumping a foot of rain on everything in its path. Doc arrived a day early and secured a cabin at Boyette's with a fishing dock on the lake. Slim and Big E drove in the pouring rain from Cincinnati, but arrived ready to fish what was billed as a first-rate crappie lake.

"Yeah, but we now have the perfect name for this Mud Daddy," ventured Doc. "I call it the Isadore Dunking. Get it?" They groaned, but with smiles on their faces.

Reelfoot had an unusual and somewhat creepy past. Legend has it that Simon Kenton, one of America's earliest land speculators, purchased the land for himself. The settlers were not going to have an easy time of it, though, as Chief Tecumseh of the Shawnee vowed to fight to his last breath. He would unite Indian tribes across the Midwest and declared to the tribes that on the appointed day he would stomp his foot and make the great Mississippi River run backwards. In 1811 a major earthquake did indeed shake the region, and the Big Muddy did run backwards, just as the chief had promised, flooding Kenton's holdings, land now under Reelfoot Lake. It wiped Kenton out financially.

Slim knew a little something about Tecumseh, one of the greatest true Americans. Years before, Slim had reason to interview the chief of Ohio's Shawnee tribe, a guy in a button-down shirt and blue jeans. The chief told Slim that the tribes had handed down many stories about Tecumseh because he and his braves were celebrities. They rode jet-black horses and wore dyed black buckskins, each seam offset with moose-whisker piping. When they rode into a village, it was in a flurry of thundering hooves. Each man wore boots, too, not moccasins – boots presumably taken in battle. These were bad-ass warriors doing the Lord's work, and nobody messed with them.

"Tecumseh, like most prominent chiefs, had a personal bodyguard," the chief said, now warming to the tale: "His name was Frog Killer."

Slim had met and interviewed many people in his time: Presidents Carter, Ford and Clinton, senators, governors, rock stars from John Denver to Bob Dylan to Skunk Baxter. He'd talked with captains of industry like they were drinking buddies and folks who simply figured out a new way to do something and were swimming in millions of dollars. Few were as interesting as this chief.

And at his back? A bodyguard.

Our cabin was in Tiptonville, Tenn., the Boyhood Home of Carl Perkins, the rockabilly singer famous for "Blue Suede Shoes," "Matchbox" and other great songs. His home was a weathered shack along State Route 78 as it runs south out of Tiptonville to the blues Mecca of Memphis. We understood why he high-tailed it out of town. It wasn't much of a house.

With the rain from Isadore falling steadily outside, we cooked spaghetti and drank vodka gimlets in tribute to Raymond Chandler's birthday. We didn't know when the great author's birthday was exactly, or even inexactly, but the gimlets, with a dash of bitters, seemed the right thing to do on a rainy night in Tiptonville. Anyway, Chandler's birthday was covered. The cabin had a television, always a welcome accoutrement during a hurricane-soaked Mud Daddy. We watched, astounded, as the heavily favored Florida State Seminoles slogged their way to an upset by the Louisville Cardinals.

In the late evening hours, Slim went on a tear because he couldn't find his alarm clock watch, which he would set so he could wake up in time to see Homer's rosy fingers of dawn claw toward a new day – the time when fishing might be the best.

"Anybody seen my watch? Have I lost my watch?"

On and on it went through the evening. Slim finally sat down, dazed and confused.

"You know, Slim" Doc said, "You remind me of the cowboy who wakes up sleeping on his saddle after a three-day drunk. He doesn't know if he lost his horse or found his saddle."

After a night of cigars and libations, the storm passed, leaving a strange calm in its wake. The air seemed not to move at all. Did dead air mean dead fishing? We rented a john boat at the local marina, ready to suffer through the inevitable lecture on the how-tos, where-fors and what-ifs of operation. Instead, an attractive, middle-aged woman wearing tight cut-off jeans and flashing an enticing tattoo above her right breast led us to the boat and tossed us the key.

"Bring it back in one piece," she said, hand on her hip and smiling.

"No problem," Slim replied.

"You want to come along?" Doc asked.

She snorted, turned on her heel and headed back into the bait shop. We watched until the screen door banged shut behind her.

With Slim at the helm, we set off, full of hope and enthusiasm, this Mud Daddy now shifting into second gear, and we hoped, winding up towards third, and then fourth and then somewhere beyond that into OVERDRIVE!

We weren't out of the little bay where the marina was situated when the motor conked on us.

"Aw, SHIT!"

We grabbed the weathered wooden paddles in the bottom of the boat and splashed back to the dock. The marina manager was there to greet us, a smirk on his face as we flailed with our paddles towards him.

"What's the trouble?" he asked.

Like we knew.

"It just conked," E said.

The marina owner with the hot wife – we assumed she was his wife, but maybe not – bent down to the motor, twiddled with it for no more than two second, then stood up.

"Your fuel line came unplugged," he explained.

Now we should have been embarrassed, but we had done so many dumb things over so many years that we were used to looking like idiots. We laugh instead of pretending to know what was wrong all along or being secretly mortified. Shit happens! And it happens to us a lot. We were relieved that it wasn't something worse.

"We knew that," Doc said with a laugh. "We were just testing you."

"I'd be embarrassed about this," Slim said, "if it hadn't happened to me about a dozen times before."

"Don't sweat it," the owner said, grinning and waving away concern with one hand. "You fellas have fun now."

We cracked our breakfast beers and headed back out onto the lake. As Mud Daddy veterans, we have learned that the way to avoid getting blind drunk or suffering a hangover is to keep the blood alcohol content (BAC) at a steady level. Not high enough for a DWI, but not low enough to bring on a killer headache either. The secret is a reasonable amount of alcohol flowing regularly during waking hours. You build it up to a BAC peak just before bedtime, get a few hours of sleep and start again in morning. The AA would not approve, but this wasn't a daily regimen, so we didn't care. We learned about hangovers the hard way, of course, and sometimes we forget about moderation, but for the most part we are now experts. We don't get really drunk, and we don't get hangovers. The crash after a Mud Daddy, however, can be quite spectacular.

For all its formidable reputation, Reelfoot is a shallow pool bristling with stumps just below the surface. Thanks a lot, Tecumseh!

It was a nightmare to navigate, and the fishing was just as bad. Hoping for a change in luck that Friday night, we drove to a floating casino in Caruthersville, Mo., on the Big River. It was called the Lady Luck. We doubted there were many ladies and knew there wouldn't be much luck as we navigated a long, covered walkway that sloped down from the shore to the boat. Not so young ourselves anymore, we still felt like kids as we passed Gray Panthers, folks in wheelchairs and walkers clanking their way to the slot machines and gaming tables. The casino looked like nothing so much as a loud and bright way to separate folks from their Social Security checks.

"This is truly depressing," said E-Dog as he bought his $5 membership card.

"I'll tell you what's depressing," Doc noted. "I just got in free cause I'm 55. I feel like there's an ice floe out there with my name on it. 'Mr. Lowery, your ride is here.' But first they need to separate me from my meager savings."

The main deck was filled with one-armed bandits, only they

don't have arms anymore. Just push a button to get the wheels turning. It's a much more efficient way to take your money. You can throw $10 into those things and lose it in less than a minute. It's breathtaking, almost like someone reaching into your pants and lifting your wallet.

On the lower deck were the gaming tables – blackjack, roulette, craps. Doc favors blackjack because he can usually play a long time without losing a whole lot of money. Slim and E like craps, because the odds are better. Slim won $35 at the craps table playing the only way he knows – place a bet, and if you don't win on that first roll, back it up, sit tight and watch. Slim won just enough to buy a round at the bar before we headed back.

"I can't believe anywhere could be this dead on a Friday night," Doc moaned. "What do folks around these parts do for fun?" Slim asked the bartender.

"They come here," he said blankly. We nodded.

On the drive back across the bridge, the Mississippi River was magical. A bright moon reflected off the water just like in a song, stirring our hearts and filling the car with "Mooon Riiiver, wider than a mile …" Andy Williams had a mega hit with that song, and Williams was born in Cincinnati, we knew, so we sang and sang and sang some more.

Doc frequently notes that he has sung "professionally." By that he means a fraternity once paid him a case of beer to sing "Louie, Louie," "Mustang Sally," "Midnight Hour" and a few other tunes with some brothers at a house party back in the late '60s. Doc likes to take the lead, and Slim and E sing background, although Slim will sometimes kick it out with an old John Fogarty number: Chasing down a Hoo Do there…Born on the Bayou.

There is a lot of history along this part of the Mississippi, almost too much for one river to bear. It was the great highway for exploring America, the route that opened the West, a way for commerce to flourish from Cincinnati to New Orleans. It was where Lewis and Clark began their expedition and where riverboat gamblers thrived. It was a creative fountain for Mark Twain and a watery grave for Civil War sailors. The Mississippi has been and remains a source of pleasure and heartache, great adventure and great tragedy. It is quintessentially American. Driving back to Tiptonville on the Carl Perkins Highway, we saw signs for Bragadoccio, Mo., and Owl Hoot, Tenn. It's a bizarre country in some ways, this little corner of America along the Great Muddy, and the Lord knows we love it.

Reelfoot is broken into two main arms, and there is a shortcut between them through a swamp. Saturday morning, as we sputtered along the canal, snakes slithered all around us. A diversion into a bed of head-high reeds to see whether there might be a pool in there ended when a snake as thick as a man's arm slithered by just off the gunwale.

"Did you see that?" Slim asked.

"Hell, yes! Get us out of here, Slim! This is too much," Doc replied.

"Too reptilianic," E added.

Reptilianic. Mud Daddies are known for word invention. Big E comes up with most of them, heard in Major League locker rooms around the country, spring training in Florida and on golf courses everywhere. A butane cigar lighter is praised, for instance, as "butanic." Big E is the one who gave Eckberg his "Slimbagger" moniker. And a mutual friend, Steve Rosen, is known as "Mr. Gripps" because to E, Steve favors jazz violinist Stephane Grappelli in name, style and cool. Plus, Steve once served for E as a chauffeur, in full livery dress, earning him the title Mister when he drove E, Tim "Hondo Von Dondo" Vonderbrink and Gary "Right Here on Our Stage" Sullivan around town on a night of drunken debauchery. A stretch for a nickname? Not to E.

Doc wants to catch up on Cincinnati sports so he asks E, the Ohio Sports Writer of the Year, about the Cincinnati Bearcats basketball team and their coach, Bob Huggins.

"So, E, how the Bearcats going to do this season? Huggins got anything?"

"Yeah, he'll do all right, I think. But his health isn't good. The guy is a walking stress test. He's gonna have a heart attack if he doesn't watch it."

"You know, I think I may have played against him in high school in a scrimmage," said Slim. Slim played high school hoops with Mike Phillips, who would go on to star at the University of Kentucky, where he won a national championship. Phillips broke Jerry Lucas's Ohio High School scoring record, in effect putting Slim into the record book for having assisted in the record breaking – at least that's how Slim tells it.

Slim's place in basketball history was once noted by world-renowned basketball commentator and raconteur Dick Vitale at a 1,000-person luncheon in Cincinnati. Slim had regaled Dickie V.

pre-lunch with his account of feeding Phillips a steady diet of soft lobs in the paint, suggesting that – because of all the great players to come out of the region, starting with the first Chuck Taylor of Converse fame – Akron was the capital of basketball for the entire nation, and then lambasting the V-man when Vitale wasn't so sure. Maybe Akron's LeBron James has convinced Dickie V by now.

"Ladies and gentlemen, we have a star in the audience today," Dickie V. announced from the podium shortly after his speech had begun, Dickie V.'s way of getting audience participation. "John Eckberg, who helped Mike Phillips set the Ohio school boy points record. John, stand up! Feast your eyes upon him, ladies and gentlemen! John Eckberg – is he a specimen or what? Is that the body of an athlete?"

Slim stood and nodded "thank you, thank you, thank you very much" to the assembled luncheon of millionaire business owners and then put both hands palm side down in that eternal gesture meant to tone down the applause, even though there wasn't any applause to tone down. In a lifetime spent before audiences – from hooping to impromptu standup comedy and rubber chicken luncheon speeches – that moment remains Slim's all-time greatest ovation. Except that there was no ovation. Slim cast at a shrub and talked about Huggins and hoops.

"You're right, E, the man is a walking coronary."

"A walking coronary," Doc agreed.

"Question is," E offered, "Can he win the big one, or will he have the big one?"

We all laughed and continued casting, hooking a few small crappie, but nothing suitable for a frying pan. Back at the cabin, we tuned the radio dial for a sporting event of some sort, then the television where a stirring game had immediate vortextual overtones. Big E's hometown team, the Syracuse Orangemen, were in a dogfight with the Auburn Tigers. The game went to three overtimes – THREE overtimes – before Auburn eked out a victory.

But the top sports story on the news – a bulletin, in fact -- was that Bob Huggins, coach of the Cincinnati Bearcats, had suffered a heart attack in the Pittsburgh airport. His heart stopped for a time, and he was effectively dead, but he was revived and hospitalized in serious condition. When the news anchor gave the time it happened, we gazed in amazement at one another. It was the exact moment we were talking about him in the boat. Did our conversation do him in?

Or was it the other way around? Did we save him? Had he passed over the rainbow, gone to see the Baby Jesus, only to have our idle conversation between casts bring him back? We were staggered and turned to one another with an unspoken question:

What *deux ex machina* was at play on these fishing trips?

Savory Steak and Onions

We know there's no big secret to grilling a steak. But the variations on the theme – like with rock n roll – are endless. Like many, we mostly just (heavily) salt and pepper the meat, let it reach room temperature, then throw it on a piping hot grill for four or five minutes a side.

Now and then we like to add a little spice to that simple recipe. Here's a pretty easy marinade that will make your steak a meal to remember. As long as you don't toast your culinary skills too enthusiastically. Here's what you need:

2 lbs of sirloin or rib-eye

¼ cup Worcestershire sauce (any pungent steak sauce will do about as well)

¼ cup lemon juice

3 tbsp red wine vinegar

2 tbsp vegetable oil

2 onions cut in rings

Toss the steak sauce, lemon juice, vinegar and oil into a thick plastic bag (freezer bags are good for this). Add onions and steak and toss it all around for a while. Get it all mixed up real good. Toss it in the refrigerator or cooler for as long as you can, say between 2 hours and a full day. Turn it all around a few times if you can.

When ready, toss the meat and onions on the grill and use the remaining marinade to baste the meat on each side once. Cook for 10 minutes, turning once. Now you're ready to slice it and serve it. Mmm good.

A power feather: I rose on that Mud Daddy morning early and alone. The boat beckoned, but its time would come later that day. Instead, I headed up the stream that fed the lake. It twisted and ran down from those West Virginia coal mountains in a crisp and clean green, but that did not necessarily mean this waterway was healthy. We were in the heart of coal country, so that meant that the water was slightly or perhaps even highly acidic, either from coal-mine runoff or the acid rain that fell from clouds seeded by deadly coal-fired power plants up and down the Ohio valley.

The acids deformed the fish or killed them altogether. But this stream seemed fresh and alive - perhaps a bass or trout could be wooed from its shallow riffles. I had the fly rod and yanked a black feathery leech through the current, and after an hour of fishing, and two slight pulls, one yielding a feisty smallmouth, it was time to return to camp to eat breakfast and get ready for another day of bad fishing and great whiskey.

Walking back to the camp, I happened to look down on the rocky shore, which is what stream fishermen must do to keep their balance, both while in the water and on land, and there it was — a red-tailed hawk feather. The Indians say no man chances upon a hawk feather because it is left for them by the bird. When we chugged out of the bay the next day, I looked back toward our campsite. There, in a tall lakeside tree, was the majestic red-tail. It watched us leave for a time, and then with several strong beats of its wings, lifted away and turned back into the deep forest. – *John Eckberg*

Our Lures

Every fisherman has his favorites, the ones he turns to out of hope and habit. Maybe they worked once or twice and he never forgot it. Maybe he caught his best fish on one and thinks it just may happen again. Maybe a favorite just looks like it ought to work. Our favorite lures compel us to tie them on and send them splashing into and through the water, though they probably don't work any better than the other things we throw. Nevertheless, we each have that special lure that we have irrational faith in, above all others, a lure that is magical. But only if its magic can be coaxed from the mystery.

Doc: I always throw a spinnerbait first. Austin American-Statesman outdoor writer extraordinaire Mike Leggett told me when all else fails, go for a green or white spinner bait. So I throw that first in most instances, usually with a white skirt and a single silver willowleaf blade. I have fancier ones, with colorful skirts and multiple blades, but simplicity is my code – until simplicity fails, then I quickly go the full monty with buzz baits, vari-hued skirts, multiple blades and more.

For top water situations (usually early in the morning, which means I don't find myself in that situation very often) I go for the Zara Spook. I like the clear body with two black eyes. If you tie it on right, it moves beautifully in the water, wiggling like a twenty-dollar hooker on a Saturday night in Tupelo. I've actually caught a few fish with it. Another favorite is the plastic twister tail worm, with gold flakes glittering in the smoke-colored body. It's been a producer on several occasions. Mine tend to be in the 4- to 6-inch range – not too big, not too small. I usually rig them Texas style, which is weight forward on the line, or with a jig head already attached to the hook so I can rig them up ahead of time. Those are my three go-to baits. When they fail, which is not uncommon, I empty my tackle box in desperation. And there are some crazy things in there.

Slim: My money lure is the golden Rapala, about six inches long, floating with three treble hooks. I rig it with three big split-shot up on the line at least 18 inches from the swivel and fish it steady and slow or with a quick reel. I really don't have any idea what I'm doing when it comes to speed of retrieve, but I know that varying the speed will catch fish: fight or flight and all that. Before changing to another lure, I will remove first one, then all the lead and twitch the Rapala across the top of the water because one time I saw Doc catch a nice fish that way, though it has never worked for me. I do it anyhow.

Next up is another Rapala, but this one is silver. Same size, same routine. Then comes the Rapala Fat Rap or a medium-diving crankbait in pearly silver. It's going to be customized with a hula skirt from a tube bait to give it extra allure and motion. Only after those lures have failed do I pull out the spinnerbaits: white or black, single leaf. Still no fish? Back to the golden Rapala for a spell and heavier shot. After that it's a motor-oil colored tube bait, jigged off the bottom to resemble a crawdad, or a faded green tube bait. I always count down my lures to start the retrieve somewhere just above the bottom of the lake and will always cast toward the seams of shade whenever possible. Two or three colors of tube baits later, I'll switch to a rubber worm – silver and six inches or so – then move to a purple worm. But worm fishing is slow and boring, so it's not something I relish.

Finally, the quest takes me to a spinner I found that has a mottled silver leaf and resembles an old tough-to-find lure called a CP Swing. I rummage around in my tackle box for the jar of pork rind and put a thin strip on the tail. This spinner has won Mud Daddy contests by bringing in a bass in the final 10 minutes of fishing. It is always the last and best hope. If I have no pork rind and it's the second day of the Mud Daddy, I'll use some uncooked fat from that morning's bacon trimmings, kept in a salt-water bottle in the tackle box. Still no fish? Out comes the fly rod and a No. 14 Adams or a little yellow popper, because this nonsense has got to end and rarely does the mosquito imitator or little yellow popper with feather tail fail to bring a fish to hand.

E-Man: My favorite lure for the type fishing we do – off points, 15 to 20 feet of water, in impoundments, in October – is a dark-colored jighead and skirt, anything to slow the descent of the lure (pork rind serves this purpose, too). I have had the best luck with this get-up in Laurel River Lake, Kentucky. It is also a highly recommended lure at Poirier Preserve in Quebec Province, Canada – where I've been venturing the last several years in late June with the fighting O'Connor clan of Lake Ontario fame. So my tackle box is full of them. I present them "Billy Westmoreland-style," with high-rod tip retrieve, then a tight-line descent, which is when the fish hit. I like taking four rods onto the boat – one too many – but I always want to keep a line wet and, besides, the clutter never fails to elicit a deprecatory comment from Doc, who fishes closest to me from amidships. Slim whines that my shit is everywhere, and he's right. I like relatively light tackle, so all my lines are six- to eight-pound test, and lures 1/4 to 3/8 ounce.

The second line I rig with chartreuse Weed Wader spinner bait, double-bladed. It's my favorite lure when fishing structure close to shore, because it's snagless and can be fished either top water with great action or at any level beneath the surface by varying the retrieve. My third line I always keep rigged with whatever lure they recommend in the marina. That can make for some space-consuming hardware in the tackle box, but it's an act of faith worth the reward, such as the time I brought home the bacon with a silver-and-blue Torpedo hauled through the hydrilla at Sam Rayburn reservoir. I don't insult the Torpedo anymore by fishing it in foreign venues; I give it the Lindbergh treatment in the Lone Star State. The fourth rod I save for natural bait. I'll use anything, but am most fond of fat nightcrawlers, rigged New York style. My personal best was a three-pound bass hauled from a weedy shoreline at Blue Mountain Lake, Adirondack Mountains, summer of aught five. The sinker is on the bottom, worm 18 inches up, unless the lake bottom is Snag City, in which case I reverse. When we commence the inevitable trolling lollygag down Highway 1, I turn to the duck-billed burnt-orange and black Wiggle Wart, for deep-water action that always brings an admiring glance from the Trotsky of the Troll, Uncle Slim, aka Slimbagger!

Chapter XXI - The Hand of God Tour

Mud Daddy tip: *Slim's father, Stanley, unlatched his old metal tackle box and let the lid slam onto the floor of the aluminum johnboat he'd rented. He didn't bang it exactly, but he wasn't quietly gentle, either. They were on aptly named Mosquito Lake in Northeast Ohio, not far from my hometown of Akron. Stanley was no longer navigator. He was too old for that. That duty now fell to Slim, and he tried to observe the unspoken rule of quiet in the boat at all times so as not to scare the fish. Slim hid his grimace and said nothing when Stanley continued to slam around in the boat. After choosing a favorite lure, a gold-colored Rapala designed by a Finnish fisherman from long ago, Stanley dropped the lid shut – again. He was a full-blooded Swede whose parents had emigrated from Lagan in Smaaland, a watery region of Central Sweden. He'd fished for all of his 70-plus years, so he should have known better than to bang around in a boat.*

"Dad," Slim scolded, "we need to be quiet."

Slim was disappointed and actually angry with his father. Fishing with your father shouldn't be like fishing with a 3-year-old.

"Naaaaah," he replied, banging the box with his foot for good measure. "Yellow Momberg always banged around on the canoe. He said it annoyed the fish, especially pike, and would make 'em strike."

Slim frowned and looked away at the jade-green hillside. Yeah, right he thought. We can forget about fish from this nice bay. Within minutes, Stanley had boated a Walleye. And then came another. "Yellow was right, too," Stanley said, as he eased the second fish back into the water.

The first sign of The Vortex had appeared some months earlier. Slim had sent a review copy of his true crime book, Road Dog, along with a stash of pictures from Mud Daddies past, to Doc's office at the Austin American-Statesman. But the book and photos never made it to Doc's desk – probably tossed out without a second thought by some clueless newsroom clerk or junior editor, Doc speculated. Slim thought malicious intent was in play. A few days before the Mud Daddy, there was a sale at the newspaper of the review books that once arrived by the hundreds each week (proceeds go to an education foundation). Doc pawed absentmindedly through the tables piled high with books and came upon the faded review copy of Road Dog, but without the Mud Daddy photos. Doc bought it for a buck.

This Mud Daddy is remembered as the "Hand of God" weekend. We were at Norfolk Lake near Mountain Home, Arkansas. We had a "waterfront" cabin with as much lakefront footage as a trailer in Lubbock, Texas. Still, it had everything thing we needed: a working TV; a screened-in back porch with a red vintage Formica-top table; and a shrine in the front room. Doc had been to the Dominican Republic and returned with a huge box of Cohiba cigars. The humidor was surrounded with Suaza tequila, Bushmills Irish whisky, Parrot Bay rum, Maker's Mark bourbon and a 55-can party-pack of Molson's ale. Ancient Romans would have been envious. Yes, we had everything but soap and hot water. A $1 bottle of Suave shampoo that Doc had bought en route on a whim would have to serve as bath soap, dishwashing soap and, well, shampoo, because that was all we had. And the hot water? Somebody's gonna fix it, right?

The first evening of any Mud Daddy should be spent finding one's sea-legs, so to speak – acclimating to the new surroundings. To do this quickly and efficiently, we recommend drinking a lot. As such, homage was paid to Doc's shrine there in the living room again and again, our celebration interrupted only briefly by a big spaghetti dinner somewhere in there, no one remembers when exactly. Eventually, all our fervent devotion paid off. BAM – er, what's that wall doing there? The next morning we concluded we wouldn't have spaghetti as the first meal of a Mud Daddy anymore. Slim and E had spent a good part of the late night and early morning kneeling in prayer to the porcelain idol.

We christened it the "vomitorium." Doc knows his history.

Strangely, we had a fish-finder on the john boat we had rented at the marina. And we hated it. With this infernal contraption we could actually see there were fish below! In all the previous years of endless hours with nary a bump, as well as out-and-out skunkings, we could take some comfort in the simple assumption that there were no fish. It wasn't our lack of skill, improper tackle or our inattention to the task at hand that was at issue. No, it was, in fact, the dearth of piscatorial denizens of the deep frequenting the points and drop-offs that had led to our skunkings – not our ineptitude. No way was it our fault.

But with the friggin' fish-finder, we could no longer indulge this delusion. And we didn't like it. The fish were clearly down there. We could see them on the screen, swimming around, their jaws clamped shut and giving us their middle dorsal fin. Our normal level of aggravation at not catching fish was pinned into the red by that damned fish finder. Finally, we turned the thing off and immediately began to feel much better about the trip. Now if we didn't catch anything, it might be because the fish weren't down there anymore.

We floated into a quiet cove that looked like every fisherman's dream, with downed trees stretching into the lake for underwater cover, a sheer drop-off at the edge of the cove and a gentle slope at the elbow. It was a luscious spot. And it yielded zip. Not a bite.

Reduced to what is usually an act of desperation – a No. 14 Adams, which looks like a mosquito – Slim whipped the fly line back and forth like a crazy man to get the fly up near the bushes along shore. "Stay Out of the Bushes," Slim commanded as he let loose the line. The others stopped fishing to berate and belittle Slim, well aware he was hoping to take the lead for the coveted Enquirer Outstanding Angler award with one, just one, puny fish. But not today. He couldn't even get a bite on a fly?

Unbelievable.

"This is bullshit," Slim announced.

The conversation drifted here and there and finally settled on the "The DaVinci Code" and whether Mary Magdalene was carrying Jesus' child when she fled to France after his crucifixion. Or did she have a toddler in tow, too? Slim contended that one of the little ones who came to Jesus when he played with the children was actually His child.

"I think that's true but I also know something else that's true," Slim said. "The fishing is so bad today that even Jesus couldn't catch a fish."

Big E, ever the practicing Catholic, cautioned Slim: "Could come back on you, Slim Man."

"Yeah," Doc reminded him, "J.C. was a pretty good fisherman, you'll recall. Cast on the other side of the boat."

Then Slim launched into his take on Jesus and fishing.

"Imagine what the disciples thought when Jesus suggested they put the nets on this side of the boat … not that side," Slim said. "They'd seen Him turn water into wine, so who would argue? But man, there must have been some griping. When you're out in open water, one side of the boat or the other? C'mon, Jesus, what's the difference? And, are YOU gonna help or are YOU just gonna sit there?

"And as for walking on the water. Jesus is always depicted as this Solemn Guy. When He came walking across the water, in that storm, no frigging way was he solemn. "Man, I bet he was goofing around, like Sammy Davis Jr. out there," Slim continued. "You know. Probably went, 'Hey, check this out!' Then threw a little Michael Jackson toe kick into the mix."

Slim took one more cast and we shut it down as it had begun to drizzle. We agreed to head over to another cove across the lake and then back to the cabin for sustenance and libations to ease the pain of the morning skunking. With Slim at the helm, we motored out into the main body of the lake. As we moved across the water, Slim spotted something in the distance disturbing the surface.

"Check it out," he shouted over the drone of the outboard.

Slim thought it might be a wounded fish of some sort, perhaps dropped by an osprey. He's excitable like that. As we drew close to it, we saw that it was a good-sized bass, and it had a fin protruding from its open jaws. It had tried to swallow a baitfish of some sort, literally biting off more than it could chew. Now the big bass was rolling onto its back and slowly dying right in front of us. On the first pass, E tried to bare hand it but missed.

E-Man rolled up the sleeve of his flannel shirt, pushed up the long sleeve T-shirt underneath and stretched out past the bow, snatching the bass on the next pass in one quick swoop. He held it up for the others to see.

"Whoa, E, that's amazing," Doc said, grabbing his needle nose pliers from his tackle box. He reached in and pulled the smaller fish out of the bass's gullet.

"It's a bluegill. Its fins were jammed into the bass's throat. He couldn't swallow it or spit it out. Man, that's something."

A bluegill! The very fish Slim had been trying to catch only minutes before was inside the mouth of the nicest bass we'd seen in years.

Doc got the camera while E tried to revive the bass, pushing it back and forth in the lake, forcing water through its gills. Soon it began slowly moving its tail fin, showing signs of coming around. Big-E pulled it back up long enough for a quick picture, then went back to work reviving the fish. After a minute or two, finding the strength to swim out of E's hand, the bass finned down and away and out of sight. Did it look at us on the way down? Slim thought so. We couldn't be sure.

"I think God turned to his right and said, 'Hey, J.C., did you hear what Slim just said about you?'" Doc said.

"A bluegill!" Slim added. "Did God go, 'Well, I'm tired of Afghanistan and Iraq and poverty and famine and all that. Check it out! Those Yahoos are on their annual fishing trip and Slim's been reduced to fly fishing for bluegills. Watch!'"

"I think we just got a warning, Slim," Doc said. "J.C. was showing us exactly what He can do when it comes to fishing."

"That was wild," said a clearly elated E, who was now in the lead for the coveted plaque. "We've had a lot of vortextual events on these trips, but nothing like that. That was unbelievable."

A killer bluegill sent from above.

We motored back in silent reflection. Later we toasted the event with Bahama Slims (recipe to follow), served meatloaf, followed by fruit cocktail cobbler for dessert, and Cohibas and Bushmills on the back porch. Life can be good if you just let it come to you.

Later, Slim created fantastic rocketry with coruscating secondary explosions in the low heavens. These awe-inspiring bursts of light and sound have a spiritual quality to them as well, especially after a few highballs. Slim's rockets come together in a flurry of tape, Styrofoam and cigar tubes. He can make a rocket while whipping up pancakes for breakfast. He can make rockets while watching football games. He can make rockets while sipping whiskey and watching the sun set behind burnished hills of autumn. When the time comes to launch, Slim applies flame to a tiny rocket engine – fuses from smoke bombs brought along just for their ignition capabilities work best. All Mud Daddy launches have this in common: Doc and E-man stand in cautious wonder, the fear of a misfire palpable. Then rockets rise in

The Mud Daddy Chronicles

a loud rush to several hundred feet – in a stunning and loud display of engineering and bravado. We usually toast successful launches – unsuccessful ones, too – and this trip would be no exception.

The Hand of God Tour at Lake Norfolk ended with the rocketry but without further fish or acts of God – unless you count the excellent bruscetta made with hoagie rolls and E-dog's Italian flair.

Bahama Slims

Equal parts cranberry juice, orange juice with slice or two of lime squeezed over the rocks

White rum or vodka to taste. Make a pitcher for boat but add 1 part soda or tonic

Sergio Mendez must be cued up on the box.

Norfolk Lake Beef Burgundy on White Rice

A good meal for a cabin with a kitchen and most of the usual appliances. We made this successfully on the Hand of God Tour.

1 lb of ground beef or chopped sirloin

1 cup sliced/chopped mushrooms (take your time washing the mushrooms and get the grit out of the caps for once in your life, why don't you)

1/2 cup chopped onions

1 can regular cream of mushroom soup

1/2 cup wine, red or white, but red's better if you haven't run out. Use beer in a pinch.

1 tbsp Worcestershire sauce

2 tbsp oil

1/2 cup sour cream

Salt and pepper to taste.

Sauté the mushrooms and onions in the oil until the onions are pearly, translucent and all that. Sing something about "Zee Weeemaan of Fraunce" as the onions cook over low, slow heat, five minutes or so. Add the beef and begin chopping it into small chunks. If the pan's not Teflon, use a fork to make the burger really small. Once pinkness is just about gone, add the soup, Worcestershire sauce, ½ cup libation, salt and pepper and stir it up good. Let it simmer covered for a while – half an hour sounds about right.

While the meat is simmering, cook the rice. It takes about 30 minutes. Use brown rice, which takes 45 minutes, if you want to think you're being healthy (which seems kind of silly considering everything else in this recipe). Plan it so the rice and beef burgundy are done about the same time. That alone will be challenge enough for any amateur chef. During the last 10 minutes, stir in the sour cream — not into the rice, into the sauce. Sheesh. Serve this sloppy beef burgundy over a mound of rice. If you use brown rice, the mixture doesn't look all that appetizing. In fact, it looks like something from the vomitorium. But it's really, really good!

Chapter XXII - The Battle of Muddy Pond

Sometimes, it feels like the Mud Daddy won't come together at all. Sometimes problems with wives, kids, work, and money, or a combination of them, seem insurmountable. Sometimes it seems like the trip won't be worth the hassle and expense. But that doesn't mean you actually stay home attempting to be a good husband, a good father or a good plumber. It's times like these that you have to be strong. Suck it up! Figure it out. Go!

While surfing the Web in 2004 for a cabin, any cabin, somewhere in central Kentucky near Laurel River Lake, Slim decided to seek a photo of the earliest fish known to archeologists and biologists. He didn't know why he wanted to do this, only that it seemed right. He soon found a skeletal sketch of the first shark, discovered countless eons ago in the Cleveland shale of Ohio. "Hmmm," he thought as he forwarded the Web photo onward to Doc and E.

The next morning, on his breakfast table is a pool toy – just sitting there, something Slim had never seen before. It was, of course, a shark, and it looked just like the photo he had sent the previous evening of that killer from the Cleveland Shale. Just like it!

"Where did this come from?" Slim asked his daughter, Rachel, when she came down for breakfast

"Oh, I was cleaning out a backpack from summer and found it inside," she replied.

So how is it that the plastic shark reappeared on a fall evening long after the swim club had closed and just when a guy was putting a fishing trip together and had sent a photo of the same ancient creature off to his pals only the night before?

Slim knew the Mud Daddy was in full force.

The 2004 return to Laurel River Lake in Kentucky, otherwise known as The Battle of Muddy Pond, was another one of those trips that almost did not come off. Only at the last possible minute, and way too late in the fall, did a window of possibility open up. Slim took the lead, found the cabin, a marina and a boat in short order, and Doc lucked into enough money to fly to Cincinnati for three days the first week of November. He was paid to undergo a medical experiment that involved needles, fasting, a formula drink and a colonoscopy. He doesn't like to talk about the details, because things went wildly wrong and there was a lot of pain. But the $300 check got him a fishing trip.

Night had fallen, and the place was deserted when we found the state park cabin that Slim had secured sight unseen.

"What the hell is this?" Doc asked in disgust. "Looks like these cottages have been abandoned for years. Don't tell me people sleep in these things."

Everybody agreed. It looked like a something out of a bad slasher flick. Bedding was on the floor. The cabin had a kitchen that was dried-up-pork-and-beans funky. Trash was in the living room. The windows were filthy, and the grill outside, well, it had no grill outside. We went looking for a new place to rent at 10 p.m. In the closest convenience store, Slim took the lead and asked the clerk whether she knew anybody with an empty RV or maybe a cabin nearby. She replied that she sure did and picked up the phone. The owner of this little grocery had a new place just down the road, and they would soon be at the store to take us to it. After looking the cabin over, cash was exchanged for a three-night stay. It was one big room, but it boasted two double beds and a bunk bed, a large dining table, a decent bathroom and a kitchen area. And it had about 4,000 dead lady bugs by the sliding glass door.

After the owners left, we came to a stunning revelation.

"Uh oh."

"What is it?"

"There's no oven. Or range. Nothing to cook on."

What were we, blind? All we had was a propane grill off the front porch. But what did we expect in the middle of the night in the Kentucky woods? We'd make it work. We would not be defeated. Not without a fight, anyway.

Fishing was another matter. We were utterly defeated. Nothing. Nada. Nil. Zip. Zero. Dead in the water. When the fishing goes so far south that you hear the call of the penguins, the mind plays tricks as one bobs on the deserted water. Several hours into the first day, it was obvious to all that a severe skunking was again at hand.

So we did what we sometimes do when the fishing dies: We went through our tackle. Decades of hope littered our boxes and bags. A generation of craziness, ignorance, expense and what-was-I-thinking acquisitions at outdoor stores from Canada to Mexico, New York to Hawaii. An insane assortment of lures presented themselves. There were Lazy Ikes made for Great Lakes angling, huge Cordell Redfins for big lake striped bass and Chesapeake Bay bluefish, tiny rooster tails for Appalachian streams and enormous baits only good for salmon fishing with downriggers off the coast of Alaska

All of it had been used, or at least purchased with the hope it would be used, on various fishing trips around the country and beyond. Going through those artificial lures was a trip back in time.

"R'member this?" Doc growled through the cigar clamped between his teeth. He held up a gray-black rubber mouse with a large hook curving from its back.

"Lake Rayburn, right?"

"Right, big man. Didn't get a single damn hit."

He threw it back in his box in disgust

"I'll see your rubber mouse and raise ya,' " said Slim, bringing forth a plastic lizard as long as his hand. It was clear but filled with red, blue and silver glitter.

"What is that supposed to look like to a fish?" Doc asked. "A lizard out for a night of disco dancing?"

"What it looks like to me," Slim replied, "is a lure designed to catch a sucker. And not the kind with fins. At the time, I just had to have it. It looked surefire!"

We produced scores of different colored plastic and rubber worms, a red rubber crawfish with a huge hook protruding from its back and evil looking green-and-black lizards that floated. None of these lures – hundreds of dollars worth – ever gained so much as a nudge from a fish. Doc had a hunk of hand-cast metal shaped like a torpedo with two red eyes painted on it with nail polish and a treble hook dangling from the end. It was, he explained, guaranteed to simply slay white bass during the March run on the Pedernales River. But he'd never tried it.

E-Dog displayed a collection of bizarre crankbaits, some of them in horrid blends of puce, chartreuse, acid orange and other shades not seen in the natural world. One was a fat thing in a sickly see-through orange color that must have weighed almost a half-pound. The three of us had a Crayola collection of crankbaits in Day-Glo yellow, orange, blue, green, red, pink and more. What were we thinking? That a bass might mistake an electric pink crankbait for real food? That fish are color blind? That it doesn't matter that millions of dollars and as many hours have been spent researching a fish's feeding habits and that candy-apple red was not the conclusion? No, we thought, "Why not?" It might just piss off a fish enough to try to kill it instantly. Or pique its curiosity enough to try something brand new, a change of pace. Adventures in eating. Since the commonly used baits haven't worked all that well for us either, might as well go for fear and loathing.

Slim favored contraptions, some of them jury-rigged by him, others purchased because, again, the man can't resist something too crazy to be believed. Every man has to believe in something, right? Slim believes he'll buy that nutty looking $5.95 buzz bait that resembles a toy submarine, heave it into the water and some fish that's grown fat and sassy discriminating between fact and fiction will swallow it.

Among other strangeness lurking in the bottom of his tackle box, Slim has a bottom-walking wire thing, crappie rigs with multiple attachments that would do a Cuisinart proud, even a rubber band to rig up a balloon to a lifesaver that melts then drops the sinker and bait far, far out into a lake.

"Helium?"

"Nah, any air will do," Slim said, though he's never tried it. It's a wonder he didn't have a kite in there to get the lure way far from the boat.

They were all here, in all their failed, fishless glory. But we couldn't part with them. Someday, someplace that rubber mouse or bottom-walking wire contraption might be the only thing that's working, the one thing the fish just can't resist. You don't know until you try.

Like the duck that walked into a bar and asked the bartender if he had any duck food.

"This is a bar, not a pet store. We don't have any duck food. Now get the hell out of here and don't come back."

Next day the duck waddles in and asks again if the barkeep has any duck food.

"I told you yesterday we don't have duck food. No duck food. None. Now get out of here. Don't come back."

Next day the duck comes into the bar and asks once more for duck food. "Damn it! I told you we don't have duck food. Now if you come back in here again asking for duck food I'm going to nail your little webbed duck feet to the floor! You understand that? So get out of here and do NOT come back."

Next day, the duck is back in the bar again and asks the bartender, "Got any nails?"

"No, I don't have any nails," he answers.

"Got any duck food?"

That night in the cabin, Slim whittled away at a cord to the boom box because there were no batteries. Sometimes the music worked, other times it disappointed. So Slim whittled. It went like this for about 20 minutes: cut, plug in to test, unplug, cut, plug in to test, unplug, cut, plug in to test, cut.

BAM-FLASH!!!

Slim got mixed up and forgot to unplug before he started to trim the box-end of the adapter. A giant fireball of electricity exploded through the steel edge of the Swiss Army knife. It blew a hole the size of a BB in the blade, turned his fingers black and shot a ball of lightning across the cabin.

"Hmmmm," Slim said. "That could have killed me. I guess they didn't wire in any fuses."

Talk soon turned to the hereafter and finally the Bible. Doc, a sometime churchgoer who goes more for the music than the scripture, said he was always puzzled by one passage. When Jesus commanded a fig tree to bring forth fruit and the tree did not, the next day the tree had withered. Why would He have done that? Doc asked. Jesus wasn't here to kill but to save. Doc said he thought he knew the answer. He said that he thought the incident with the fig tree was when Jesus finally realized the extent of his awesome power. This wasn't turn-water-into-wine-to-please-Mom. No, if He was annoyed, His petulance could kill.

At that exact moment, the small Magna-light flashlight on the table, which had been converted to a candle, winked out, as if the Holy Spirit was tuned into our talk and wanted to let us know that Doc was right. The conversation froze as we all recognized that like the Hand of God fish from the year before, the Lord is always near on a Mud Daddy.

The next morning there was one last place to try. Behind the cabin was a stagnant, muddy pond about 50 yards across, surrounded by sloping, red clay banks.

Slim looked at E and Doc. "Why not?"

"Okay," Doc agreed. "We fish for 30 minutes and no more. Anyone catches a fish, he's the Outstanding Angler winner and we leave. First fish or half an hour, whichever comes first."

It was ugly. Three guys casting like mad men, thrashing the murky water with whatever they had on, using three rods each, in quick succession. Doc and E feared the fly rod. Slim had won several EOA awards by enticing some puny bluegill to swallow a tiny dry fly at the last moment. And he was determined to do it again. But the others had reason for hope – Slim had managed to entangle his fly line on about his third back cast in the only tree near the pond, and while he wrestled with the scraggly little maple, his line became more and more entangled. Doc and E fired cast after cast, walking the pond's edge. The more Slim worked to get the line out of the tree, the more entangled it got.

It took Slim several minutes to untangle and then, with time running out, only minutes left, he finally cleared his line to make one last cast near a concrete block in the muck at the shallow end of the pond.

Fish on!

A sickly bluegill, color drained completely from its scales, decided at that moment to commit suicide and swallow the fly. Slim had won again, taking the trophy from E, who had claimed it the year before with his Hand of God fish. The Battle of Muddy Pond was over.

"Yeah! I got your duck food!" Slim crowed.

The Magic Bag

The contents of Slimbagger's magic bag, from which 23 scrumptious desserts have been created over the years: mini-chocolate bars, caramel candies, hard candy, raisins, granola, Twinkies, Maker's Mark bourbon/tequila, apples, pears, oranges, raspberry jam, oatmeal, coffee creamer, ricotta cheese, bananas, margarine, maple syrup, pancake mix, cookie crumbs, doughnut crumbs, crescent rolls, lime juice, purloined sugar packets and cream cheese.

Bull Shoals Meatloaf

We made this delicious meatloaf in a cabin near Bull Shoals Lake, a cabin that didn't have a bread pan. Slim came up with a delightful Mud Daddy improv. And it worked. He has also made meat loaf in a saucepan. Whatever it takes.

One-and-half pounds of ground round/sirloin (if using hamburger or ground chuck, half-fry the meat, then drain off the grease)

About 1/4 cup of salami, chopped into small pieces

1/4 cup or pound or handful of sausage. Whatever you have.

½ cup of picante sauce or medium-heat salsa from a jar (ketchup is good, too, best if purloined from fast food coffee-stop)

Small bunch cilantro (if you have any — you might)

Leftover or drained half-can of corn, misc. vegetable

1/4 cup onion

Clove minced garlic

One egg

Half cup or less of bread crumbs (toast stale, purloined bread then crumble) or cracker crumbs

Salt and pepper to taste

Mix everything together into a big gob of goo. Stir it up real good. If you have no bread-loaf pan (and we didn't) then build one from a double sheet of no-stick aluminum foil. You must make it double or even triple to ensure no spillage. Put the loaf into the pan and reshape loaf with pan. Be careful poking around after the stuff starts to cook. You don't want a leak. Put the pan onto a cookie sheet or other baking dish as a precaution. Make sure the foil edges go up above the meat. Cook for 45 minutes at 325 degrees or until bubbly at the top. Smear the top with more picante sauce (drained) or small diced tomatoes that have had the seeds and liquid stuff removed. Bake another 15 minutes. Serve with Merlot and eat with gusto. There shouldn't be any leftovers, but if there are, stash slices for toasted meatloaf sandwiches for the next day or chunks to put on crackers for a floating brunch.

Chapter XXIII - Call Me Tishomingo

Jim sounded normal enough on the phone, though maybe a little too chatty, his conversation thick with cornpone and molasses, a little too cloying. Jim managed a three-house complex at Pickwick Lake in Mississippi near the Alabama border and rented boats, too. Pickwick had been good to us in the past, so why not try it again? Slim thought the combination of Jim's place, his boat and the lake would make a great trip in September 2005 – except that Jim wanted the cash for the boat and house, both sight unseen, wired to him direct, rather than paid at the time of arrival. The terms made Slim less than comfortable.

But, because it was late September, and the time left for a Mud Daddy was quickly slipping away, Slim agreed to Jim's demands and closed the deal. With much anticipation, he and E-Dog left Cincinnati on a weekday afternoon, bound for the Nashville airport, where they would pick up Doc, who was flying up from Austin. All the stars seemed in alignment after they snagged Doc and drove through the Tennessee night and into the next morning, listening to great songs by Otis Redding and others that Slim, in a Vortextual moment, had discovered at a neighborhood garage sale only days before the Mud Daddy. Cool music at garage sales in his Cincinnati subdivision go together like bin Laden and mercy. It doesn't happen. Except this time, when Slim found tables, literally tables, full of great tunes: from Robert Cray to Southern Culture on the Skids, Emmy Lou Harris to Sergio Mendes. These were Dead Man's tunes, Slim thought, figuring that nobody would willingly part with all this music, all this gear, unless they'd gone over to the other side. So Slim snagged a dozen CDs, a pair of pliers and left elated.

Despite the long night drive, the boys – actually old men by now – were in high spirits. The last time they visited Pickwick, everybody caught fish. This trip should be the same. Upon arrival the next day, they found the first problem was one that was completely out of their control. His name was Jim. He was clearly nutso-bananas and full hilljack. He drove a white American luxury car, smoked discount light cigarettes, and lorded over this lake from his bedroom/office near a marina that mysteriously did not rent boats but had great minnows. Why wouldn't they rent boats? Jim had a ready answer.

"Everybody tears 'em up. Can't afford the insurance anymore. I'm the only guy on the lake who rents a boat," he said. And then he repeated himself, almost like an idiot savant.

"Everybody tears 'em up."

That would become a Mud Daddy mantra.

Everybody tears 'em up. Much like the mantra from two decades before: Rigid Taiwanese Standards.

So Jim had an outboard monopoly on this lake – the only guy left who still rented john boats – and we had no choice but to deal with him. Then the conversation took off in a surprising direction as Jim limped back to his desk.

"I limp when the weather gets me because of this. See it right there? The scar? And I got it from this catfish," he said, pointing to his knee and then reaching for a picture of a man in blue denim shorts who was 30 or more pounds heavier. Next to him was a very, very large catfish.

Now, a 100-pound catfish is truly an awesome and marvelous creature. Bigger than a large dog, a giant catfish is no easy animal to catch and then kill. A big catfish looks like pure malevolence, too, with a permanent frown for a mouth and spurs on just about every fin. The catfish that got Jim got him good, and left a karmic residue that haunts this loony guy on this lost arm of a lake in Mississippi to this very day. Jim soon described how he hauled it in and took it down to the killing tree where it was nailed fin up.

"Somebody took that picture just before we gutted it. Now what happened was somebody nailed the fish to a tree and didn't do a very good job of it. So when I pulled the knife down to spill out the guts, the nail gave way and that fish came off and the spur got me. It went into my knee and then broke off," Jim said.

"I was flopping around there screaming. Somebody called the EMTs. When they came up, they thought I was having a heart attack so they cut my jeans off and right where they cut was where the catfish spur had broken off. So I screamed some more."

It was the ultimate fish wound story – or at least the best we had ever heard. Finally, he was through with his story, through with Slim signing a half-dozen papers and releases, and now he was ready to give us motorboat boot camp. His version of it, anyhow. He wouldn't let us leave the dock unless we went through motor technology step-by-step. Why? Well, he didn't want anybody "tearin' up the motor," and in good faith we couldn't disagree with him because many people are indeed huge screw-ups. Also, it was a Mud Daddy.

Jim looked down his nose at our gear. He told us he doesn't fuss with casting lures for fish or baiting hooks with minnows and fishing with a bobber. Why? Well, because he was above that. For one thing, the fish were too small. And besides, he was a jug fisherman. He made that clear from the first phone call. And if he liked you, he said, he might invite you to come out jug fishing with him at night. But he wasn't sure yet if he liked us enough, he said on that first phone call.

Now, American men are dedicated to many things in this world. Some men are dedicated to their families, to their wives and to their children, every waking hour. Some men are dedicated to their church, to their local high school, to their V.F.W. Some are devoted to grandparents, parents, brothers and sisters. Other men are committed to golf, to softball, to NASCAR, to hunting, to fishing, to camping. Some men live to play poker, blackjack or Texas Hold 'Em at the closest riverboat casino. Some men are dedicated to model trains, slot cars, woodworking, or to music, to NFL football, to Major League Baseball, to college football, to college hoops, to prep sports, to ballroom dancing. Some are dedicated to kayaking, canoeing, boating, hiking and camping. Don't forget bowling and croquet. Some men are committed to flowers, to landscaping, to gardening. Hell, some men are even dedicated to mowing the lawn.

Well, Jim was dedicated to catfishing. But not just any sort of catfishing. No, Jim, like he said for the fifth time, was a jug-fishing catfisherman. We soon realized that he went after catfish the way Ahab went after white whales, and, in fact, he even limped like Ahab because of that catfishing mishap that he told us about and wanted to tell us about one more time but we wouldn't let him.

Jim had been the self-crowned king of nighttime catfishing in these parts for a long time, having won the local tournament something like six years straight – until they started having it in the day, which pissed Jim off beyond belief. The guy was the Stephen Hawking of the Catfish Universe. Did we say he fished with jugs? Jim detailed how he has 75 or more of them, each about the size of a gallon container of milk, and a couple of nights a week, he chugged a pontoon boat out onto the vast water of Pickwick Lake in the deepest dark of a misty night to put out jugs at key places that only Jim knows about. (By the way, don't ask him about foggy boating because if you do, get ready for his personal foggy-boating story that lasts through a couple of cigarettes and a cup of coffee. Your eyes will glaze over. You will be begging for somebody to spray you with lighter fluid and set you on fire because that would be better than listening to a foggy-boating story.)

Out on the lake he lays out the jugs rigged with a sinker on a line tight to the bottom and then a 75-pound test stainless-steel swivel, leader and hook on another line that might stretch out behind the jug for 40 yards or more to a hook baited with shrimp. He puts jugs over underwater channels and above underwater stumps. It takes about two hours to get all the jugs out. Then, Jim and whatever sucker or two he's convinced to come along, wait for about three hours until it's time to haul the jugs in. On the other end of the line on about 10 percent of the jug-rigs is a giant catfish, which Jim cleans and gives to the local police and fire departments for their catfish dinners.

Across the drive on the walkway around the boat barn, Doc pounded the water: cast after cast after cast. Nothing. Slim and E were mesmerized by Jim's tale, but now they wanted to get out onto the water because, after all, it was 10 a.m., the fog was slipping away and so was this Mud Daddy. Finally, Jim let the boat go and we headed out for a day on the water. Slim got a bass on a crankbait dressed with a tube bait tail and grabbed the lead in the competition for the Mud Daddy plaque. Action was light until E jerked back on his rod.

"Whatcha got there?" Doc asked E, as all eyes in the boat shifted toward E's rod, which was bent in a U-shape and pointing straight down as the line sliced here and there through the water. E-Dog reeled in until he could reel no more and his drag engaged.

"I don't know what it is," E replied and then the fish surfaced – a giant bluegill, as big as a frying pan and its eyes black and deep. As E hauled it in, the fish mouthed a silent song, and the gills flexed for oxygen. Its sides glowed deep green and its back several inches across. We knew immediately we would be keeping this one. It was a $700 appetizer – about what the trip had cost so far.

We avoided Jim for the rest of the trip. After dinner Doc headed back to the dock. He refused to give up in his quest because he knew that one or two fish would put him in the lead. He cast at the water until the moon had risen and crawled above this shallow back bay, its reflection dancing across the water. As a chilly fog settled over another Mud Daddy, a lone man stood near a boathouse in the moonlight, pounding the dark water with casts.

Splash… after splash… after splash…long into the night.

Grinnin' Parrot Cobbler

Peel, core and dice three pears into thumbnail-sized chunks.

Stir in sugar from 10 or so sugar packets (purloined from fast food restaurant on the way into the lake. Remember, international hospitality companies want you to be happy. Take as many as you think you'll need because you'll probably have forgotten to bring your own sugar)

Juice from a lime

Crescent dinner rolls from a tube

Tab or four of butter or margarine (see purloin tip above).

Put sugared pears into baking dish that has already been greased with butter. Add juice from a lime. Open the tube of crescent dinner rolls and slice rolls into half-inch strips. Create an interlacing pattern across the top of the pears with the strips of crescent roll dough. Crumble cookies or create cobbleresque topping from butter and crumbs and sprinkle across the top where the crescent rolls do not cover. Bake until done, about 45 minutes in 350 degree oven. Serve with ice cream, Half & Half (purloined, of course), drizzle of whiskey. Now that's good eatin'.

Chapter XXIV - The Greer's Ferry Follies

It wasn't the vortex that brought the crew back together after years of neglecting their Mud Daddy duties.

It was the taunt.

Doc sent Slim and E-man an email with a picture of the Enquirer Outstanding Angler Award in a prominent position on his bookshelf. He said that after seven years the award would be fully retired in his possession, as the rules stipulated. There are no rules, obviously, but their only recourse was to cobble together another Mud Daddy or concede that Doc was in fact the Enquirer Outstanding Angler and owned the hardware to prove it.

Doc laid out some possible locations – mostly in Arkansas, since that was halfway between them – and Slim found a nice looking cabin right on Greer's Ferry Lake in the Central Arkansas Ozarks. It was without a doubt the most luxurious, and most expensive, lodging they had ever procured for a Mud Daddy.

It was a three-bedroom, two-bath layout with an open floor plan, a large-screen TV and a back deck with a stunning view of the lake just beyond the trees. It was mid-September and the weather was still warm when everyone arrived. There were greetings, cigars, beers and – mirable dictu – barbecue acquired from a joint on famous Highway 61 that E and Slim stumbled into on the long drive in.

"So you got this in a place where Robert Johnson met the devil then?" Doc asked.

"Either that or a place where Dylan revisited," Slim said.

"God said to Abe, kill me a son. Abe said, man you must be puttin' me on.

"God said no, Abe said what

"God said you can do what you want Abe, but next time you see me comin' you better run.

"Abe said where you want this killin' done"

"Out on Highway 61"

Thursday night was a marathon of catching up. Where kids were living and working, how the new careers outside of newspapers were going. And for E, a decision to be made. The abominations at Gannett were making E and most others at the Enquirer reapply for their jobs. Never mind his nearly 40 years of award-winning work on their behalf. His columnist job was going away and maybe his employment altogether. E didn't like the looks of that, so he took a buyout and said AMF, with middle finger pointing toward McLean, Va.

Although it was a long time coming, it was still a Mud Daddy, so of course the weather turned on us overnight. A strong cold front blew in lowering clouds and a surprisingly cold rain. And, following a long-standing practice, Slim forgot to secure a boat for us. First, we got a late start. Then we couldn't find a marina that was open – in fact, there wasn't another boat to be seen on the water. We worried we were too late in the season for rentals. When we finally located a marina with rentals, all they had was pontoon boats, more expense than we usually bear.

"Don't you think that's Bill Clinton's brother?" Slim asked, nodding to the dark-haired guy writing up the paperwork for the rental.

"Too young," E noted. Sagely.

"Maybe an illegitimate son, then."

"No, Slim," sighed Doc. "Just because we're in Arkansas doesn't mean everyone we see is related to the former prez."

"But the resemblance is uncanny."

"No it's not."

The pricey pontoon turned out to be something of a blessing. We had a radio and some cover from the cold rain. Slim had his hands full maneuvering the clumsy thing, which acted like a sail with every wind gust blowing us this way and that. And no one else was fishing. We cast and cast without so much as a follow-up, and getting soaked in the process.

Still, the lake was beautiful. Steep rocky cliffs with expensive homes perched on top, numerous fingers of inlets, some stretches of sandy beaches and some drop-offs that simply had to hold fish.

But the combination of bad weather, bad timing and our general ineptitude did us in. Not a bite.

"Well, hell, let's take a break for lunch," said E.

"Do we have any food?" Doc asked.

Silence. No one had thought to bring so much as a slice of bread. We had been away from these trips too long. Lost our chops. But not our appetites. We each had a few vending machine crackers to carry us through, but that was it. A few hours later we limped back into not-Clinton's-brother-or-son's marina – cold wet, hungry and skunked. It was a true Mud Daddy.

After cleaning up, snacking and drinking to alleviate the pain of a skunking, we headed out to dinner in E-dog's new car. Now there's a strange fact about a guy who's probably related to Columbus – he has the worst sense of direction ever. Pulling out of the driveway, E started to turn right.

"Where you going?" Slim barked.

"It's left E," Doc reminded him.

E let go with a belly laugh. "I really have a problem with directions." At the main highway he started to go left when the town was to the right. We'd just been through all this a couple of times already.

"Damn, E-man, you really don't know where the hell we are, do you?"

"How the hell do you get around?" Slim asked, truly baffled by E's lacking sense of direction.

"I'm like Wrong Way Corrigan," E said, laughing at his own inability to find his ass with both hands. He then regaled us with the story of Wrong Way Corrigan, the pilot who landed in Ireland when he was supposed to be flying to California. It was a good story. But he never did figure out when to turn right or left that weekend.

Saturday dawned with the same foul weather, but we were better prepared with some funky rain gear and a cooler with not only beer and flasks of whiskey but a bit of food. Slim located a different marina – we'd had enough of not-a-Clinton's place. As we drove into the parking lot, a guy in a pickup was hauling around an auburn-haired girl in a little flatbed wagon usually used to haul gear from trunks and truck beds down to the boats. He was driving in big figure eights to her squeals of delight. She was about 10, with an infectious smile and a fun way about her. A spirited dog ran alongside as she swung around the parking lot. It was a mottled herding pup of indistinguishable origin, but it was having as much fun as the girl. In many parts of this country, that sight would have had some overly concerned adult speed dialing Child Protective Services. But here, in the Arkansas backwoods, it was just good fun. And a delightful sight.

We headed across the gangplank to the office with the frisky pup nipping at our heels like he was herding sheep and the little girl running ahead of us and yapping a mile a minute. Inside, it was a better deal than the not-a-Clinton's marina. We got some advice, a map with good fishing spots marked for us, and a happy little girl and her dog running around having fun. We gathered our gear and ourselves into the pontoon – the pup kept jumping into the boat with us, then out again – with Slim at the helm and set out with high hopes for a better day all around.

A cold drizzle fell most of the day and the fishing was still lousy. Greer's Ferry is a sizeable lake and we weren't ever sure exactly where on the map we were. In the afternoon we got the Texas Tech-Arkansas game on the radio – but it was a rout, much to the chagrin of Doc's son Evan, who has three degrees from that august Harvard of the South Plains. The fish may have been rare but the scenery was breathtaking. Tall bluffs diving into the clear water. Jagged rocks rose to strange table-top formations. These flat wedges of rock balanced on precipices one after another.

In the afternoon, the sun broke through and so did Slim. After two full days of zilch, we turned to desperate measures. Slim rigged up a contraption with a large sinker at the bottom and a plastic bait tied on above it: a Strike King Structure Bug. Slim bought the crawfish imitator because they were highly touted by Karl Kalonka, The Extreme Angler on the Outdoor Channel and had sold out in some stores. Slim bounced that mess of motor oil plastic flecked with purple glitter down the sheer wall of jagged rock bluff that was the shore and immediately hooked a nice bass. It shook free before he could boat it, however. Slim went right back at the same place with the same rig, and quite soon he hooked another one. This time, he got it in the boat and made sure everyone got to admire it before he released it.

Now, none of us is prone to high-end gear. We aren't good enough anglers for that, so the juice would never be worth the squeeze of a $500 rod and reel set. But Slim goes really, really cheap. His reel was one you'd buy a child of eight or so for his first fishing trip. It had already fallen apart once out of pure cheapness, and Slim had to piece it back together but then the handle fell off for sure. So Slim rigged a casting rod to a spare spinning reel and was back in business. And after his catch, it would fall apart again.

We kept trying baits on and near the bottom, but we never got another bite. That was the only fish to be had that weekend.

"Oh, shit!" Slim was peering over the back of the boat at the engine. Doc and E leaned over to see what he was looking at.

Somehow – and we'll never know exactly how – Slim's fly rod had loosed about 70 feet of line that was now tightly wrapped around the boat propeller. We knew instantly what this meant: Someone was going to have go in and untangle the line from the prop. There was no alternative.

"Well, it's my damn line, so I have to go in," said Slim, stripping down to nothing and sliding into the clear green water. Fortunately, the water was warmer than the air, so being immersed wasn't too awful.

But the boat was rocking and Slim was having trouble hanging onto the ladder with one hand and unraveling the fly line with the other. It was tricky and tedious.

"I think you're going to have to cut it," said Doc. He pulled his filet knife out of his tackle box and reached down to hand it to Slim. He stopped. He couldn't hand it blade first or the bobbing Slim might lose a finger or two. And he couldn't hand it to him handle first or HE could lose some digits. While Doc was pondering this conundrum, the knife poised just out of Slim's reach, they both realized at the same time that this was not a good solution. There would almost certainly be blood. Slim wished he had thought to slip the blade between his teeth before splashing down into the water but only had that wish for a moment before he realized how stupid that could have been. No need for a knife.

"I think I'll just keep unwrapping," Slim said, kind of laughing, but kind of not.

Eventually the line was untangled and a naked, wet and cold Slim was hauled back into the boat. It was not a pretty sight. Far from it, in fact.

One great thing about autumn fishing in the cold is that few boats are on the lake so seclusion is easy to find. In one bay, however, the quiet of the lake was broken by the sound of a chain saw. Some old guy was taking down a tree in the back lawn of his lakeside retreat.

"I never mess with chainsaws anymore," Doc said. "Too damn

dangerous and I'm too damn old."

As daylight faded, we started back to the marina. They were closing shop at 5 and we had to have the boat back before then. We motored back to the main channel and up an arm we thought led to the marina. Soon we could see it and felt relieved we'd made the deadline. But as we drew closer, it didn't look right.

"Is this the right marina," asked E.

"Has to be," said Slim.

"I don't think so," Doc added. "I'm pretty sure it isn't." And it wasn't.

Doc grabbed the map and quickly divined where we were and where the right marina was. We had taken the wrong arm, but we weren't far away from where we needed to be. We got back just in time – and just as a driving rain hit. We unloaded the boat in a soaking downpour and a palpable sense of rue. One fish. One damn fish.

We agreed to dine at the finest restaurant we could find in Greer's Ferry, and it wasn't bad. But we had to buy a "the scenery membership" to order wine and drinks. We did so without complaint. Well, without too much complaint. The night at the cabin was spent with football on the TV, cigars and drinks on the deck, and discussing the impending end of E's newspaper career. Slim and Doc had left that business years before, and with little – make that no – regret.

There was some desultory casting in the lake behind the cabin Sunday morning, but nothing came of it.

The news of the morning? Vortextural.

Golfing great Greg Norman had suffered a terrible accident the day before while working with a chain saw. It happened at about the same time that Doc had offered his cosmic caution.

"How is it, Doc, that you have this ability to whammy celebrities on these fishing trips?" Slim asked.

"It's a gift," Doc deadpanned.

The highlight of that morning was E's fritatta mundatta, made with a strange assortment of stuff scrounged from around the cabin. Delicious it was. Then we held the ceremony: the Enquirer Outstanding Angler Award passing from Doc to Slim for – again – one fish. At least it was a nice one this time. Then the long drives back to Texas and Indiana. At least there was the NFL on the radio and a mix-tape CD of soul tracks Doc had made for E.

Here's what it came down to: gas for the trip, cabin rental, two pontoon boat rentals, cigars, food and libations. We guessed that one fish cost about $2,000.

And it was worth every damn penny.

Grilled Fish En Papillote

This is a dish you can prepare ahead of time as long as you have a cooler and cook it the first evening. Or the second if you are brave, hearty, foolish or don't fret about possibly spoiled fish.

Now papillote means 'parchment' in French. Maybe. At least we think so. But Mud Daddy veterans though we are, we aren't foolish enough to try to cook something in parchment, which is just paper. Anyway, we don't know where to get parchment. We thought that went out with quill pens and sealing wax. Ask E about parchment and he'll say something like "Didn't he catch for the Washington Senators?" Ask Slim and he'll probably say, "It's that hilltop temple in Athens, I'm sure of that much." Use aluminum foil instead. Much less chance of catching everything on fire.

Here's what you need:

Fish fillets – 6 to 8 oz. each (salmon works best)

Ripe tomato

Asparagus tips

Garlic butter

Salt and pepper

Here's what you do:

Place each fillet on a sheet of double thick foil. A little veggie oil on the foil will keep the fish from sticking. Lay a pretty-thick-but-not-too-thick slice of tomato on each fillet. Lay about three asparagus sticks on the tomato slice. Add a dollop – you decide how much is a dollop – of garlic butter on top of the stack. Salt and pepper to your liking.

Now comes the tricky part. Fold the foil around the fish, making a little tent. Bind the sides of the foil so that it makes a solid seal – you want to keep the heat inside the foil with the fish, not let it escape because you're too clumsy to make a solid seal.

Now set the sealed foil packets on top of a hot grill and leave it there for 22 minutes and 31 seconds. Or so. Now here's the good part: you've got a whole meal – with veggies – right there in a packet. You don't even need a plate.

Unfold the foil – *DON'T TEAR IT!* – and dip your face into the wonderful steam rising from inside. It's a joy to behold.

Rod Case/Tater Cannon

Materials

4 feet of 3 inch PVC water pipe (rifling optional)

(3) 4 inches of 4-inch PVC water pipe

4-inch to 3-inch PVC pipe adapter

4-inch PVC rounded pipe end cap

4-inch PVC pipe end with threaded/removable fitting

4-inch PVC T-joint fitting (three open ends)

Female end of garden hose replacement fixture (discard clamp)

Small hose clamp (like those used to clamp rubber tubes to fitting on cars)

Butane disposable charcoal grill lighter

PVC glue

Self-tapping screws.

Duct tape as needed

Tennis balls – sliced in half

(For Rod case capability: Two PVC pipe ends for 3-inch pipe that have insets that can be screwed on and off.)

Tools

Drill, saw, gloves to protect your hands if you're an idiot. (Figure it out.)

Assembly

Glue the four inch sections of 4-inch PVC pipe into the three ends of the T-joint. Follow directions on PVC glue bottle. Drill a hole into the rounded end cap that is no bigger in diameter that the pipe fitting from the garden hose. Slip garden hose end piece into hole, glue it with the threaded part inside the curvature of the end piece, affix hose clamp to outside protruding nipple, then glue the entire PVC end cap to bottom part of "T." Glue the 3-inch-to-4-inch adapter to the left arm of the "T" and the fitting that has a screwable, removable insert to the right arm of the T.

Fit 4 feet of 3-inch PVC (barrel) into adapter, drill two small holes through adapter into barrel section, then anchor with two screws long enough to protrude into barrel. Cover joint with strip of duct tape. Insert Butane lighter into hose fixture, clamp with screw clamp.

To fire: Squeeze sliced tennis ball and push down into the barrel with flyrod as plunger. Do not push beyond end of barrel. Affix typical valve from propane blowtorch to butane tank (from portable BBQ grill), unscrew back of contraption, and direct gas into chamber for no more than five seconds. (Most failures occur because too much gas is in chamber.) Click igniter. Vavoooom! Tennis ball will fly. To use tater, sand/file top of barrel into edge so potato is cut to fit as it smooshes into the device. Taters are expensive, though. We shoot tennis balls.

The Longest Epilogue Ever

And that's how the days of our fishing trips turned into years and the years into decades - one atop another. We started in the morning of our lives and now evening has come to us. After more than two decades of three- and four-day trips, we figured we had pilfered about 90 days of adventure and fun from life. We'd stolen a boy's endless summer from our adulthood, and now three men and two other close friends in late middle age looked back upon a lifetime of annual adventures on the water and wondered: How did young guys with gumption turn into old guys with guts? How did it happen so fast? Where did the time go? Out trips went from time on the water into memories and then they became scenes in dreams. The hair that wasn't already gray fell out or grew in mysterious places like the inside of ears or way too thick between our shoulder blades. And eyebrows really went crazy, not quite nutsobananas, like 60 Minutes' Andy Rooney, who had little terrier tails up there where his eyebrows are supposed to be, but long enough to be troublesome.

We found daily reminders of the passing and pressure of time.

At work, what used to be a bite turned into a growl. At home, we dutifully did the dishes, mowed the lawn, put up and took down Christmas lights and waited for the spring thaw. And we always thought about fishing. We took comfort in the regularity of tasks, the clockwork of the seasons of our lives and duties because we knew that one great fishing trip awaited us each fall – even if it came and went without a fish on the line – and we savored the thought of that upcoming pilgrimage. Would this be the year the Mud Daddy would become something truly special, perhaps one that brings to the boat a fish as big as a big man's leg?

The prospect of unlimited annual adventures on the water seemed to be fading, too. Friends and family members had already stepped over the rainbow. How many of these Mud Daddies were left? We rarely ask the question because we don't know the answer and whatever the answer was, we weren't going to like it. Perhaps 10. What if there were only one or two? And as for the newspapers that employed us, they were sick, with advertising revenue disappearing like the snows in the Spring. Doc retired early in Austin and Slim moved over to the private sector. Big E bailed out of the Enquirer in 2014, the last to leave among our crew, and the Raging Bull retired the same year.

Whatever happens, we believe we will head out for open spaces and open water to play and become worry-free kids again, though we also know in our hearts that our best days on the water were behind us and that the best fishing, which was never really very good, are probably gone, too. How could it not be the case? We never had the money for jaunts to Alaska or Belize, or even Bozeman, where the trout are huge. And though the years have taken their inevitable toll on us, time has been harder still on many of those wild places that we had visited, or yearned to, through the years.

This much we know: our favorite fishing destinations are under a threat far worse than those glaring, orange slabs of plastic E-dog would tie onto a line and cast into the mist on a mirror-smooth lake. Those lost eddies and riffles, the quiet waves coursing across so many Midwestern and Appalachian rivers and lakes, places that usually took a nightlong drive to find, are in an awful mess. Our environment is waging a daily, terrible losing battle. The polluters have clearly been winning this fight, and though we had media platforms that reached hundreds of thousands of newspaper subscribers every day, it wasn't enough. So we concluded there was one thing we could do: write this book, tell our tale, put words down on a page, stack the paragraphs together like trout on a stringer in a sepia photo from the 1930s. Perhaps telling the story of the Mud Daddy Chronicles can turn things around just a bit. Stranger things have happened. And what about all those mystical vortexes, those signs from the One Enthroned in Heaven Who Laughs? He or She surely has been watching this degradation and maybe all the time was calling on us. Why us? Like the basketball player asked by the coach whether the team was playing poorly because of ignorance or apathy: "I don't know and I don't care." We were like that, too, when it came to the

Vortex and its mysteries. We don't know or care. We aren't absolutely certain it means anything at all. All we know is that it happened, happened regularly and happened to us.

We have chronicled our time on the water because we know that words can make a difference. We've seen it. So our words might help explain our friendship, the food we cooked, the fun we had, and then tell about the threat to our nation's lakes and streams. Is it ignorance or apathy that traded clean rivers and lakes to maximize profit at any cost? The venal underbody of the Great American Dream can be an immense and terrible thing.

We often speak about that first Mud Daddy so many years back, a trip to the South fork of the Shenandoah River. We can laugh now about facing death on a rainy mountain curve, Doc insisting to this day that he saved all our lives with his split-second heel-toe brake work and delicate whirl of the wheel. E-dog and Slim can swear that he damn near killed us by negotiating a hairpin curve on a rainy highway at 45 instead of 25, a debate that never ends. And there was Slim's bunny-hop with death as his waders filled with water, wondering if he could make the shore or if the end was only seconds away. E-man shed Mud Daddy blood when he went down into a hole in the riverbed and surfaced with a deep gash on his knee that was filled with river water, dirt and gravel. He wound up with a puss-filled, infected leg that kept him on his back for two weeks and could have led to amputation.

Those recalled adventures led us to wonder: was it time to return to those Virginia moonrises, to Doc's corner of the river where he caught a fish on every other cast. After all, we know that unless things change future generations may never know the incredible thrill and rush that comes from catching a fish on every other cast. Or what seemed through the mists of time, every cast. We were connected to the memories of Slim's dad, Stan Eckberg, standing waist deep in a Menominee River feeder stream in Michigan's Upper Peninsula back in the 1930s, doing just that – catching a different species of fish on successive casts. To a young E-dog and his brothers headed out in the rain of upstate New York in the 1950s, bare feet slapping on a wooden dock as they hauled in one fat trout after another. And to Doc, who began fishing from a bridge over the muddy Bannister River in Halifax County.

We'd go back to Virginia and the Shenandoah, we decided, and relive that glorious, messed up first Mud Daddy.

Then we learned the terrible truth.

The forks of one of America's iconic rivers were sick, and its lively smallmouth bass and flashy sunfish were dying or dead. Our spiritual home waters were sick. Thousands of fish have died each spring, floating belly-up in eddies and through sparkling riffles. Five minutes of research showed us that. What was even more tragic, nobody knew why. Or if they knew why – manure run-off from farms, hormones injected into steers – nobody was willing to point fingers and make the changes that needed to be made to save the Shenandoah.

The dying started around 2002, happening every year since and starting sometime around late spring. By 2005 it was clear to local landowners and state biologists that something needed to be done. You just can't have a river of dead fish greeting the spring green of Virginia each and every year. What was the problem? One could guess pollution, and the full impact of decades of pollution was summed up succinctly in a 2008 report from the Virginia Department of Environmental Quality. Its opening line is remarkable for its clarity and for its sad implications:

"A fish kill resulting in the loss of an estimated 80 percent of the adult smallmouth bass and redbreast sunfish occurred in more than 100 miles of the South Fork Shenandoah River in Virginia between April and July 2005. Nearly identical fish kills were observed in the South Branch of the Potomac in 2002 and the North Fork of the Shenandoah River in 2004."

One hundred miles!

Most of the fish that were lost were adult smallmouth bass and redbreast sunfish. It was not an easy death for the fish, either. Mortality was preceded by bacterial skin lesions, and the fish suffered plenty before they gave up. The kill area occurred through the entire length of the river, with no upstream or downstream boundaries. Task forces were formed, but still the fish kept dying. It got worse. In 2006 a task force concluded that something really whacky was going on: fish had both male and female characteristics. These intersex fish were found with testes that contained immature eggs. Imagine that. Scientists began to test the water quality for ammonia, dissolved oxygen, pH and temperature. And though the testing occurred every hour around the clock, nobody was looking for the obvious cause: hormones in cattle feed to induce better milk and muscle growth. Those hormones had made their way into the watershed, and as a result, our home waters were dying.

Virginia didn't exactly break the bank to fund the research, either. In October 2006, Gov. Timothy M. Kaine announced that he had located a whopping $150,000 for a scientific investigation into the cause of the Shenandoah fish kills. By 2007 researchers concluded that the spring fish kills that had affected the Shenandoah, James, Cowpasture and Maury rivers were abating. Here's a news flash for the researchers. Maybe it was because there were few fish left to die? By late 2007, the agencies could no longer avoid the obvious: "Many of the water quality tests so far have been evaluations of river water and have focused specifically on nutrients and ammonia, which are normally associated with agricultural wastes. A plan is under development for expanded, comprehensive testing of waste streams and sources connected with agricultural land uses." Note that no action was being taken, rather, "a plan was being developed." Chemical compounds and biological agents (a euphemism for hormones) would be the focus of the 2007 study. And then, before the study could be launched, an April 2007 fish kill on the Shenandoah's North and South forks decimated the fish population for dozens of miles around Woodstock, Bentonville, Elkton and Front Royal. Throughout 2007 the fish continued to die, and the roster expanded to include sucker, rock bass and largemouth bass. Authorities asked anglers to help but found there weren't many anglers left because there weren't many fish left.

The decimation of the Shenandoah was all but complete by 2008: "Fish kills are occurring in Virginia rivers again this year but have developed more slowly than in past year." And of the ones still swimming around, reported the few anglers still casting for them, about one in three had lesions. By the summer of 2008, the fish kills in Virginia had expanded to touch the Jackson River downstream of Covington and Craig Creek, a tributary of the James River at Eagle Rock. Lesions were also reported on fish in the Mount Jackson-Edinburg area. There was a note of optimism: "The North Fork from Woodstock to the mouth is producing very good catches this year. The South Ford also is supporting excellent catches in areas that previously experienced Big fish kills."

But the report ended on a sour note: "causes of the fish kills remain unknown."

Suspects for fish kills everywhere are hormones in cattle and manure run-off. Agriculture is Virginia's largest industry with an economic impact of $55 billion that provides 357,100 jobs across the state. The three top categories of farming are broilers, cattle, calves and milk, with fresh market tomatoes rounding out the list, according to the Virginia Department of Agriculture and Consumer Services. The mega-farms are clearly the big guns, accounting for 82 percent of farm income. The top counties in farm employment? Not surprisingly they are Rockingham, Washington, Augusta, Pittsylvania and Scott, which account for one-fifth of employment and likely one-fifth of the state's beef and milk output. It's no coincidence that some of those counties are also the watershed counties of the rivers and creeks that are dying.

Milk, the official beverage of Virginia, is also an industry addicted to hormone supplements in feed. U.S. regulators have approved synthetic hormones zeranol, trenbolone acetate and melengestrol acetate under a variety of trade names, including Compudoze Implants, Heifer-Oido, Posilac, Steer-oido, Ralgro and Synovex and MGA Premix. Critics claim that hormones used as growth and milk production enhancers also cause breast cancer and may be the main reason that girls are reaching puberty early. The products can increase milk production by 10 percent over the span of 300 days. But the public was outraged that hormones were in their milk, and after much public pressure, including Wal-Mart dropping the sale of milk from cattle injected with the stuff, Eli Lilly &Co.'s Elanco Animal Health bought the rights to Posilac and its use abated.

Hormones were not the only threat, and perhaps not the gravest, to fish in waters that course through farmland and field. It was clear that run-off from livestock waste lagoons killed more fish than anyone realized. And livestock farms are universal in the U.S. In Ohio, between 2000-2003, according to the American Society of Agricultural and Biological Engineers, there were 98 recorded incidents of manure spills, which happened, mostly because buried tiles on farm fields led right to the streams. Big farm operators did not fuss with a sewer plan for the manure. Anyhow, who is going to enforce and how could they possibly put teeth into that law? So, four of five farms that had a sewer plan did not bother to abide by it – year after year after year.

In Doc's adopted home waters in Texas, authorities found hundreds of dead carp, gizzard shad, channel catfish and Gulf killifish on the Pecos River in March 2007 as a poisonous golden alga bloom grew unabated. Tests found 100,000 algae cells per milliliter of river water, an alarming level, particularly considering that 20,000 will bring a fish kill. Texas was not alone. North Carolina had 4,000 livestock farms in 1992, and 800 of them violated water standards with impunity with 20 causing "severe impact" on nearby waters, according to a 1992 study. Livestock waste killed fish everywhere by creating algae or phytoplankton blooms that choked the oxygen from rivers and streams and pathogenic micro-organisms that decimated fish populations. One 2003 study from the EPA found that cattle farms caused at least 30 percent of the catastrophes for the nation's waterways from manure run-off.

There have been too many to recount here, but it helps to list a few. In Wabasha County, Minn., in 1997, a dairy manure release killed 17,000 minnows and white suckers. A year later in Kitchen Creek, W.VA., just upstream from our beloved Shenandoah, more than a mile of stream was polluted from a heavy rain run-off at a manure pond, leading to the death of 13,693 fish including a bunch of Mad Toms, the original Mud Daddy namesake for all these adventures. The specificity of that number? There's only one way to get there. Somebody counted them. In Iowa in 2008, a fish kill in South Big Creek in Henry County near New London was investigated by the Iowa Department of Natural Resources. In that one, a hose supposedly ruptured from a manure pond pumping truck then flowed into a ditch and tributary before reaching Big Creek. Once authorities were alerted, the manure was pumped onto a nearby farmer field. And the next big rain? Back into the stream. When streams are low, just about any amount of run off from a manure lagoon is deadly. These spills were not necessarily in out-of-the-way corners of the map, either. One in June 2001 came on Black Earth Creek in Wisconsin near the village of Cross Plains. It has long been a first-class trout stream for the state and Midwest with naturally reproducing brown trout that makes it one of the best trout streams in the nation where "anglers could fish for wild, 'stream bred' trout in a rural landscape that still is relatively pastoral in nature" and similar to a classic English trout stream, according to a report from the Wisconsin Department of Natural Resources.

The creek had at least 12 miles of quality trout fishing . . . until dead browns began to float into and through the eddies. Manure washed into the river from a heavy rain led to the kill. About 150 trout were collected and later electroshock samplings found that populations in some branches had been decimated, as just one-fifth the number of trout lived in those waters compared to a known population from years before. The culprit? Investigators found a nearby 900-head dairy farm and run-off from the concrete floor those cows stood upon. How bad was it? A nearby farm gully was three to four feet deep with manure.

Other lost corners of the Midwest, where we had had delightful Mud Daddies through the years, were also under attack from other threats: fly ash dams – pools of discarded waste from coal burned at electric generating plants. Those festering swamps of utterly unregulated poison are everywhere. America's coal-fired power plants produce an incredible 131 million tons of the stuff annually and store it in more than 1,300 dumps. While some is redirected into concrete and ends up in floors of the local new Wal-Mart, most is dumped in lagoons near the nation's 600 power plants. How much are we generating? Think of it this way: a million railroad tanks cars full of the stuff. That's a train that would stretch from Washington, D.C., to Melbourne, Australia, according to the environmental group Earthjustice.

One fly ash pond erupted in late 2008 and swamped more than 300 acres with a billion gallons of toxic sludge in Kingston-Harriman, Tenn. It was a watershed we had fished before and remembered fondly. There was Crazy Jim who put out scores of jugs to snare catfish in the night, a huge blue-gill E-dog landed that was as big as a frying pan, a smallmouth Bass Slim nailed late one afternoon and a striped Bass Doc snagged in the dorsal fin while trolling. We knew that place and loved it.

Similar dumps are on the shores of Lake Erie, Lake Michigan, the Mississippi River and the Ohio River. There is a dump somewhere near you. These collections are particularly insidious to humans as ash can leach toxins that may cause cancer and birth defects. Fly ash clearly decimates fish, bird and frog populations. The Environmental Protection Agency has identified 63 sites in 26 states where groundwater was contaminated by heavy metals from fly ash dumps. Three of those were managed by the Tennessee Valley Authority, the same agency that managed the dam that broke in Kingston-Harriman. Environmentalists have added another 17 cases to the list of sites where dumps have contaminated water supplies.

Elsewhere, coal mining to fuel those power plants decimated more than 1,400 miles of mountain headwaters as industry leadership in this space means peeling the top off mountains and taking what's under it. Think Pittsburgh to Vicksburg. That's 1,400 miles but this 1,400 miles is, rather, was pristine mountaintop.

Everything about fracking or gas and oil fracturing is awful. The water consumption to operate just one fracking well is staggering: anywhere from a million to 8 million gallons of water. When mixed with corrosives and chemicals, about 40,000 gallons of chemicals are used per fracking. The chemicals are a soup of carcinogenic metals and substances: hydrochloric acid, formaldehyde, methanol and the like – more than 600 in all. With 500,000 active gas wells in the U.S., some estimates go as high as 360 billion gallons of chemicals to run current gas wells. That's in addition to 72 trillion gallons of water.

Methane concentrations are reportedly 17 times higher in drinking water near fracturing sites than untainted wells. There have been over 1,000 documented cases of harmful ground water near zones of gas drilling as well as cases of sensory, respiratory, and neurological damage from ingesting contaminated water. About 30 percent, at best, of the fracking water stays in the ground. It does not biodegrade.

Sometimes, it was all just too damn sad.

And so, we wondered. Were these Mud Daddy trips just a sad Requiem for the destruction of America's rivers, streams and lakes? Is that why we were given front row seats? Why we were given a chance to see the Hand of God Fish swim back to the deep? Is that why we were able to marvel at the amazing tenacity of Pete the Patoka terrapin, who broke out of his pen on a bone-chilling Indiana night? Why that skunk looked Bob "Ragin' Bull" Rankin right in the eye in Missouri and his resulting weekend that was free of fish? On each trip we smoke cigars like there was no tomorrow, because when you think about it, no one is promised tomorrow. Sometimes the laughter was so deep and heartfelt that it turned into tears, and usually it was about something incredibly stupid – like Edog trying to sing and the song ending up a howl. And all those vortex coincidences?

Did they come to us because we were supposed to bear witness to this terrible environmental calamity that was touching every corner of our nation's wild places? Could it truly be the end of an American outdoors experience, though at the time we were only vaguely aware of how devastating the pollution had become? The San Juan River where Slim's brother, Dale, pulled trout after trout from the current was gone - poisoned.

Or was it the beginning of a season of restoration? Who could say? So, we wrote a book and then went fishing. Year after year we cast those lures into quiet pools and did it on misty mornings and sizzling summer afternoons alike.

We laughed about our memories and antics – faces lit by campfire and thoughts fueled by whiskey neat as cigar smoke twisted toward the moon and the firmament of 90 billion galaxies. We eventually put some words down and in our heart of hearts told what we knew was true. We had done what we could. We prayed it would be enough.

Appendix

Whatever it Takes

EMAIL Monday, June 9, 2003 2:18 PM

E-Man,
Slimbagger tells me you're out for the Mud Daddy this year. And after I toiled to make that nice scrapbook for you! Some gratitude. There are some things you obviously have not considered.

1 – 'Cuse (Syracuse) won NCAA this year. Which means you obviously ought to go on a fishing trip and brag about it. Particularly since they beat Texas. See, that Syracuse-Austin connection keeps coming up. You ignore it at your peril. The Lord of the Mud Daddy is trying to tell you something. Best to listen.

2 - As I was e-mailing Slim about my brother's place on Cumberland Lake, the Bull was e-mailing me about wanting to go fishing with the three of us this year. Vortextual, no?

3 - This would be the 20th anniversary of the famed and fabled Laurel River Lake Mud Daddy of '83 with You, Me, Slim and Bull. Where we saw that huge bass tail-walking across the water. Don't ignore 20th anniversaries of any kind. This one means something.

4 - This is the year that the Slimbagger turns the big FIVE-OH. He's 50 years old, dude. We gotta celebrate that in true Mud Daddy fashion, no?

5 - Whatever "problems" you can come up with as an excuse must be laid next to mine, and they will be found wanting, if not positively piddly:
(a) Barb lost her job this year and we are subsisting on one income.
(b) Jason was nearly killed in a dog attack that has cost me $5,000 in

medical expenses.

(c) Jason's college rent in Santa Barbara is $500 a month, his tuition is $5,000 and that's just for openers. Doesn't count bail money and lawyers.

(d) Jason totaled my car last week when he hit a deer at 2 a.m. We know how much damage that does, don't we? And is it significant that he hits a deer with my car just as I'm e-mailing you about a Mud Daddy? I think so.

(e) Evan turns 16 this week and goes on my insurance at $350 a quarter. That's in addition to Jason, me and Barb.

Now, I suggest to you that these "problems" that occur in real life would overwhelm most men, but will they keep me from a Mud Daddy weekend? I think not. Need more?

6 - Ohio State won the national championship in football, and we know who went to Ohio State. So we can "discuss" whether the Bucks or Orange get top billing at the next MD.

7 - Texas won the national baseball title – so with UT, SU and OSU, we got all 3 national titles and a STRONG – maybe the strongest – MD connection in a long time. It may not top nearly killing Bob Huggins by talking about him in the boat last year, but it is still Major League. Now that we are all in our 50s (some of us in our mid 50s) we have to confront the reality that the last round-up may be just around the corner. We should fish while we can and enjoy each other's company while we can 'cause it can all come to a cold, dark close in a sudden, single moment of pain and violence. So, search your soul. Peruse the Mud Daddy book I toiled over and sent you gratis. Consider whether you really want to blow this off or go have a great weekend.

Yours in Mud Daddydom,
RX

EMAIL reply – From Big E, one day later:

Strong points all, Docteur, and I would agree that the Huggins-Mud Daddy connection is the strongest of all. If I don't make every effort to make it, it is likely I will wind up dead, given the Karma this magnitudinous event has associated with it. I am not one to tempt the fates. I shall make every effort to be there. … By the way, that was a helluva scrapbook you sent. I loved it all, but was especially pleased with the inclusion of my letter to McLaughlin about his slipup on referring to Schwartzkopf as Schwartzwalder – a Mud Daddy Classic. … It's an event that is bigger than us all, no doubt about it.

- 30 -

Other Books by the Authors

John Eckberg is the co-author of *Road Dog* (Federal Point Publishing 2002); and author of *The Success Effect* (Sterling & Ross 2005, trade paperback in 2008); *Have a Crumby Book* (Clerisy 2007); *Fascinating Ohio* and editor of *Pot of Gold* (both Kindle books from Success Effect Publishing 2009)

John Erardi is the author of *Pete Rose 4,192* (Enquirer Publishing 1985); and co-author of *The First Boys of Summer* (Road West Pub 1994); *The Big Red Dynasty* (Road West 1997); *Opening Day* (Road West 2004); *Cincinnati's Crosley Field* (Clerisy 2009);*The Wire-to-Wire Reds* (Clerisy 2010);

David Lowery edited *The Untold Story of the Lower Colorado River Authority* (A&M Press 2015)

www.ingramcontent.com/pod-product-compliance
Lightning Source LLC
LaVergne TN
LVHW011221080426
835509LV00005B/245